9

SEEING AROUND CORNERS

SEEING AROUND CORNERS

How to Spot
Inflection Points in Business
Before They Happen

Rita McGrath

Houghton Mifflin Harcourt
Boston   New York
2019

For information about permission to reproduce selections
from this book, write to trade.permissions@hmhco.com or to
Permissions, Houghton Mifflin Harcourt Publishing Company,
3 Park Avenue, 19th Floor, New York, New York 10016.

hmhbooks.com

Library of Congress Cataloging-in-Publication Data is available.
ISBN 978-0-358-02233-6
ISBN 978-0-358-23707-5 (international edition)

Book design by Chrissy Kurpeski

Printed in the United States of America
DOC 10 9 8 7 6 5 4 3 2 1

In one of my last conversations with my mother, Helge-Liane Gunther, she made a big effort to say something that was clearly important to her: "I'm proud of you." It shouldn't have mattered that much, but it did. A lot.

She was extraordinary. A scientist, when that was rare. A path-breaking researcher whose work was cited for decades after she completed it. And the heart and soul of our family.

I'd like to pass her thought along.

To our daughter, Anne, and the amazing women coming into their own along with her: I'm proud of you.

Contents

Foreword   *ix*

Introduction   *1*

1. Snow Melts from the Edges   *13*

2. Early Warnings   *39*

3. On the Lookout for Weak Signals:
   Defining Your Arena   *65*

4. Customers, Not Hostages   *78*

5. What Must Be True?
   Creating a Plan to Learn Fast   *101*

6. Galvanizing the Organization   *127*

7. How Innovation Proficiency Defangs the
   Organizational Antibodies   *144*

8. How Leadership Can and Must Learn
   to See Around Corners   *167*

9. Seeing Around Corners in Your Own Life   *191*

Acknowledgments   *211*

Notes   *217*

Index   *247*

Foreword

As hard as it may be to remember now, there was a time, not so long ago, when no one was talking about disruption. Innovation, back then, was a niche topic of interest to only a few. The consequences of digital transformation were only dimly anticipated. Thirty years ago, that was the world we lived in.

Even then, however, the early warnings were clear to a few of us. Rita McGrath and I were both pursuing our doctoral degrees in the late 1980s — she at Wharton and I at Harvard. Both of us intuited that the assumptions underlying theories of success in business at the time were on the brink of major challenge. In my case, the big idea was that assumptions about "good management" would lead to corporate disaster as leaders faced what I came to call the "innovator's dilemma." In her case, the big idea was that approaching highly uncertain projects as though they were business as usual was a trap. Both ideas were published in the *Harvard Business Review* in 1995.

We were challenging orthodoxy — in fact, we are still challenging orthodoxy.

This orthodoxy is based on assumptions that in today's competitive environment are simply not correct. Big market share is good, for example. Rita and I would ask, Market share, meaning what? The very concept of "industry" is an artificial categorization. Often the most important competition any business will face is from entrants who are not hamstrung by assumptions about what their "industry" expects of them. Addressing this reality may be challenging, but it can be strategically navigated with a useful theory — a statement of what causes things to happen, and why.

The terms "theory" and "theoretical" often connote "impractical." But theories are statements of cause and effect — which actions yield which results, and why. As such, a good theory is consummately practical. Every time a manager makes a plan or takes an action it is predicated on a belief that they will get an expected result. Managers, therefore, are voracious consumers of theory. The more we understand what causes things to happen, the more we can help managers understand that in *these* circumstances you should do *this,* but in *those* circumstances you should do *that.* These cause-and-effect relationships offer clarity and predictability to what otherwise might seem like a game of chance.

The first step toward developing any useful theory is getting the categories right. In my previous work, I realized that product or demographic segmentation were the wrong categories when trying to predict purchase behavior. As Peter Drucker famously said, "The customer rarely buys what the company thinks it's selling him." This led me to discover the theory of jobs to be done, which asserts that people buy products and services because they are trying to make progress in their lives. Once people realize they have a job to do, they reach out and "hire" (or fire) a product to get that job done.

Rita McGrath insightfully builds on that research to introduce a new category that basically rips apart decades of strategic thinking in which where you are in an industry determines your fate. Thinking in terms of an *arena,* rather than an industry, McGrath suggests, means that markets are no longer defined by product category but rather by the jobs that people are trying to get done in their lives. This concept offers a much more powerful categorization scheme for managers navigating disruptive change.

She then goes a step further to illuminate not just the *what* but the *how* of successful innovation. Her theory of discovery-driven planning helps managers discover the future while simultaneously containing risk. I've long been convinced of the power of this theory — it is required reading in my course at Harvard Business School and is used extensively in our strategy consulting work at Innosight.

Innovation doesn't have to be a painful hit-and-miss effort. Though disruption is constantly on the horizon, managers don't need to be blind when charting their course. *Seeing Around Corners* will help those of us who seek to better understand — and even anticipate — what innovation will bring us next.

Clayton M. Christensen
Spring 2019

SEEING AROUND CORNERS

Introduction

Some years ago, Andy Grove introduced the concept of strategic inflection points in his landmark book *Only the Paranoid Survive*. A "strategic inflection point," he observed, "is a time in the life of a business when its fundamentals are about to change." And that is how many of us experience inflection points – as a single moment in time when everything changes irrevocably.

When you look at the true nature of strategic inflection points, you see a different story. It is similar to the way in which Hemingway's character Mike Campbell in *The Sun Also Rises* responds to being asked how he went bankrupt. "Gradually," he says, "then suddenly."

An inflection point is a change in the business environment that dramatically shifts some element of your activities, throwing certain taken-for-granted assumptions into question. Someone, somewhere, sees the implications, but all too often they are not heard. That someone might be you!

This book will help you see the opportunities represented by strategic inflection points and help you, your team, and your organization take advantage of them. There are three major ideas to grab hold of here.

- What you experience as a big, dramatic inflection point has almost always been gestating for a while.
- This creates opportunity: if you see it early – or even better, spark it – an inflection point can be a strategic boon.
- You can use tools from the discovery-driven growth playbook to maximize your opportunities.

Let's take a concrete example.

Imagine a sector that effectively serves only one in five potential customers. Now imagine a massive change that would allow competitors to capture all that unmet demand in a highly profitable way and without taking on a lot of risk. Imagine that the sector as it is generates about $8 billion in revenue annually. The post–inflection point sector could be five times that size, meaning that some $40 billion or so in revenue could potentially be unlocked for those competitors adroit and farsighted enough to be at the right place when the inflection point does its work.

Though they are often depicted as disruptive destroyers of existing businesses, inflection points create vast new spaces even as they destroy outdated technologies and models. Famed economist Joseph Schumpeter said it decades ago — incumbents in a sector are always vulnerable to the "perennial gale of creative destruction," which sweeps away the old and outdated, and introduces the new and more desirable.

CAN YOU HEAR ME NOW?

The sector I just described actually exists. It is the business of manufacturing, prescribing, and fitting hearing aids. Judged by the standard of making sure people who need the help get it, the sector is doing a terrible job. According to researchers, 80 percent of adults between the ages of fifty-five and seventy-four who might benefit from a hearing aid don't have one, and many who do have one don't use it. Anyone who has ever tried to persuade an older person whom they care about to get help with their hearing (and who hasn't?) is all too familiar with the negative aspects of how this corner of the healthcare market is organized.

For starters, hearing aids are expensive. In 2017, the *New York Times* reported prices ranging from $1,500 to $2,000 or more per ear. Medicare does not cover hearing aids. Barbara Kelley, executive director of the Hearing Loss Association of America, reports that "the number one complaint we get in phone calls every day is, 'I need help, I can't afford hearing aids.'"

But that isn't the only problem. The traditional hearing aid business is regulated by the US Food and Drug Administration (FDA), and access to the technology is tightly controlled by incumbents. Audiologists, their lobbying associations, and the few (six — actually, soon to be five) companies that manufacture hearing aids have strictly limited the options available to patients. The incumbents insist that what all patients want is the "gold standard." As one observer described it, this involves buying a hearing aid only after a thorough diagnostic evaluation that includes otoscopy and bone conduction testing, speech-in-noise testing, real-ear measurement/speech mapping, aural rehabilitation, and hands-on hearing aid fitting. Even if they have the means, for many people this seems like overkill.

Finally, we have the social stigma factor. People don't want to wear aids for fear of looking "old." Despite strong evidence that they could use the audible help, admitting it is tough. The often ugly, obvious, and occasionally noisy traditional hearing aids are whatever is the opposite of cool.

I know this firsthand. When I asked my mother-in-law about a whistling noise I heard at a family gathering, I didn't realize that she had finally started to use her hearing aid and that it was the source of the unfamiliar noise. She yanked it out of her ear, stuck it back in a drawer, and didn't use it for the rest of our visit. Sadly for her (and distressingly for me), the benefit of using an aid to fully participate in the conversations she craved was no match for the "embarrassment" of wearing the device. Had I only known that this was a common feature of hearing aids, I would have kept my mouth shut!

This is serious stuff. A study by Frank Lin of Johns Hopkins found that hearing loss is associated with an increased risk of developing dementia, of social isolation, and even of an increased risk of falling. Uncorrected hearing loss makes it even harder for eventual treatment to be successful and increases the cognitive load on the brains of people struggling to make out what others are saying. Clearly, this is a social and health problem of epidemic proportions.

THE GATHERING INFLECTION POINT

Problematic as it is, the hearing aid business model has remained more or less the same since the FDA classified hearing aids as medical devices in 1977. Before then, hearing aids were generally treated as a consumer product, with some hilariously bad and misleading advertising and celebrity endorsements to go along with that positioning.

Meanwhile, in-ear hearing aids — which needed to be fitted to individuals' ears — were often sold by audiologists, and that became the norm. Due in part to misleading claims and some shoddy practices, interest groups began to raise alarms about hearing aids, prompting the FDA to classify them as medical devices with extremely strict protocols for their manufacture and dispensing.

The current inflection point for the highly regulated (and profitable) hearing aid business had its roots in two citizen petitions filed with the FDA in 2003. An FDA citizen petition is a process that was originally intended to allow individuals and community organizations to make requests for changes to healthcare policy. While the petitions themselves had no immediate impact on the way hearing aids were regulated, they were early markers of a shift in sentiment that would move these devices toward the same over-the-counter access currently available for "reading glasses" — corrective lenses that can be sold without a prescription.

The incumbents aren't eager to back down. No less than the American Academy of Audiology suggests that any device that amplifies sound should be subject to FDA regulation. Taken literally, this position could be seen as requiring such regulation for everything from earbuds to headsets.

The academy aside, the cost to consumers and the intransigence of incumbents have led to an odd coalition of bedfellows determined to change the system. In 2017, for the first time, the regulatory structure that the academy has been trying so hard to preserve began to be dismantled. In a classic Clay Christensen–style disruption, new technologies are proving to be "good enough" and are expanding the pool of consumers who might benefit from an improved ability to hear. This is what Christensen has often described as "competing with non-use."

THE DISRUPTERS EDGING INTO
HEARING ASSISTANCE TERRITORY

Although they are not — heavens no, absolutely not — selling *hearing aids,* there is no shortage of companies offering what in the industry are called "personal sound amplification products," or PSAPs. These products are not regulated by the FDA and are readily available over the counter to anyone who wants them. And even more worrisome to the conventional hearing aid manufacturers, in many hearing assistance applications, PSAPs do just as well — or even better.

For instance, Bose, the iconic manufacturer of speakers and noise-canceling headphones, is making a product it calls Hearphones that sell for around $500. Despite advertising that makes it sound an awful lot like the product is directed at people suffering from hearing loss ("We want to help you hear every word of your conversations"), at one point, Bose was emphatic that these devices were most definitely *not* hearing aids, thus avoiding FDA oversight. In 2018, however, the company received approval for an over-the-counter version of a self-fitting hearing aid. Other heavyweight players are crowding into the market, including Samsung with its Gear IconX earbuds and Apple with its AirPods — wireless earphones that can allow you to listen to music, time exercises, and, incidentally, connect to hearing aid apps on a phone or other device. In addition, dozens of new companies are piling into the aid space, with aids like Fennex, Petralex, and Here One. And on the startup side of things, a product called Eargo took its inspiration from fly fishing to create an actual hearing aid that you fit yourself, buy over the Internet, and charge the way you might charge one of your more familiar electronic devices.

YOU THOUGHT $8 BILLION WAS A BIG NUMBER?

But, really, all this excitement and energy about a market that hasn't historically been seen as all that interesting? Well . . .

Experts have projected that even under the existing regulatory regime, the hearing aid business could be an $8 billion business by 2019. Some say that by 2023 it could be in excess of $9 billion. This is an interesting aspect of strategic inflection points. When something that used to be complex and expensive becomes convenient and cheaper, one result is often an explosion in demand. If we extrapolate from the statistic that only one in five people who could use help with their hearing have hearing aids today, the market size in short order could be five times greater – perhaps as big as $40 billion – after the inflection point that allows anybody to get a discreet, self-adjustable hearing device.

Moreover, you might even see quite dramatic changes in the use case for hearing devices, along the lines of how the smartphone changed the way people use mobile phones. People might find themselves purchasing more than one device, as they now do with glasses. Perhaps one look and functionality for a Friday dinner out, something completely different for the Sunday afternoon sports game, and maybe even something else for watching TV at home. Once something becomes inexpensive enough, the possibilities are endless.

As you will see throughout this book, weak signals of an impending shift – *when recognized early enough* – can give you a head start to prepare to take advantage of it. Right now is exactly the moment when companies interested in entering the over-the-counter hearing aid business should begin preparing and making plans. Not investing in a huge big bang, mind you, but investing in preparations.

An inflection point occurs when a change – what some people call a 10X change – upends the assumptions that a business is built on. When the moment of crystal clarity arrives, that is the moment to mobilize the troops, bring focus, and bear down hard on preparing the organization for the post-inflection world, just as Bose, Samsung, and others are doing in the over-the counter hearing aid (sorry, *not* hearing aid) space.

GRADUALLY, THEN SUDDENLY

Inflection points can take a surprisingly long time to unfold. Wilbur and Orville Wright made their first twelve-second historic flight near Kitty Hawk, North Carolina, on December 17, 1903. The first mention of their accomplishment in the *New York Times* appeared three years later. In fact, it wasn't until May of 1908 that serious reporters began to pay attention and the public realized that manned flight was not (as an expert predicted in 1902) too far in the future, but that it had actually arrived. In short order, industries as varied as passenger travel, consulting, logistics, and even defense were fundamentally altered forever.

Inflection points create dramatic shifts in the competitive dynamics of a functioning system. They have the power to bring about exponential change. Perhaps 10X larger, 10X cheaper, 10X more convenient, and so on. The sources are seemingly endless. Some common triggers for an inflection point can be found in:

- Technological change
- Regulatory change
- Social possibilities
- Demographic change
- New connections (among formerly isolated elements, common to digital disruption)
- Political change
- And many others

Inflection points have the power to change the very assumptions on which organizations were founded. Changes in the environment in or around organizations can create new, entrepreneurial opportunities – and result in potentially devastating consequences for those still operating under the old model or assumptions. The effects are often compounded because institutional rules typically lag what is possible.

For example, if you look at companies that have navigated inflection points superbly in recent years (Amazon, Aetna, Cognizant, Adobe, Fujifilm, DSM, Gore), you don't see huge, wrenching reorganization for the most part. That takes place in companies that recognized the changing circumstances too late (IBM, A&P, Sears, Hewlett-Packard, Dell). And when an inflection point goes the wrong way, the entire organization can crumble or become irrelevant (Toys "R" Us, Blockbuster, RadioShack).

The progress of inflection points, moreover, is not linear. They proceed in fits and starts, and while they are emerging, it is normal for reasonable people to disagree about their importance and likely impact.

The great entrepreneurs and innovators, however, don't just allow an inflection point to happen to them. They connect emerging possibilities, deepen customer insights, and explore new technologies to spark the changes that can get them — and keep them — on top.

THE FOUR KEY STAGES OF HOW INFLECTION POINTS UNFOLD

There are four basic stages in the development of inflection points: hype, dismissive, emergent, and maturity. These are similar to the phases in the Gartner Hype Cycle methodology used to understand how technologies are commercialized.

In the earliest stage of a likely inflection point, the most productive thing you can do is to identify early warnings of what might be important and to pay attention. It is still too early to make big bets.

As things progress, the early stage gives way to the *hype stage*. At this point, pundits will start proclaiming that the entire world order is likely to be completely overturned. The result is often a bubble — believers invest heavily and a "land grab" mentality takes hold. The 2013–2016 run on blockchain currency like Bitcoin is a good example. Everybody charges into an emerging arena, each hoping for a small share of what they assume will be massive growth.

Academics who have studied this stage call it "capital market myopia." In a famous 1987 case study, William Sahlman and Howard Stevenson showed how dozens of entrants into the then emerging Winchester disk drive industry blew through a mountain of investment, each hoping for a small share of a vast market. Such phenomena occur when players make decisions that are individually sensible but fail to take into account the collective consequences of everybody making the same decision.

Like a Greek tragedy, the hype stage almost always ends in disaster — sometimes dramatically. This brings us to the *dismissive stage* in the life cycle, in which those who sat out the hype take an "I told you so" perspective, saying, "That's never going to happen." This stage, however, is often where the real opportunities lie. In the dismissive stage, a few of the initial entrants will have survived the shakeout and begun to set the foundation for major growth. They will be building viable business models, finding new customer needs to address, and potentially even beginning to make money. At this point, you should be thinking about some toehold investments, exploring where there might be opportunities, and giving the inflection point some emergent attention.

Dismissal is often followed by the much quieter but more "concrete" *emergent stage.* In this stage, those who are paying attention can clearly see how the inflection might change things. This is the point at which you need to generate lots of options that position you for whichever model will eventually emerge.

Finally, the inflection point comes into its own in the *maturity stage.* It is now obvious to everyone how it will change the world. Those who are not prepared will see their businesses go into decline. Hopefully, your organization will be well positioned to take advantage of the growth opportunities this stage represents.

Post-inflection, the change is incorporated into everyday life assumptions. Indeed, by this point there are plenty of people who have completely forgotten what things were like before the inflection took place. Your agenda now is to make sure you jettison resources that are no longer relevant and enjoy the growth that successfully transitioning through an inflection point can yield.

HOW THIS BOOK IS ORGANIZED

The first part of the book is about "seeing" inflection points coming. It describes how organizations can create the early warnings of a pending inflection point and then organize to take action on those insights. Chapter 1 builds on Andy Grove's observation that "snow melts first at the periphery" to describe how agile, responsive organizations create fast, horizontal flows of information so that decisions can be made quickly and responses to environmental challenges can be processed in real time. Chapter 2 describes how you can create your own early-warning system, which can help you not only spot a pending moment of inflection but also decide when the right time to act is, a key strategic decision.

Chapter 3 offers a point of view about the elements of strategy creation and its integration with the innovation agenda of an organization.

It also shows how people at every level in the hierarchy can provide value to the creation and execution of a strategy. Given the pace and speed of change, strategy creation is no longer an activity that is confined to the executive team. Rather, it is an effort to galvanize the entire organization to act around a common point of view about the future.

The second part of the book explores how organizations can create opportunity in the face of a major inflection. Chapter 4 describes mechanisms to home in on customer arenas, which are often invisible to those hemmed in by traditional industry-focused logic. An arena consists of a customer's "job to be done" at a specific time and location and shows how you can become the provider of choice to help customers succeed, and do so at a profit.

Chapter 5 shows how you can release constraints on customers that keep them stuck in an unsatisfying experience, allowing them to flee previous solutions and flock to yours. Chapter 6 illustrates a way to plan ahead to the capture of opportunities by generating many hypotheses and dismissing many of them quickly. In this chapter, you will learn the critical importance of falling in love with a problem faced by your customers, rather than settling on a particular solution. In design terms, this is the difference between helping people who are tired of standing and designing a chair. The first concept allows far greater room for your imagination.

The third part of the book is a general guide to personally managing in high-velocity, high-uncertainty environments full of potential inflection points. The challenge is often not seeing a change coming. (*Fortune* called out the potential of Amazon in 1996!) The challenge is doing the transformational work required to rewire the organization. This is equivalent to the "innovator's dilemma" — the very systems and processes that served you well pre–inflection point can be the biggest barriers when you need to transform.

Chapter 7 describes the way in which organizational systems resist responding to a nascent inflection point and what levers change agents can use to shift them. This chapter also examines how imminent failure, or actual failure, can coax an otherwise unwilling organization to make the changes needed for its own self-preservation. Chapter 8 focuses on the behaviors of leaders in ambiguous and uncertain environments and offers examples of how you need to get beyond the "command-and-control" mindset and move toward a very different kind of leadership behavior.

Finally, Chapter 9 ties the idea of organizational and systems inflection points to how you can leverage them for your benefit in your personal life. It makes the point that an inflection at the level of society or a large organization has ripple effects that touch your personal life in meaningful ways.

Although it is quite normal to be apprehensive about a strategic inflection that changes major aspects of our lives, my hope is that as you proceed through this book, the excitement and opportunity of a major inflection point will also shine through.

Onward!

1

Snow Melts from the Edges

Christ, this guy has the fate of European democracy in his hands and he doesn't know what to do.

—Molly Scott Cato, British member of Parliament,
on Facebook CEO Mark Zuckerberg's testimony
before European lawmakers, May 23, 2018

If ever there was an inflection point worth anticipating, it would surely be the change in business assumptions spawned by the dominance of social media platforms. In short order, "social" has upended marketing, turned company and customer interactions into two-way streets, given previously obscure voices a platform, and connected databases that used to be safely separated, with outcomes that nobody anticipated.

Social media—whether it be Facebook, Google, Twitter, or others—had a difficult 2018. It included the spread of "fake news," false accounts, election and voter manipulation, the hijacking of online accounts, selling individuals' most personal information to third parties, racial profiling, allowing the impersonation of celebrities, and targeting vulnerable populations. Google, which failed to even send an executive to represent the company at congressional hearings, is facing all kinds of regulatory and business model pushback.

As a society, we are now collectively scratching our heads at how this all came to pass.

This chapter uses the rise and ongoing struggles of Facebook and other social media platforms to illustrate the dilemma of "seeing" the real implications of unfolding inflection points. Whether you are a powerful CEO or someone far lower down the food chain, blind spots are dangerous. Toward the end of the chapter, there is a discussion of practices that facilitate, as opposed to block, the early detection of such important signals. The central idea here comes from Andy Grove's prescient observation "When spring comes, snow melts first at the periphery, because that is where it is most exposed."

Evidence of an emerging inflection point doesn't present itself neatly on the conference table in the corporate boardroom. It is the people who are directly in contact with the phenomenon who usually notice changes early. It is the scientists who see where a technology is going and when it might shift. The salespeople who are talking to customers each and every day. The people on the customer service calls who are learning firsthand what's on customers' minds. The people who sound the alarm about something that is broken in a system. The people who have an uneasy feeling about the implications of an impending decision down the road.

These are the people — maybe you are one of them — who see it first and most clearly.

THE RISE OF SURVEILLANCE CAPITALISM

When I was young, the go-to source for important information was a reference book, like the *Encyclopaedia Britannica*. It kept its secrets about what I read in it, which sections got my attention and which didn't, and even who I was. Those who watch over reference books, librarians, are the custodians of human knowledge embedded in the materials in their care. They have long been admonished to maintain an ethic of "facilitating, not monitoring, access to information." Indeed, the right to privacy with regard to my utilization of library resources has been affirmed again and again in myriad court cases throughout the years. The risk of librarians being able to tell others about my personal interests was considered so great that it was actually addressed in their code of ethics.

Today, that perspective on privacy seems almost quaint. Indeed, the digital advertising business, in which firms such as Facebook and Google use what they know about their users to finely target advertisements, is huge. One estimate put the value of advertising channeled through these platforms at $88 billion in 2017. The business model underlying this vast revenue source is completely opaque to many who, data brokers argue, willingly give up their information to obtain the benefits of using these platforms for free. Most of us, however, are oblivious to the specifics of how our most personal data is being used in ways that were not economically or physically feasible before the digital revolution.

Unlocking the Secrets of Formerly Private Databases

Back in the days of before the digital revolution, information about people was stored in all kinds of places. The credit-scoring people knew about your financial transactions. The motor vehicles department knew about your driver's license and car ownership information. The criminal justice system knew about your arrest record, were you unfortunate enough to have one. Your doctors and medical providers knew about your health, medications, and any procedures you might have had. And so forth. But imagine if some kind of über-database could know and combine all this information to create a comprehensive picture including everything about you? Guess what? Not only does that capability exist, but hundreds of organizations are actively profiting from it.

In the pre-digital era, information about where you lived, how you drove, what diseases you had, what run-ins with the law you may have had, what you liked to spend your money on, and your political leanings were to some extent available to third parties with an interest in finding out. It was effortful and expensive, though, and the depth and quality of the information were often questionable. In contrast, today's data brokers can compare multiple databases against one another cheaply and at lightning speed. Further, as formerly manual databases are digitized, the cost of accessing these records drops dramatically.

Tim Sparapani, an expert on the data broker industry, says that most of us would be stunned to discover the amount of personally identifiable information about many of our most intimate behaviors that is freely available to anyone with the budget to buy it. And you don't even have to get to Facebook scale to benefit from people volunteering to share their information with you. A *60 Minutes* investigative broadcast in 2014 found that data brokers are perfectly happy to set up websites such as GoodParentingToday.com, whose "community" members offer specific details about their lives in response to questions such as "Are you expecting?," "Do you have adequate life insurance?," and "Do you have pets?"

What Take5 Solutions, the company behind this site and a whole bunch of others, *doesn't* tell you is that once you've told them something about yourself, they can cross-match the clues you've given them against other, massive databases that can fill out the picture in much more granular detail. Scarily, there is no particular protective consumer oversight about what information these organizations store or whom they are prepared to provide it to.

Individual databases on their own may contain innocuous information. But harness the power to combine them, and entirely unanticipated outcomes can occur. And we've known this for a long time. For instance, in 2009 researchers were able to predict individual Social Security numbers by combining data from different subsets — without a data breach and without accessing any privileged information. In a particularly sleazy new business model, websites such as Mugshots .com make people's arrest photos available online, without regard to whether the person was ultimately found guilty or convicted, and then charge these people hundreds of dollars to have the photos removed from the site. Thousands of people have reported having their job prospects and personal lives disrupted by such disclosures. Law enforcement has found it extremely difficult to prosecute the operators of these businesses, which are essentially accountable to no one.

Traveling Amidst the Throng

When logging on to a website, most of us think we're just, well, logging on to that website. What we don't realize is that third parties with whom we may not have any relationship at all are watching us, tracking our movements and capturing that information in their own databases. They know how we move through the site, what we click on, what we read, what we skip over, and combining this information with what is already in our dossiers, they can create a much richer view of who we are.

And while this is pretty much an open secret, the average person seems to have no idea that telling any website anything may put that information out there in the public domain.

Moreover, just logging on to the Internet creates a digital footprint that tells interested parties about your online behavior. While users are dimly aware that websites track them using cookies, what many are not aware of is what are called "third-party cookies." For instance, if you log on to a news site and that site has a Facebook "like" button on it, a cookie is placed on your computer that Facebook can access. So even if you have never visited Facebook or don't have an account, the social network still receives information about what you've been doing on the web. So much for all those folks who say, *I don't have a Facebook account, why should I worry about the network having my data?*

Social media leaders promised, promised, and promised some more that tracking people all over the Internet would stop and that users would be put back in control of where their information would show up and with whom it would be shared. In 2019, Katherine Bindley, a *Wall Street Journal* reporter, thought she would just test out how well the companies were doing in keeping their promises. She downloaded What to Expect's pregnancy app, and, as she reports, "in less than 12 hours, I got a maternity-wear ad in my Instagram feed. I'm not pregnant, nor otherwise in a target market for maternity-wear. When I tried to retrace the pathway, discussing the issue with the app's publisher, its data partners, the advertiser and Facebook itself—dozens of emails and phone calls—not one would draw a connection between the two events." She goes on to elaborate on the many ways in which companies breach people's privacy without their knowledge, including tracking their locations when location services are turned off, using secretive algorithms that govern why people see certain ads, and showing users ads based on activity that takes place outside of Facebook even if they opted out of Facebook being allowed to do this.

In an even more disturbing study (if that is possible), another *Wall Street Journal* inquiry found that health and wellness apps were sharing highly personal information with Facebook. In their testing, they found that a heart rate app sent information to Facebook immediately after users keyed it in, an ovulation monitoring app sent information about when a user was having her period and whether she intended to get pregnant, and a real estate app sent data about what homes a user was looking at and which the user marked as favorites. Even worse, as the authors note, "none of those apps provided users any apparent way to stop that information from being sent to Facebook." And even worse than that, the data can often be traced to a specific device and IP address, making it possible for Facebook to match it up against its existing trove of personal information, all for the benefit of advertisers who are willing to pay for targeted ads.

There is clearly a huge gap between the data sharing people think they are permitting and what is really going on.

Your Environment Is Watching You

Most of us know that the Internet is a bit of a Wild West when it comes to our privacy, and we can only hope that our information doesn't leak out to the wrong people. But what about when the rest of our world starts to take on Internet-like tracking?

The *New York Times* reported in 2018 that in millions of households, so-called smart televisions are set up to track what you're watching, and not only that, they also track information from all the other devices (such as a smartphone) that are linked to the same network as your TV. Samba TV, for instance, as part of its smart-TV setup process, asks for permission to send information about you back to its mother ship. That includes not only information about your viewing habits but also all the information flowing through any other device connected to the same network.

This is a holy grail for advertisers, because they can capture immediate information about the effectiveness of television ads based on subsequent visits to their sites by people being tracked in this way. As Christine DiLandro, a former marketing director at Citi, discussed at an industry event, the ability to connect people's real-time viewing behavior with their digital activity is "a little magical." Companies can pay Samba to target individuals with specific pitches after viewers have seen a competitor's ad, one of their own ads, or a particular show. And this is all perfectly legal, as long as the companies can claim to have provided consumers with information that accurately describes the tracking — even if it is buried in a thousand-page acceptance policy.

For the 47.3 million people with access to a smart speaker like Alexa or Siri, it's a guarantee that the device is listening elsewhere in their homes. And in incident after incident, it is very clear that the speakers are collecting and capturing data in the background of our lives. For instance, an Amazon Echo recorded private conversations between a husband and wife in Seattle and sent snippets of the recordings to an acquaintance hundreds of miles away. More and more for the dossier.

FAST, EXPONENTIAL, AND UNCHECKED: FACEBOOK'S RISE AND . . . ?

As an example of the challenges likely to face all the big advertising-supported social media platforms, let's focus in on Facebook. From its founding in 2004 as an online social network at Harvard (and soon other colleges and universities) to its current ability to reach over a third of the world's population, Facebook's growth has been exponential and its influence eye-popping. Its attitude toward its use of personal data, however, has not changed much since the start. Its blind spot was failing to recognize that eventually the public, regulators, competitors, and others would catch on to what the social network was doing.

Signs of what we could expect from Facebook with respect to privacy were available from the beginning, as the following instant message exchange between Mark Zuckerberg and a friend, first exposed by the podcast *Silicon Valley Insider*, reveal.

> **Zuck:** Yeah so if you ever need info about anyone at Harvard
> **Zuck:** Just ask.
> **Zuck:** I have over 4,000 emails, pictures, addresses, SNS [Social Security numbers]
> **[Redacted Friend's Name]:** What? How'd you manage that one?
> **Zuck:** People just submitted it.

Zuck: I don't know why.
Zuck: They "trust me"
Zuck: Dumb fucks.

When the network was opened up to people outside academic institutions in 2006, the company's leaders reportedly began to think of it as "the directory of all the people in the world," which they hoped would "dominate."

Fast-forward to Facebook's IPO in 2012, when, as one observer noted, the pressure to make money from Facebook's vast number of users became intense, precipitating its forays into targeted ads. This was only the beginning of a series of well-documented mishaps basically stemming from Facebook's unprecedented ability to mine user information and provide automated access to advertisers.

By 2016, the signals that the use of certain types of targeting were unacceptable became so loud that you would have needed earplugs to avoid hearing them. In just one egregious example, Facebook allowed advertisers of housing to prevent the ads from being shown to members of "affinity" groups such as African Americans, Asian Americans, and Hispanics. When ProPublica broke the story (after buying an ad in the housing category that specifically excluded ethnic affiliations), a prominent civil rights lawyer said, "This is horrifying. This is massively illegal. This is about as blatant a violation of the federal Fair Housing Act as one can find."

In a Faustian bargain, consumers have accepted that they can get services for free by agreeing to hand over personal information. The result is an entirely lopsided economic arrangement. What started out as a relatively modest and fun idea (*Share pictures of your friends! Share photos from your vacation!*) has now become a social force, fueled by billions of advertising dollars.

Other data brokers pursue problematic practices as well. Google, for instance, has run afoul of the EU, which fined the company $5 billion for practices such as requiring manufacturers to preload Google apps on their devices and to sell only unaltered versions of Google's Android software. Unlike Google's leaders, who don't deny the data collection but argue that it creates "more choices for everyone," Facebook's key executives have professed shock and ignorance at how the data that users have placed in their care have been deployed.

Facebook's CEO has now been hauled before elected representatives on two continents. The company's response to the Cambridge Analytica revelations has been critiqued in terms of poor crisis response. That scandal involved the company selling information on over 50 million people without their knowledge for the purpose of targeting political ads. A mini-movement of people who want to abandon its ecosystem has emerged. Pundits are now saying that Facebook might well go the way of Myspace. And even luminaries such as Apple cofounder Steve Wozniak and Brian Acton, founder of WhatsApp, declared #DeleteFacebook.

Social media companies face a significant inflection point, with Zuckerberg declaring that his company is "at war." Billionaire investor George Soros went so far as to announce at the 2018 World Economic Forum meeting in Davos, Switzerland, that Facebook's "days are numbered."

THE CASSANDRAS OF THE
PERSONAL DATA BUSINESS

We can't say Facebook wasn't warned.

As I have found with virtually every major inflection point I've studied, there was early evidence of this one's potential long before it landed on our doorsteps. Let's examine the early signs that are particularly relevant to Facebook (while recognizing that the whole data brokerage/social media space is likely to be affected).

Observers have long considered a significant risk of the World Wide Web to be how information on it could be used. Indeed, in 1996 no less a luminary than web inventor Tim Berners-Lee wondered about the effects of the Net:

> Will it enable a true democracy by informing the voting public of the realities behind state decisions, or in practice will it harbor ghettos of bigotry where emotional intensity rather than truth

gains the readership? It is for us to decide, but it is not trivial to assess the impact of simple engineering decisions on the answers to such questions.

Facebook and Google didn't even exist at the time this futuristic question was raised. Both, however, were growing rapidly when a now prescient warning was issued in 2006. Danah Boyd, a technology and social media scholar, and a principal researcher at Microsoft, warned about the privacy dangers represented by Facebook's News Feed feature. She observed at the time that although individual bits of data were readily obtainable by those looking for them, News Feed created feelings of exposure, in that information users had provided to the website was now being pushed to everyone they were connected to, in a way that they had not anticipated. This isn't helped by Facebook's blunt characterization of who counts as a "friend." By lumping together everyone from the guy you see regularly at the coffee shop to actual friends and family, Facebook makes it difficult to be selective about who sees what. This contributes to what Boyd called a feeling of "invasion."

As she said then about News Feed, "It is unhealthy, socially disruptive, and far worse for the users than the lurking employers ready to strike down upon thee with great vengeance for the mere presence of a red plastic cup . . . I also think that it will be gamed." Poignantly, Boyd's warnings had to do with information users knowingly shared with Facebook. Even she wasn't thinking about the use to which private data could be put when bought and sold. Her warnings went largely unheeded as the company grew exponentially. The torrid rate at which Facebook added users continued unabated.

Another series of warnings that went unheeded were about the presence of bad actors on the platform. These people created fake accounts, initiated scams, and otherwise weaponized the relationships people established there. The presence of fakes was so pervasive that a 2011 article in *Adweek* advised people on "7 Surefire Signs Your New Facebook Friend Is a Fake." Facebook's assumption that requiring users to sign up with their real names would be a deterrent seems to have been wrong.

More interesting than the warnings of outside observers such as Boyd were the calls to action from Facebook insiders. They warned that the data the company was collecting could be used for purposes no user ever intended. Sandy Parakilas, a platform operations manager at the network from 2011 to 2012, said in a 2018 televised interview that he told senior leaders at Facebook about inadequate protections for the sensitive data users had given it, but that he was basically ignored.

As he said in the interview, "It was a few weeks before the IPO, and the press had been calling out these issues over and over again . . . pointing out the ways in which Facebook had not been meeting its obligations." He went on to describe how "horrified" he was to discover that he, just nine months into his first job in tech, was responsible for the security of Facebook's user data. As he observed, "They were not concerned about solving the problem, they were concerned about protecting their reputations inside the company."

In a growing chorus, ex–Facebook employees have taken issue with the societal effects of the platform. Chamath Palihapitiya, a former Facebook executive, has bemoaned the addictive nature of what Facebook has created, blaming it for "ripping apart society."

Some ex–tech executives have gone even further than issuing verbal critiques. In founding the Center for Humane Technology in 2018, former executives at places like Google and Facebook were trying to create a unified institutional response to what they see as the negative social consequences of social media addiction.

THE BEGINNING OF A TIPPING POINT?

It has been in the interest of the data collectors to keep people in the dark, legally covering their behavior with terms of service that run into the thousands of words. Today, data brokers can cavalierly buy and sell your most personal information (Do you smoke? Are you gay? Do you like the 50 Shades series?), virtually without oversight, and most of us don't even know it. With the sight of company executives being hauled before Congress, the introduction of the General Data

Protection Regulation (GDPR) in Europe, and ever more examples of how personal data in the wrong hands produces horrible outcomes, I believe we will look back at this time as a major inflection point in how the use of personal information is governed.

Antonio García Martínez has his thumb on the pulse of the problem. In his Silicon Valley tell-all, *Chaos Monkeys,* he describes how he helped create the third-party advertising programs that follow users all around the Internet. His jaundiced perspective on Facebook limiting how its data is used? "The hard reality is that Facebook will never try to limit such use of their data unless the public uproar reaches such a crescendo as to be un-mutable."

There are many signs that such an uproar has arrived. In a 2016 report of Americans' attitudes about data privacy, the TRUSTe/National Cyber Security Alliance (NCSA) Consumer Privacy Index found that more people were worried about privacy than about losing their primary source of income.

Governments, likewise, are waking up. According to the *New York Times,* no fewer than fifty governments have put measures in place to claw back access. Once technology platforms became networks for peer-to-peer communication, free from governmental constraints, governments began to feel threatened and to respond accordingly. Indeed, Facebook has been banned in China since 2009 (after it was thought to have played a role in communication among protesters) despite a major charm offensive, including Mark Zuckerberg's learning to speak Mandarin.

It is also not inconceivable that in exchange for permission to continue to operate at all, governments might insist that Facebook be split up. With growth in its core News Feed platform flattening and all the growth taking place on WhatsApp and Instagram, that would be very bad news indeed for Facebook's business. With data being characterized as the "new oil," analogies are being made to the breakup of the big oil companies in the early 1900s, or to the innovation that blossomed in the 1980s after AT&T could no longer exercise monopoly power over what services and equipment consumers could buy.

Government officials are also starting to use legal mechanisms to throttle the business models of so-called smart-TV manufacturers that use services such as Samba to pad their thin margins.

Even more serious for Facebook in particular is its declining attractiveness to its own current and prospective employees. In late 2018, only about half said that they felt the company was making the world better, and 52 percent said that the company was on the right track. Another report said that many employees were turning to outside contacts to find work at other organizations.

Another big challenge to Facebook's business model is competition. While it has a deep and sticky relationship with its users, it doesn't make money from them. It makes money by selling information about them to advertisers. And the information is all indirect — who you are, what you like, what you click on, and so forth. Imagine how much more powerful advertising on a platform such as Amazon could be. Not only does Amazon have a lot of information — much of it far less creepy than what Facebook collects — but it also knows what you actually buy. Observers expect Amazon to siphon off a fair amount of traffic from both Google and Facebook as it leverages the information it has to provide advertisements users can quickly turn into purchases.

Competition might also emerge for Facebook from other platforms. Just to speculate, the founders of Instagram left the company in 2018 after reported disagreements with other company officials. In a statement that would give me pause if I were on the management team, Kevin Systrom, Instagram's cofounder, said he was looking forward to starting "something new." Think about it: Here's a guy who has already created a hugely popular social media channel, out in the wild. And unlike other founders whose companies are likely to be vulnerable to being acquired by Facebook, its normal anticompetitive activity, Systrom is not likely to be tempted by any dollars Facebook might dangle in front of him.

So my basic argument is this: the inflection point has arrived for Facebook and other advertising-fueled data-gathering organizations. The company and its peers may yet figure out how to maneuver through the inflection, but we can be fairly certain that they will look quite different as this movement unfolds.

INSIGHT FROM THE EDGES: EIGHT
WAYS TO ADDRESS BLIND SPOTS

Facebook is at a pivotal moment. As of this writing, the network, with its more than 2 billion active users, $40 billion in revenue (2017), and ubiquitous presence virtually everywhere on the Internet, seems unassailable. And yet, giants have fallen before. The failure to see the storm clouds coming plays a huge role in a lurch toward irrelevance. Consider Nokia.

In 2007, it had a 49.4 percent share globally of the smartphone market. Its CEO was on the cover of *Forbes* in November, accompanied by the headline "Nokia: A Billion Customers — Can Anyone Catch the Cell Phone King?" And yet, the early warnings of its collapse were already in place since the introduction of Apple's iPhone and the commercialization of the Android platform earlier that year.

I know, because I was working closely with the company in the early 2000s. I started to get emails from people in the know, saying that the bean counters had taken over at Nokia and the talented folks who used to be so close to the market were being squashed. That even though I held in my hand a device that would be recognizable today as an Internet-connected tablet, no customer would ever see it. And, most dispiritingly, that the venturing and growth processes that I and others had worked so hard to put in place were being dismantled. Nokia's leadership had lost touch with the edges — with the places in which negative inflection points for their business were gathering force. A similar success-fueled ignorance seems rife at Facebook.

Facebook's data collection and targeting practices have led to extraordinarily troubling outcomes. And if spokespeople for the company are to be believed, this has all come as a terrible, terrible shock.

Leaving aside cynicism about such claims, we can identify a consistent pattern of ignoring external concerns that characterizes challenges for Facebook. Whether Facebook eventually extends its competitive advantage (as it has done before, with the acquisitions of fast-growing WhatsApp and Instagram) or not, it's clear that its leaders would have preferred not to be "at war" in 2018.

In the next chapter, I'll introduce a methodology for spotting and interpreting weak signals that things may be changing. Here, I focus on how you can detect those signals before the news is obvious to everyone, using some examples from the Facebook saga to illustrate.

BEING PRESENT AT THE EDGES

If snow melts from the edges, it behooves you to have mechanisms in place to see what is going on there. This is a prescription widely made by futurists, such as Amy Webb in her brilliant book *The Signals Are Talking*. And yet, when I consider how many executives I work with spend their time, getting to the edges is one of the last things on their agenda. Citing the pressures of the day-to-day, the need to deliver to the current quarter, or even a lack of concern because of tremendous ongoing success, they stay safely at headquarters and surround themselves with internal team members.

Consider, then, the following eight practices that can help you make sure there isn't something brewing at the periphery of your organization that could have an explosive impact on the company before you realize it.

1. Create Mechanisms That Direct Information Flows from the Corner Office to the Street Corner

A very common reason that leaders miss potentially important inflection points is that they are isolated from the people who could tell them what is really going on. By closing themselves off from critical communication with people who may disagree or who may have different vantage points, such leaders develop a false sense of what is going on in the world.

This seems to be part of the story at Facebook. At this highly successful company, it isn't surprising that its leaders have kept to a fairly narrow circle. These leaders, many of whom have been at the organization for a decade or more, have often described the senior team as a "family." On the positive side, they report strong, trusting ties and relationships of long standing that allow the company to move fast. One indication that the inflection point has arrived for Facebook is that many members of this tight-knit team have announced their departures.

Some observers, however, have not been so complimentary about this cozy arrangement. One has said that "Mark Zuckerberg is surrounded by sycophants and people who think just like him; that he's unaware of the negative impact his company has had on the world." Some have gone so far as to argue that Facebook is "cult-like," a workplace in which dissent is discouraged — a surefire recipe for creating blind spots.

Organizations looking for the early warnings of an inflection point have practices in place that allow the information and trends bubbling up far away from headquarters to be seen and heard. One practice is the deliberate creation of information flows that reach directly from leaders' offices to the front lines of the business. This can take many forms. When Lou Gerstner was running IBM, he spent his first months in office visiting customers and talking to frontline employees to get a feel for what was really going on. In a very hierarchical system, he drove staffers crazy by organizing "deep dive" sessions to which participants were invited depending on how much information they had, regardless of their hierarchical level.

Level-skipping conversations are another source of unfiltered information. One practice I've observed is a leader who regularly invites various employees, chosen at random by a computer program, to breakfast. Another, famously in use at Citibank's credit card division, is to regularly ask leaders to report on one insight they have learned from an actual customer that month.

The key here is to provide a methodical but organizationally safe way for those with decision rights to get exposed to what is changing at the interface between the organization and its external environment.

2. Make Sure You Are Leveraging Diversity of Thought

For better or worse, human beings draw their expectations about the world from their own frames of reference. Facebook's founding team, and its initial sets of users, had not just a collegiate frame of reference, but an Ivy League one at that. This led to their missing the implications of what could be done with their platform once all of humanity —

with different cultural norms, different institutional expectations, and different motivations — had access to it.

Or, put more bluntly by Anil Dash, a blogging pioneer and the first employee of Six Apart, the creator of Movable Type: "If you are twenty-six years old, you've been a golden child, you've been wealthy all your life, you've been privileged all your life, you've been successful your whole life, of course you don't think anybody would ever have anything to hide."

Lack of imagination and the inability to see how other people might take advantage of a situation in a way that you never would is a typical blind spot. For instance, the optimistic souls behind the LinkNYC project, an effort to put abandoned pay phone booths to better use, created public places to access the Internet in them. In the minds of the project's founders, the terminals would be used by tourists looking for local information, by people tracking down good restaurants, and for other relatively benign purposes. Imagine their dismay when reports started to come in of people watching porn on the street, setting up outdoor living rooms around the terminals, and using them in conjunction with other unsavory conduct!

Ask yourself: Am I inviting diverse viewpoints into our discussions? Are we listening to people whose life experiences and views are different from our own? Are we all homing in on one scenario to the detriment of even being able to imagine others?

3. Balance Type 1 and Type 2 Decisions: Empower Agility but Create Balance

Amazon founder and CEO Jeff Bezos has famously observed that there are two basic decisions that an organization needs to make. What he calls type 1 decisions are those that have huge implications for the organization, are potentially highly risky, and are irreversible. Type 2 decisions, in contrast, are reversible, low risk, and rich in learning potential. A well-documented success at Amazon is Bezos's use of small teams to act on type 2 decisions.

This approach reflects the popularity of "agile" methods as an alternative to conventional bureaucracy. One principle is that teams should be small and empowered to make decisions about low-risk activities under their control. At Amazon, Bezos instituted his famous "two pizza rule," meaning that no team should be so large that it could not be adequately fed by two pizzas. In his view, a team of ten, perhaps twelve people is as large as teams should get, since they don't require much coordination and can work together fluidly. He also describes delegating authority in making type 2 decisions. Such decisions, Bezos argues, should not have to be made under the heavy scrutiny of corporate bureaucracy.

As an example of how this feels, consider this description of the difference between an agile, connected team and conventional corporate action. In 2015, consultants Chris Zook and James Allen of Bain & Company observed the practices of John Donahoe, the CEO of eBay. Donahoe regularly convened meetings with employees who were under thirty (who often came in through acquisitions). One of them, Jack Abraham, had an idea for a major redesign of the company's web page. Donahoe told him to figure out what resources he needed to make it happen. Abraham took the five best developers out for drinks one night and convinced them to take a two-week trip to Australia the next day to work on a prototype. Donahoe was blown away. "Had we asked a normal product team," he said, "I would have gotten back hundreds of PowerPoint slides and a two-year time frame and a budget of $40 million. Yet these guys went away, worked 24/7, and built a prototype. These guys build. They do no PowerPoint. They just build."

Empowered and trusted people at the front lines of a business are hugely important, which has been a big part of Home Depot's turnaround — after forgetting this most critical lesson for a while. The way *not* to achieve this goal is to hire a bunch of expensive consultants who talk to the people who actually know what's going on, and then have the consultants report back to the decision-makers what they heard!

I would argue that Facebook has gone overboard on the use of small, empowered teams to make decisions that in retrospect are actually of the type 1 variety. Consider the company's many hugely public mishaps, from the introduction of its advertising service Beacon, to the permissions and access granted to developers, to charges of emotional manipulation, to the Cambridge Analytica fiasco, to accusations of election meddling. The truth is, the "move fast and break things" mantra that serves organizations well for exploring and making type 2 decisions can be deadly in the execution of type 1 decisions. Facebook itself seems to have recognized the dangers of using type 2 processes when operating at the scale it does. In 2014, Zuckerberg announced the retirement of "move fast and break things" and instituted the implementation of "move fast with stable infra." While this was aimed at the developer community, I would argue it would have been useful to apply this discipline to the consequences of Facebook's external activities.

4. Instrument the Edges: Foster Little Bets

Facebook gets this one right. The recommendation follows Peter Sims's notion in his book *Little Bets*.

As another example, Adobe uses its Kickbox program to solicit ideas and input from people throughout the organization who normally wouldn't be heard at the strategy or innovation planning meetings. Their philosophy is that the most creative ideas can easily die fighting corporate bureaucracy for the chance to be discovered. Hence, the Kickbox — a red cardboard box with a "pull in case of ideas" graphic.

Inside is a set of instructions to "beat" the box, a Bic pen, two sets of Post-it notes, a timer, a Staples mini-notebook for "bad ideas," a slightly larger spiral notebook, a World Market caramel and sea salt chocolate bar, and a $10 Starbucks gift card. The latter two because all good innovations depend on a steady stream of sugar and caffeine. One thing that distinguishes the Kickbox from suggestion boxes or innovation boot camps is that it also comes with a $1,000 prepaid Citi card that employees can spend however they like, without ever justifying any purchase to a manager or filing an expense report.

The idea of Kickbox was developed by Adobe chief strategist and vice president of creativity Mark Randall. In the midst of the company's transition from shrink-wrapped-on-premises software to a cloud-based offering, Randall took advantage of this major shift to take a hard look at how Adobe brought new ideas to the surface. He used a best practice for getting insight from the edges — in this case, interviewing dozens of employees to find out what obstacles were in the way of their pursuing promising ideas based on insights that they might uniquely have about customers and next steps.

What he found is consistent with my thesis here: Often, the big problem was not coming up with interesting ideas. The problem was fighting one's way through the bureaucracy to get the approvals necessary to move forward. Randall had a world-class insight: for the price of funding just one $1 million project, he could fund one thousand $1,000 little bets. Any employee can request a Kickbox, and there are no deadlines or penalties if the idea doesn't pan out. Participants are urged (but not required) to attend a two-day course that teaches them about some of the basics of vetting an idea and nurturing it, such as gauging customer interest. The curriculum that comes with a Kickbox consists of six levels, each of which has its own suggested next steps and a few questions. Complete all the levels, and you "beat the box."

Of the roughly one thousand people to have obtained a Kickbox so far, relatively few have made it to the next level, although Adobe credits insights developed through the Kickbox program as instrumental in its acquisition of the content company Fotolia for $800 million. Some twenty-three Kickboxers have, however, made it all the way through the six levels. At that point, they have everything they need to sell management on their idea and to receive a prized *blue* Kickbox. The contents of the blue box are a mystery, but that transition represents a journey from the edges of the organization (the red box) to key decision-making roles (the blue box).

Adobe has, moreover, made the Kickbox program open-source, so that other organizations can give it a try.

5. Get out of the Building

Whatever their motivations, it is relatively clear that what might have begun with good intentions on the part of the data marketing firms has had any number of unintended consequences. I would assume that Facebook never intended its targeting to extend to political manipulation or tyrannical citizen suppression. But the inability to see how things work "in the field" creates blind spots that can be readily exploited by bad actors.

Alert leaders make it a point to personally connect with the external environment, looking for what is changing and how. As serial entrepreneur, educator, and inventor of the "customer discovery" process Steve Blank is fond of saying, "There are no answers in the building." His encouragement is for everyone in the organization to get out and find inspiration and ideas from customers outside their normal interactions. This is complicated because frontline employees often unintentionally hide information from their leaders in a misplaced effort to give a good impression.

In a *New York Times* story that is ostensibly about worker hours, you can see how this happens. The main point of the story is that the Gap had seen some business benefits from offering workers more stable and predictable hours. Not all managers, it reported, were finding this to be easy. Indeed, one store manager said that he had "probably extended two to three shifts every day in the run up to the visit" by an executive.

Let that sink in for a minute. The laudable effort on the part of the executive to experience his organization's contact with customers in the field was completely undermined by the manager's decision. The store he was experiencing was not the one that customers normally encountered, but one with staffing levels significantly higher than were budgeted for. No wonder the leader overlooked the signals that all might not be well: there was no opportunity to see them at all. Not that the store manager was to blame. In many company cultures, this would be standard operating procedure. It's kind of like straightening up the living room when you are expecting guests. We all know the living room doesn't usually look like that!

Another example of this pitfall is an executive from a wireless telecom company who attended one of my classes. At the time, the company was famous for spotty coverage and generally poor network performance in many parts of the country. He mentioned to me that one of their executives from headquarters (which happened to be in Europe) was going to be coming to the United States the following week. I asked him, "How do your executives react to the poor quality of the service here in the States?" He responded, "Oh, they don't have those problems. We know their itineraries, the routes they take to get from place to place, and where they'll be working. Our technical guys always make sure that the signals they get are nice and strong and that they don't have those problems. After all, they have work to get done while they are here." Once again, a deliberate, if unintentional, decision to shield decision-makers from the reality of how their organization feels to its customers.

The encouragement here is to make sure that you don't disappear into the safe spaces at corporate headquarters, but instead let yourself experience direct exposure to what is actually going on in the connection between your customers and your organization.

Another way of guaranteeing that this will happen is to put leaders in a position where running into customers occurs naturally. For instance, consider moving your desk to be near where the action is, or make a point of being present when critical conversations are taking place.

A number of "get out of the building type" exercises can be very helpful here. One I like is borrowed from my colleagues at Solve Next and is called Brand Takeover. Basically, what you do is imagine that your organization was taken over by a different one. Then you ask yourself: What would they have you start doing? Stop doing? If you had vastly more marketing money to spend, how would they want you to spend it? Just imagining that you are part of an entirely different organization can be immensely liberating.

6. Create Incentives That Reveal Useful, If Awkward, Information

Given that Facebook's business model relies on selling personal information, it isn't surprising that reports that this process was deeply flawed were not exactly welcomed with open arms. Facebook executives simply did not want to listen. These executives brusquely dismissed questions regarding privacy, arguing that users "gave their consent."

As NPR's Aarti Shahani observed, a real issue for Facebook is putting engagement of users ahead of any other metric. "People who've worked at Facebook say that from Day 1, executives have been fixated on measuring engagement: how much you like, click, share, up to what second you watch a video," she reported. "In product meetings, current and former employees say, any suggestion to tweak News Feed – Facebook's signature product – must include a deep analysis of how that would increase or decrease engagement. This dogged focus on metrics is also apparent from the company's own blog posts and research."

The lesson here is that powerful business incentives can thwart the willingness to take in and absorb uncomfortable lessons. Indeed, when not carefully designed, powerful executive incentives can lead to results that nobody wants. Consider Enron, the disgraced energy trading company. Even as its business performance destroyed shareholder value, it lavished massive rewards on executives, which in turn incentivized them to keep bumping up the stock price, which in turn ultimately led to not only unsavory but illegal behavior.

It is worth remembering that it is entirely possible for companies to cease operations if what they are doing is found to be illegal. Consider, for instance, Aereo, a startup that attempted to resell broadcast television shows over the Internet. A coalition of powerful plaintiffs were so wound up about the company's business model that they sued it, in a case that went all the way to the US Supreme Court. Facebook has by now attracted so many lawsuits that it actually mentions them in a special note in its quarterly Securities and Exchange Commission report.

7. Avoid Denial

While there is no shortage of evidence that something is seriously wrong at Facebook, the company's public statements continually downplay just how bad things are. From its comments denying that anyone could think the platform could have influenced the 2016 presidential election to a later defense of the right of Holocaust deniers to spread their stories on the platform, there seems to be little genuine willingness to take responsibility for the use of Facebook for immoral, if not illegal, ends. This is doubly interesting because 2010 research done by Facebook itself showed that the social network had a big impact in turning out voters in the midterm elections.

This type of behavior is not new. Leaders turn a blind eye quite deliberately because it is just more convenient not to take in news that things might be changing. For instance, when Robert S. Apatoff, CEO of the iconic mapmaker Rand McNally, was interviewed in 2006, he basically dismissed the likely effects of the digital revolution:

> Anyone who thinks old-fashioned folded maps are going away should think again, according to Apatoff. "It's kind of like saying newspapers are going to disappear," he said in an interview at the company's headquarters north of Chicago. "There's going to be some changes in how they're used, but people still want to open them and read them with their coffee. Same thing with trip

planning. People will continue to want to be able to consume maps this way," he said, even if they use maps or atlases together with hand-held devices or the Internet.

Rand McNally was acquired by distressed-asset investment firm Patriarch Partners in 2007.

8. Talk to the Future That Is Unfolding Now

According to a quote widely attributed to science fiction writer William Ford Gibson, "The future is already here — it's just not very evenly distributed." One of my colleagues at the consultancy Innosight, Scott Anthony, has turned this concept into a practical prescription: Identify the places where you could go to talk to representatives of the future.

For instance, if you want to know how the twentysomethings of ten years from now will be looking at the world, you can be absolutely certain that you could have a conversation with the ten-year-olds of today. If you are interested in cutting-edge developments in almost any sector, there are bound to be conferences at which people present their ideas at an early stage.

For instance, one of my colleagues at Columbia University, Frank Rose, runs an amazing program called the Digital Storytelling Lab, dedicated to exploring how digital technologies are influencing the stories and experiences we share with one another. Among the lab's initiatives is the Digital Dozen competition, in which awards are given to people who have engaged in developing "innovative approaches to narrative." Frank's reason for creating the competition was his belief that each revolution in human communication takes about twenty years to assume its mature shape. He has observed, for example, that when moving pictures were first commercialized, nobody knew what a "movie" was. So what did they do? They filmed stage plays! I would make a similar observation about online education. We don't know what it really is yet, so we film professors talking at the front of the classroom. This is highly unlikely to be where the new medium takes us, but we don't yet know what that will look like, and so experimentation and trial and error are essential.

With movies, it wasn't until many years had passed that the elements of what we would consider absolutely normal aspects of the moviemaking business became standard practice. Filming out of sequence, using different camera angles to capture a similar scene, cutting and editing, and myriad other techniques were still to come when moving pictures were first invented.

The Digital Dozen competition pulls together digital works that, at the moment, defy classification. One contestant for the 2018 awards featured a hilarious series of ads and montages by the direct-mail processing company Mailchimp. Mispronunciations of its name are brought to life in montages such as "Mail Shrimp" (featuring a singing shrimp sandwich in a post office) and "Kale Limp" (showing kale-covered puppy dogs), all done with hugely immersive video and sound, and reflected in real-life billboards and other concepts, such as "Fail Chips," which tie the messaging together.

Another entry immersed the viewer in the experience of visiting the US-Mexico border. Yet another was a cartoon-based project exploring what it was like to be in the Danish secret service in World War II. And so on. Don't take my word for it; visit the Digital Dozen website at http://digitaldozen.io/2018-awards/ for an eye-opening look at the future of digital communications and storytelling.

The main point here is that the future doesn't just happen all at once. It begins to unfold unevenly. If you can "interview" where it is starting to take place now, you can begin to develop an early point of view on it.

SOMETIMES CASSANDRA IS ONTO SOMETHING

The still unfolding drama around Facebook's utilization of personal data to support its business practices continues to draw out the dangers of failing to pay attention to what is going on at the edges of your organization. It also highlights the importance of paying attention to those who are directly in contact with the emerging inflection point, as they may be in the best position to help you understand it.

If you are one of those people on the edges, keep this thought: *Your time may be coming sooner than you think.* Sitting ringside at a change that is about to unfold can give you tremendous insight into what actions to take now, before the outcome is obvious to everyone.

Key Takeaways

Snow melts from the edges. The changes that are going to fundamentally influence the future of your business are brewing on the periphery. To avoid being taken by surprise by an inflection point, you need to be exposed to what is happening at the edges.

The upheavals created by major strategic inflection points usually take quite some time to unfold. They are also not "complete" when you first see them. But if you are paying attention, you can begin to see the implications of their trajectory early on, when it is still possible to influence them.

Eight practices can help you make sure you are seeing what is going on along the edges.

1. Ensure direct connection between the people at the edges of your company and the people making strategy.
2. Go out of your way to include diverse perspectives in thinking about the implications of the future.
3. Use deliberate decision-making processes for consequential and irreversible (type 1) decisions. Use small, agile, empowered teams for reversible (type 2) experimental decisions.
4. Foster little bets that are rich in learning, ideally distributed across the organization.
5. Pursue direct contact with the environment—"get out of the building."
6. Make sure your people are incentivized to hear about reality, not the reverse.
7. Realize when your people are in denial.
8. Expose yourself and your organization to where the future is unfolding today.

You do not need to be a CEO to see how an inflection is likely to unfold. In fact, you are probably more likely to see it the closer you are to the external trends that make your business possible.

2

Early Warnings

There are far more possible catastrophes than
will actually happen.

— Patrick Marren, principal, Futures Strategy Group

Weak or faint signals of an impending shift, when recognized early, can give you a head start to prepare to take advantage of a coming inflection point.

An inflection point occurs when a change — what some people call a 10X change — upends the basic assumptions that a business model is built on. When the moment of crystal clarity arrives, that is the moment to mobilize the troops, to bring focus, and to bear down hard on preparing the organization for the post-inflection world.

This chapter is not about what happens *after* that moment of recognition. Rather, this chapter focuses on the ambiguous, messy, primordial soup of potential changes, threats, and, yes, opportunities that precede an "Aha!" moment. It is a confusing, frustrating period, when people can legitimately have major differences of opinion about how important, consequential, dangerous, or valuable a shift in the environment might be.

DIGITAL DOUBTERS

In a now hilarious repudiation of the early Internet hype, *Newsweek* published an article by Clifford Stoll in February of 1995 entitled "Why the Web Won't Be Nirvana." In it, he writes:

> Visionaries see a future of telecommuting workers, interactive libraries and multimedia classrooms. They speak of electronic town meetings and virtual communities. Commerce and business will shift from offices and malls to networks and modems. And the freedom of digital networks will make government more democratic.
>
> Baloney. Do our computer pundits lack all common sense? The truth is no online database will replace your daily newspaper, no CD-ROM can take the place of a competent teacher and no computer network will change the way government works . . .
>
> How about electronic publishing? Try reading a book on disc. At best, it's an unpleasant chore: the myopic glow of a clunky computer replaces the friendly pages of a book. And you can't tote that laptop to the beach. Yet Nicholas Negroponte, director of the MIT Media Lab, predicts that we'll soon buy books and newspapers straight over the Internet. Uh, sure.

It should not be lost on us that the very publication, *Newsweek,* that used to churn out forty print editions a year itself went belly-up in 2012, a victim of the massive change that Stoll suggested would never occur.

Even so, seeing a shift coming does not always mean you should go rushing headlong into investments in it.

For example, in 1995, the same year Amazon made its first sales and Stoll expressed his skepticism, researchers did a study of what kinds of companies were using the Internet and for what business purposes. They found, upon looking at some three hundred companies that had created web pages at that point, that commercial use of the Internet was primitive at best. While some respondents were indeed positioning themselves for a "land rush" as the technology matured, the majority agreed with this sentiment, voiced by one of the study participants:

Sales are dismal and barely cover the cost of maintaining the Web page site through my Internet provider . . . I do not see the Internet being a viable marketing tool for products other than computer products for at least 20 years.

Recall that the Internet shopping experience of 1995 was radically different than it is today. Even in 1997, less than 40 percent of American households even owned a computer, and less than 20 percent had Internet access, which was provided mostly by slow and glitchy dial-up modems, often through the services of America Online. At that point, AOL was still charging its users an hourly fee to provide access. It changed to an unlimited flat-rate charge of $19.95 per month in 1996, which, while lessening the anxiety customers had about running up their Internet charges, also led to a flood of traffic. Many customers ended up dropping the service, which was plagued by constant busy signals.

In the early days, there were few trusted, convenient ways to pay for things over the Internet. The whole idea of e-commerce had not yet gone mainstream. Even finding what you were looking for was not simple. Competing search engines used different business models, some of which included pay per search — limiting customers' interest and enthusiasm for them. Let's not forget, while other early search engines existed, the advertising-supported, algorithmic, free-to-the-user model Google has leveraged so effectively was still years in the making.

Always-on, fast broadband as we know it today really only got started around 2000. It took until around 2007 for half of American households to have both computers and broadband connections. That year is also notable, of course, as the year Apple released the first iPhone, putting the equivalent of a broadband connection in everyone's pocket.

In fairness, from the perspective of a traditional retailer in 1995, it would have been foolhardy to make significant investments in Internet capabilities, given the immaturity of the technology at the time. This is a very confusing period in the unfolding of an inflection point. While the AOL–Time Warner merger in 2000 spooked a lot of people into thinking that they should perhaps make a big bet on the Internet, the company's rapid unraveling persuaded many that big Internet investments could only lead to no good. There is little joy in moving too soon to try to take advantage of an emergent inflection point.

The early web illustrates one of the sneakier aspects of inflection points. When they first emerge, although it is possible to speculate about what they could become, in the early stages they are inevitably incomplete in some way. Ecosystems can't form until they have a complete enough solution to offer. Take blockchain, for example, a technology that is currently in the shiny object stage of development. While it offers promising solutions to some vexing long-term problems, such as the creation of trust in a distributed manner, the institutional framework for blockchain's full deployment is incomplete. We don't have agreed upon protocols, standards, or rules of the road for it to be mainstream — yet. That doesn't mean we should ignore it, not at all. It just means that we need to develop a point of view on what would be necessary for the technology to be useful and when that might happen.

As of this writing, inflections represented by the emergence of big data, artificial intelligence, virtual reality, gamification, and many other innovations are all interesting but incomplete. Many observers quite sensibly conclude that they will never come to much of anything. In fact, there have been many superhyped potential inflection points that have indeed amounted to absolutely nothing (the paperless office, 3-D TV for the home, intelligent appliances . . . the list goes on).

By the middle of the first decade of the 2000s, the Internet had gone from being frustrating, disorganized, and chaotic to being a place that people turned to for useful information (Yahoo), to clean out their closets (eBay), to send and receive email (AOL), to connect with others in their local community (Craigslist), and to actually buy things (Amazon). Digitization and its potential impact on creative work was no longer a brand-new phenomenon.

In other words, the signals and drumbeat that this was going to be big were by then very strong, creating a clear and present promise of major change and a powerful impetus for those affected to take action. The quest in this chapter is to explore that period before the signals of an inflection point become obvious and strong. When there are so many things that could represent a potential inflection point, picking out the weak signals that actually matter is no small challenge.

In a delicious bit of irony, Bill Gates published his book *The Road Ahead* in, you guessed it, 1995. In it, he observed, "We always overestimate the change that will occur in the next two years and underestimate the change that will occur in the next ten. Don't let yourself be lulled into inaction." The problem is something Gartner calls the Hype Cycle, in which some kind of shiny new object captures the public imagination and creates a lot of buzz, then fails to deliver any near-term change in anything. This in turn leads people to dismiss the emerging shift, discounting its importance. While Gates did anticipate an information superhighway, ironically Microsoft ended up being surprised by an Internet that eventually put the company on the defensive.

In 2000, Gates selected his longtime number two, Steve Ballmer, to succeed him at the firm. While the company was extremely profitable, in 2016 Steve Blank observed that during the Ballmer era, Microsoft failed to understand the five most important technology trends of the twenty-first century: "In search — losing to Google; in smartphones — losing to Apple; in mobile operating systems — losing to Google/Apple; in media — losing to Apple/Netflix; and in the cloud — losing to Amazon. Microsoft left the 20th century owning over 95% of the operating systems that ran on computers (almost all on desktops). Fifteen years and 2 billion smartphones shipped in the 21st century and Microsoft's mobile OS share is 1%."

These are the risks of overlooking weak or faint signals that other competitors are able to see.

The reason weak signals represent strategic opportunities is that the earlier you can spot an inflection point in progress, the more easily you can design your strategy to deal with it effectively. I am fond of an analogy to driving: When you can see far ahead, you can adjust your trajectory with a small move of the steering wheel. But when you see only after the inflection point is upon you, it requires a big jerk of the steering wheel.

Put another way, when you can see an obstacle far down the road, you need to make a very small adjustment with your steering wheel. But when the obstacle is suddenly in front of your car, you have to quickly and drastically turn the wheel in a big, big way.

LAGGING, CURRENT, AND
LEADING INDICATORS

A good many managers pride themselves on being data-driven, obsessed with hard numbers and fluent with the facts. As a friend of mine who is a senior executive at Infosys is fond of saying, "In God, we trust. Everybody else brings data!" Indeed, in many organizations, the preparation of bulletproof slide decks, exquisitely detailed spreadsheets, and precise references to sources of data occupies stupendous amounts of managerial time.

The difficulty with such an emphasis on facts is that, unfortunately, facts are often a lagging indicator of what could potentially be important. By the time you are dealing with a fact on the ground, whatever led to it has already happened.

Lagging Indicators

A *lagging indicator* is an outcome or consequence of some activity that came before. Many of our most utilized metrics in business are lagging indicators. Profits, revenues, returns on investment, and even earnings per share are all lagging consequences of decisions made at some previous time.

Many companies I work with are strongly biased toward using lagging indicators to make their most important decisions, which itself can create incredible blind spots. Despite research that shows that even seemingly unambiguous metrics such as accounting numbers are influenced by personal preference, we have an almost magical belief that numbers will not deceive us. Thus, we are systematically biased to prefer lagging indicators in our strategic decision-making, which is problematic. By the time an inflection point has handed you a new reality, it's a tad late.

Hard numbers can be helpful if they can help you to identify a trend or discontinuity by looking at patterns over time. In and of themselves, however, they are not particularly helpful if your goal is to understand the future and to see around the corner.

Common lagging indicators include:

- Operating margins: how much profit you make on sales at the moment
- EBITDA: earnings before interest, taxes, depreciation, and amortization (meant to convey how much a company is earning absent extraneous information)
- Revenue/turnover: total amount taken in by the company in a given time period
- Revenue growth or decline: change from a prior period
- Return on net assets: net income divided by the assets used to generate it
- Operating income change: change from a prior year period

As you can see, every one of these numbers represents an *outcome*. It is a reflection of actions taken that produce that number, but it doesn't shed any light at all on what you might need to do for the number to tell a different story in the future. Focusing so much on lagging indicators is one reason many strategists and long-term thinkers find the quarterly profit obsession of many publicly traded companies to be so depressing. In striving to make a quarterly lagging indicator look good, factors that might make it look better over the long term are sacrificed.

Current Indicators

Current indicators give you data about the current state of things. One reason so many real-time systems are popular is that it is valuable to know exactly where you are — a bit like a directions app showing your location and how long it will take to get to your destination. Entire industries — from sensor-linked monitoring to enterprise resource planning (ERP) systems — have been built on being able to answer the question, What is going on right now?

Many current indicators are based on the proven recipe for success in a given business — that is, on conditions at one point in time. Managers learn to pay attention to these indicators. Analysts are trained to study them. Employees and leaders focus on them. And they are often simply taken for granted as predictors of what will drive success in the future.

For instance, in the traditional energy business, a number of key performance metrics have grown up over time based on the assumption of a centralized, grid-based power supply network. Examples include:

- Power cuts and average duration: How much disruption are customers currently experiencing?
- Consumption by sector: Who is consuming your energy and when are they consuming it?
- Operating cash flow: How much cash are you generating from operations?
- Production costs: What is it costing you to produce your energy? How do different sources compare?
- Availability factor: How readily can you meet current energy demands?
- Asset utilization ratio: How efficiently are you using your assets?

As long as the key constraints of a grid-based, largely regulated utility arrangement for energy companies remain in place, these metrics (key performance indicators) make sense. However, such metrics are not going to tell you very much that will prepare you for the future of the energy business. As we'll see later in this chapter, the advent of renewables, the idea that power can be generated in a distributed manner and sold back to the grid, the possible implications for energy consumption of electric vehicles, consumption changes led by "smart" thermostats, and the very idea that in the future customers will have a choice of suppliers and interaction mechanisms are not reflected in these current indicators.

With employee incentives often tied to their performance with respect to driving current indicators, it isn't surprising that many people don't bother to look beyond them. And yet, this approach can be a source of significant blind spots in a changing environment. As I've said previously, an inflection point changes the nature of the key metrics that reflect the taken-for-granted assumptions in your business. Just paying attention to the current indicators is not going to be all that helpful.

Leading Indicators

Leading indicators represent things that are not facts yet in your business. They have the potential to lead to facts later on, but at the moment you're looking at them, they are only suppositions, conjectures, and assumptions. They are often qualitative rather than quantitative. They are often told as narratives and stories rather than in meticulous PowerPoint charts. For that reason, executives are often wary about basing important decisions on them. This can be folly of the highest order in a world of strategic inflection points, because the leading indicators are where ideas about the future are to be found.

Sanjay Purohit, who was a leading figure at Infosys and head of planning for more than a decade, made it a core part of his role to spend significant amounts of time looking for leading indicators that go beyond today's key performance indicators. As he told me,

> When I have seen an organization anticipate the inflection points, there has always been a proactive effort at modeling leading indicators . . . I'm looking for knowledge that sits at the periphery of the organization. I ask myself: How do you engage with the periphery? I used to spend significant time with the salespeople. It involved being in the market, listening, looking for cues – are they seeing something they can't necessarily express but lives are starting to change? . . . It's a lot of signal processing, if you will. I spent considerable time in trying to catch these signals.

Purohit saw Infosys through a number of inflection points, most recently (2014) as the founding CEO of an Infosys-owned startup, EdgeVerve Systems, which was designed to explore the promise of platform strategies as opposed to Infosys's traditional core business. This was in direct response to the early warnings represented by the rise of Amazon Web Services, Google, and other platforms that were becoming increasingly powerful.

Relationship Between Indicators and Outcomes

Let's have a look at the relationships between these different kinds of indicators and outcomes in the following table. Say the outcome (the fact) that you want to understand is customer churn – how many customers are deserting your business in a given time period. Just knowing that information gives you little guidance on what to do to reduce it. In your quest to get to the bottom of this, you find a distinct correlation between period 1 customer satisfaction and period 4 customer defection. Customer satisfaction might, therefore, be a proximate indicator of future customer intention.

Lagging	Current	Leading
Customer churn	Customer satisfaction	Employee engagement
Employee turnover	Employee engagement	Management effectiveness
Revenue from new products	Customer usage	"Customer love"

What, in turn, underlies customer satisfaction? Many studies suggest a powerful role for employee satisfaction and engagement. Employee engagement thus becomes a leading indicator of later customer propensity to defect, and something you can take action to influence.

If your attempt was to understand a different outcome — say employee turnover — levels of engagement might be seen as a different kind of indicator, in this case a current one. Highly engaged employees are less likely to depart your organization than disengaged ones. A leading indicator might be the effectiveness of how those employees are managed. In particular, the element of psychological safety in a team is highly correlated with employee engagement and propensity to remain, as Amy Edmondson discovered years ago and massive research by Google more recently reconfirmed.

As a third example, consider the tack taken by Satya Nadella, who replaced Steve Ballmer as CEO of Microsoft in 2014. Rather than continuing to focus on Windows-driven profits that characterized the Ballmer era (and which Blank so roundly criticized), Nadella has framed his leadership entirely around leading indicators. As he said in a 2015 interview, "We no longer talk about the lagging indicators of success, right, which is revenue, profit. What are the leading indicators of success? Customer love."

Essentially, Nadella is making a big bet that if he can get the right leading indicators in place, the rest will follow. Several years into his tenure, he is receiving major kudos for transforming the software giant and making it relevant to the new growth areas in technology, even pitting its Azure cloud offering against the powerful Amazon Web Services.

This brings us to the question, How do you develop leading indicators of a potential inflection point in the early, pre-recognition phase?

THE INVERSE RELATIONSHIP
BETWEEN DEGREES OF FREEDOM
AND SIGNAL STRENGTH

A useful model for thinking about obtaining leading indicators was created by a consulting firm once known as the Futures Group and now known as the Futures Strategy Group. The model begins by assessing the "signal strength" of a given piece of information about the future.

As you can see in Figure 1, in the early stages the signals are weak. The signal-to-noise ratio is quite high, and it would be a mistake to make any big strategic move at this point, because there is still an enormous amount of uncertainty.

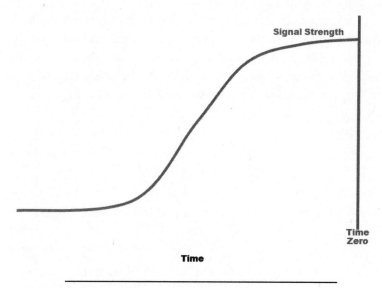

Figure 1 Increasing Strength of a Signal over Time

Information, however, has a way of gathering steam in a nonlinear way. Thus, to recall my earlier Internet example, in the 1995–2000 era the signals that the Internet was going to have a major impact on retail (or anything else) were very noisy. Some people believed the hype, others dismissed it, but the reality of the impact of the Internet during that time was that companies were still struggling with ecosystem deficiencies (slow and expensive dial-up modems, limited bandwidth, few lucrative business models, and so on). By the time 2000–2005 rolled around, the survivors of the initial dot-com bust had figured much of this out.

Email had become commonplace. Broadband and always-on connections had become widely adopted. In a relatively short period of time, what was once a question about which reasonable people could reasonably disagree, the signals that the Internet was indeed going to create dramatic change in the world were indisputable. You can think of the rapid increase in signal strength as taking place in that 2000–2005 period. After that, people could easily see that digital technologies were going to have a major impact on the consumption of any kind of good that could be transmitted digitally. By the time period labeled "Time Zero" in Figure 1, the digitization of books, music, and other products would be mainstream.

The dilemma for the strategist is that while we would like to be making decisions with the kind of specific and clear information that will be available at time zero, that is much too late. By that time, the inflection is obvious to everyone, and the chance to respond early has been lost. You can think of this in terms of the model in Figure 2.

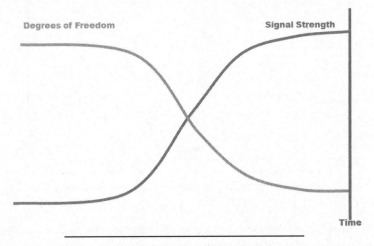

Figure 2 Inverse Relationship Between
Degrees of Freedom and Signal Strength

As this figure shows, the relationship between strategic degrees of freedom and signal strength is practically inverse. In the unfair way in which life operates, the moment at which you have the richest, most trustworthy information is often the moment at which you have the least power to change the story told by that information.

This brings us to the critical notion of building an intelligence system to detect early warnings. As we've already seen, you don't want to be making big strategic moves when the signal-to-noise ratio is very high, or too early on. You also don't want to wait until the facts are plainly obvious to everyone. Instead, you need a way to get information with respect to what is sometimes called the period of *optimum warning,* around the middle of the chart, as shown in Figure 3.

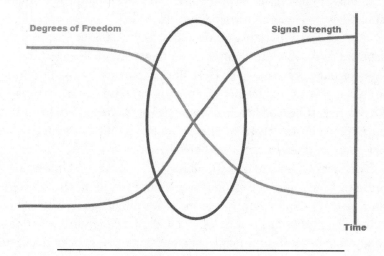

Figure 3 Period of Optimum Warning

This brings us to the role of constructing scenarios to identify potential time zero events.

EXPANDING THE FUTURES YOU CONSIDER: SPARKING IMAGINATION

Because inflection points undermine the very assumptions on which a business is based and which have come to be taken as "facts" by most decision-makers, it is often difficult for leaders to imagine a different world. It is this failure of imagination that so often leads to strategic surprise.

Consider, for instance, the shift in the US restaurant business toward take-out food that is consumed off premises. Today, some 63 percent of all meals purchased from a restaurant are not actually eaten in that restaurant. This came as a surprise to many restaurateurs who went into the business not just to prepare food but also to offer guests the experience of hospitality. As one restaurant owner has observed, "It's a completely different business," adding, somewhat wistfully, "I didn't do this to put food into boxes."

What would be useful, therefore, are some straightforward ways of expanding the possibilities you are prepared to consider. Some organizations turn to scenario planning for this.

There is a vast literature on very advanced techniques for scenario planning, and some excellent ideas on how you can envision the future. For our purposes, which is to identify potentially significant future time zero events, elaborate scenario exercises aren't necessary. What I suggest instead is using simple two-by-two matrices to outline future possibilities. These matrices should be different enough that they point to different time zero outcomes.

Two key elements to avoid in doing this work are (1) imagining a future in which only one thing changes but everything else stays the same, and (2) thinking only in terms of linear change. One of my favorite examples of this is the classic TV show *The Jetsons,* which featured robot servants and flying cars, but portrayed gender roles and work arrangements firmly rooted in 1962!

Andy Grove's 1997 discussion of indicators signaling that a change may be afoot is a reasonable point of departure. He suggests considering three future scenarios.

1. Your key competitor is about to change. If you had only one silver bullet, whom would you aim it at?
2. Your primary complementor is about to change. The ecosystem will be different.
3. Management's ability to make sense of what is going on "out there" has diminished in some significant way.

Let me give you an example. For a traditional energy distribution company I was working with in 2017, two major sources of uncertainty were future demand and future configuration of capabilities.

First, I was surprised to learn that, for a variety of reasons, energy consumption had been in slow-growth mode in much of the world for some time. This was an inflection point that many — even the vaunted General Electric — got very wrong. For GE, the result was massive overinvestment, losses and layoffs in their power business, management churn, and a toppling from their spot as one of America's best-run companies.

Further, the power distribution model that the sector had used for years — consisting of large generating plants and distributed power lines — was moving toward distributed networks, called distributed energy resources, or DERs. In that model, power comes not only from the traditional power generation plant but also from renewable sources such as wind and solar, making the one-way traditional approach obsolete. Another threat to the centralized grid was presented by advances in battery technology. In many parts of the world, a grid is either unaffordable or will result in infrastructure that will be so vulnerable to theft and malfeasance that it won't be reliable. Even with today's battery technology (powered by solar cells), some power for some of the day is better than no power at all, making the grid less desirable for those locations.

Using just these two uncertainties, we considered the following scenarios:

	Centralized grid dominates	Decentralized networks that also use solar and wind
Highly increased demand	Steady as she goes: investment in large-scale generating and distribution equipment merited	The smart-grid future: technology and channels highly likely to dominate
Demand slow, flat, or declining	Victory to the efficient: investment in smaller-scale, more efficient systems merited	Tidal wave of disruption: need to completely rethink industry economics

Now, for each scenario, we came up with a few time zero considerations. A time zero event should be a crisp articulation of a specific outcome in the future that could represent the inflection point at the moment it occurs. In the example we ran for the energy company, the time zero events looked something like this:

	Centralized grid dominates	Decentralized networks that also use solar and wind
Highly increased demand	Time zero: 80% of capacity provided by high-end, expensive machinery	Time zero: two-thirds of all energy investment made in solar and wind technology
Demand slow, flat, or declining	Time zero: more than 50% of power provided by smaller-scale or remanufactured equipment	Time zero: 50% of all grids become markets where energy comes and goes based on supply and demand

You can do this for as many uncertainties as you think merit serious consideration, but try not to come up with too many. Three to five are probably enough to digest.

Time Zero Events

It's important to have a variety of scenarios to think about, which will broaden the range of potential futures you anticipate. The next step is to begin putting some early warnings around those potential futures. Generally, we ask the question, What would have to be true at six months, twelve months, or eighteen months before the scenario could occur? Then we create indicators of this outcome becoming more or less likely.

Based on the previous example, let's take as a case the time zero event that two-thirds of all energy investment will be made in solar and wind technology.

Time Zero Case: Two-Thirds of Energy Investment Is Made in Solar and Wind

Six months before:

- Battery prices make renewable-based grid solutions as cost-effective as conventional energy supply.

- The order pipeline for new equipment is consistent with this event.

Twelve months before:
- Capital budget allocations shift resource requests from conventional to renewable technology.
- New energy storage capabilities make it possible to cost-effectively store energy generated by renewable sources at scale, eliminating the need for conventional peaker plants (which are run only when there is high demand).
- Renewables are at parity with other sources of energy — so-called grid parity.
- Legal schemes laying out who benefits and who pays with respect to DERs begin to be put in place.

Eighteen months before:
- Significant government transitions are made from conventional to renewable supply in emerging markets.
- Changes in incentives favor renewables, such as investment tax credits and production tax credits.
- Lots of newcomers, whether startups or established firms, enter this space.
- Significant retirements of nonrenewable capacity, such as coal, occur.

Now:
- Predictions of increased investment in solar and wind, leading to two-thirds of all energy investment in renewable sources within a few years.
- Predictions of rapidly increasing demand.
- Predictions of rapidly increasing efficiency, so demand can be met without increased investment.
- An enormous amount of legal scuffling around who pays and who benefits from DERs.

Having created a set of indicators, two key actions follow. The first is to make it someone's job to stay on top of that emerging time zero event and to let everybody with the potential to come upon relevant information know who that person is. The reason for this is that I often find in firms that are surprised by an inflection that the knowledge about what was going on was actually plentiful in the organization — somewhere — but no one had a complete enough picture to make sense of it.

Having one person who is explicitly keeping an eye on a particular future event increases the likelihood that whatever knowledge is in the organization has somewhere to go and will be seen holistically. And remember to incorporate feedback from people who may not be sitting in the executive suite. Go back to the periphery for information and insights about these events.

The second key action is to devote a set amount of time in the management meeting agenda to freshen your team's knowledge of those early warnings. The indicators should be tracked and updated regularly. At the regular review sessions, you can also adjust the scenarios and time zero events as new information becomes available. An additional benefit of doing this is that it creates a learning record, which can help people recall why specific decisions were made at given times. This can be helpful in testing assumptions about things that may have changed.

It is crucial in these meetings that data that challenge embedded orthodoxies be presented along with information that supports the common view. Otherwise, this effort is a waste of time, as people will continue to do business in the echo chamber of their existing assumptions.

SCHOOL'S OUT . . . OR IS IT?

Let's take another example of a sector that promises to be disrupted in some way by the digital revolution.

Education was supposed to have been thoroughly disrupted by now. Why is it proving so resistant? Because it's still very hard to prove to others what you know. For that, you can't beat a credential from a respected institution.

But what if we could have credentials *without* a degree? Think of the music business. When music began to be sold (or stolen) by the song and not by the album, the resulting unbundling, together with the increasing popularity of streaming services and live performances, created a major inflection point for the established industry. Imagine if something similar happened in higher education, with credentials offered for the level of a skill rather than a degree?

HIGHER EDUCATION: EARLY WARNINGS OF A LONG-OVERDUE INFLECTION POINT?

Predicting the disruption of education has a long history, with experts forecasting that motion pictures, then radio, television, and, of course, computers and the Internet, would overturn the existing model for education. Some went as far as to say that motion pictures would entirely take the place of education.

Many decision-makers saw the advent of the Internet as a credible threat to the model for higher education. In 2000, an online educational platform, the ill-fated Fathom, attempted to be a first mover on the World Wide Web. Now we have massive open online courses (MOOCs), with millions of learners flocking to platforms like Udacity, Coursera, and edX. Even more people regularly get their knowledge free from YouTube, with "classes" of 400,000 not being at all unusual.

Yet despite their popularity, MOOCs and their ilk have not yet prompted an inflection point that could disrupt higher education. They struggle with how to make the experience personally relevant, how to make money, and, most significantly to me, what kind of credential a student should receive.

Degree Inflation

The university degree may well be the last barrier standing between traditional education models and a major disruption. One reason is sheer laziness. Degrees are a handy shortcut. Want to reduce the number of résumés sitting in your in-box? Easy — make some kind of credential, like a bachelor's degree, a requirement. Boom! In one fell swoop that list of candidates will get a lot shorter. In fact, according to

the Bureau of Labor Statistics, 21 percent of entry-level jobs today require a four-year degree.

While it does make life easier for the personnel department, the degree requirement has a large number of unanticipated negative consequences and unintended side effects. It knocks out as many as 83
percent of potential Latino candidates and as many as 80 percent of potential African American candidates. That is a lot of talent to overlook.

Harvard's Joseph Fuller and Manjari Raman have put numbers to
what they call "degree inflation." In an exhaustive analysis of 26 million job postings, they found that

> the degree gap (the discrepancy between the demand for a college
> degree in job postings and the employees who are currently in that
> job who have a college degree) is significant. For example, in 2015,
> 67% of production supervisor job postings asked for a college de-
> gree, while only 16% of employed production supervisors had one.
> Our analysis indicates that more than 6 million jobs are currently
> at risk of degree inflation.

In addition, making a four-year degree the barrier to obtaining a
good job creates a vicious cycle. Students find themselves taking on seriously debilitating education loans. That, in turn, makes them more
expensive for employers to hire.

For the price employers are willing to pay, the economics of education debt repayment means that there are fewer candidates willing
to take what Fuller and Raman call "middle skill" jobs — supervisors,
support specialists, sales representatives, inspectors and testers, clerks,
and secretaries and administrative assistants. This makes it hard to
hire for these roles, leaving companies without the workers they need
to grow and people without access to the opportunities that might get
them a start on a middle-class life. As Fuller and Raman point out, employers are effectively locking the two-thirds of Americans who do not
have a four-year degree out of workplace opportunities.

It isn't for want of trying that people lack college degrees. Forty-
four percent of new high school graduates enroll directly in a four-
year college, according to the *New York Times,* but less than half of
them will earn a degree within four years. And college is not getting
any cheaper. One study found that tuitions rose 498 percent from 1985

to 2011, nearly four times the overall consumer price index. In 2017, Americans owed $1.3 trillion in student debt, more than two and a half times what was owed a decade earlier.

College or a Dead End?

The difficulty of matching qualified candidates without a degree to jobs they could do that don't require a degree is leading people in the United States to look for alternatives such as apprenticeships. In Switzerland, for instance, 70 percent of students who have completed the ninth grade elect to go on a vocational track. As the *New York Times* reported in 2017, "Beginning in 10th grade, students rotate among employers, industry organizations and school for three to four years of training and mentoring. Learning is hands-on, and they are paid. Switzerland's unemployment rate for the young is the lowest in Europe and about a quarter that of the United States." In contrast, in the United States "most students are offered a choice between college or a dead end."

In the Swiss system, an apprenticeship is considered as valuable as a college education for the establishment of a good life, and college is meant for those who have careers (such as law, medicine, or accounting) that genuinely require advanced classroom instruction.

A great many participants in the American system are not being well served. Many students are taking on debt they will struggle to pay off. Employers can't find the kinds of employees they need. Opportunities are closed to millions of people who could quite adequately perform a particular work role. And all because we continue to use a degree as a proxy for other things we really care about — soft skills, the ability to write cogently, the ability to interact with technology, and so on.

SO WHY AM I REVIEWING CURRENT ISSUES IN EDUCATION?

Whenever a system has a sufficient number of badly served constituents, an inflection point has fertile ground to take root. I believe that alternative forms of credentialing, in which some kind of respected accreditation body certifies skills based on the *level of the skill,* rather than the *degree,* are beginning to gain real traction.

There is definitely demand. The presence of so many online resources and other tools that individuals can use to learn is creating a hunger for alternative certification systems. Considerable experimentation has been conducted with students using online badges and verified certificates to complement their traditional transcripts. While these things have been around for a while, the notion that they might substitute for a conventional degree has been met with ongoing skepticism.

This is changing. Evidence from a LinkedIn insiders' survey of knowledgeable learning and development specialists shows a softening of the traditional model. Sixty percent of those surveyed believed that employers are well on their way to skills-based-hiring — in other words, "choosing candidates based on what they can do, rather than degree or pedigree." Fifty-seven percent of respondents said they believe employers will start to place more value on nontraditional credentials, with one respondent going so far as to say that traditional credentials are "boring."

We are starting to see business models that support alternative credentialing emerge. Pearson, a leading supplier to higher education, has an entire business line devoted to helping institutions create alternatives to traditional degrees. This is gaining traction as educational institutions pick up on the need and incorporate alternatives into their curricula. Pearson's Acclaim platform partners with companies to provide respected credentials of achievement for their workers.

Startups such as Degreed are also building a business out of certifying people for skills they possess. With competencies ranging from change management to public speaking to HTML coding, the Degreed process provides a certificate verifying that a candidate has gone through a rigorous evaluation process by experts in that particular field of study. It also certifies the level of a candidate's mastery of the skills evaluated in that process.

Another innovation that could prove disruptive to the traditional education model was introduced by Purdue University in 2016. It's called the income share agreement (ISA), by which schools offer free or heavily subsidized tuition in exchange for a share of students' future earnings. While such programs are not without controversy, the fact that they are attracting increasing attention is another signal that the existing model is working poorly for a good many stakeholders.

WHAT ABOUT THE UNIVERSITIES?

The current state of higher education institutions today reminds me of the integrated steel mills that suffered a major disruption at the hands of mini-mills, particularly when I think of large research universities. Clayton Christensen has, of course, been talking about this issue for some time and published his ideas in the book *Disrupting Class*.

As in the integrated steel mills, the economics of higher education exist because there are few alternatives. Students in the United States feel they have no choice but to attend college in order to access opportunities, just as steel customers had few alternatives to buying from integrated mills. Students must take a full slate of courses, some of which are required, regardless of whether they are interested in the topics or not.

Professors are not rewarded for being inspired curators of the social learning process, but rather for their research prowess. Teaching in many of our institutions is seen by many professors as somewhat of a nuisance. For instance, with respect to research in business schools, Michael Harmon of Georgetown University wrote a delightfully titled article, "Business Research and Chinese Patriotic Poetry: How Competition for Status Distorts the Priority Between Research and Teaching in U.S. Business Schools." In this piece, he fiercely criticizes the business of producing scholarly research in business schools, which has "obliterated any evident connection between research productivity and the furtherance of any praiseworthy social, practical, or intellectual values." More recently, my colleague Steve Denning took business schools to task for offering obsolete lessons to their students.

Normally, when a system doesn't create results for its constituents, it goes out of business. The university system, however, is buffered by its dominant control over that all-important credential, the degree.

Just as mini-mills started at the "low end" of the steel market, basically making the worst-quality steel for the most unattractive and price-sensitive customers, alternative credentials are starting at the "low end" of the education market, with boot camps, online programs, and short training events. Just as with mini-mills, however, we can predict that their quality, reach, and access will improve and that the effect on established institutions will be greater over time.

As this change starts to have an impact on more universities, several outcomes are likely. The first is the shrinking of the research-based model for faculty deployment and incentives and the shift to what we might think of as the celebrity model. Schools are already relying more heavily on adjunct faculty in their classrooms at an increasing rate. As a result, popular instructors are more likely to be in demand than those who focus on scholarship.

Another effect, which Christensen predicted, is that the "brands" of universities may well become less important than the "brands" of individual superstar professors. It may well matter more in the future that you have a credential attesting to the completion of Christensen's course on disruption or Lynda Gratton's course on organizational design than that you have a degree from Harvard or London Business School.

Similarly, we may well see rankings and accreditation drop to the level of individual course modules or programs. So rather than ranking the "best business schools" overall, journalists and observers may instead rank individual educational programs. The Thinkers50 biennial ranking of thought leaders in management has already demonstrated a version of this. The group identifies and ranks management thinkers whose ideas have had a major impact on the understanding of management and presents awards for distinguished achievement in specific categories. Notably, Thinkers50 salutes individuals, not the institutions from which they hail.

MAKING SENSE OF WEAK SIGNALS

This brief overview of the state of play in credentialing in higher education illustrates several of the major themes of this book. The first is that pending inflection points can often take a long time to have an impact. The second is that while observers often anticipate such a major change, it can take a while before a complete ecosystem is in place that fully disrupts the status quo in a meaningful way. And the third is that moving too early, as the ill-fated Fathom did, is tempting but often ends up badly.

WHAT WON'T CHANGE

With the mind-numbing pace of change that seems to be all around us, it is also worthwhile to consider what is highly *unlikely* to change as you consider your strategy.

To return to higher education for a moment, it is highly unlikely (and not actually desirable) for the university system as we know it to disappear. There is still a role for the liberal arts and the "coming of age" experience that so many college-educated people reflect on with great fondness. What is more likely to happen is that trusted alternatives to the degree will emerge, initially for easy-to-measure skills such as coding, but eventually for more advanced creative and communication skills. The optimist in me would like to think that this would open up opportunities for people who are perfectly prepared to make a contribution, but for whom a four-year commitment is unachievable or undesirable.

To quote Amazon's Jeff Bezos, "It's impossible to imagine a future 10 years from now where a customer comes up and says, 'Jeff I love Amazon; I just wish the prices were a little higher,' [or] 'I love Amazon; I just wish you'd deliver a little more slowly.' Impossible." His point is that if you know something is going to be true over the long term, you can put your efforts into maintaining that truth.

We'll return to this way of thinking in detail later in the book. To foreshadow briefly, the things that won't change are what we call the customer "job to be done." In other words, human needs and preferences are remarkably stable, even as the technologies for meeting those needs change. From smoke signals to the written letter to the pony express to the telegraph to the landline phone to today's smartphone, the "job" of conveying information over long distances has hardly changed at all, even as our abilities to get that job done have completely transformed.

This is a powerful insight, one that is central to going through an inflection point and coming out the other end even stronger.

Key Takeaways

An inflection point happens when a 10X change alters the basic assumptions upon which a business is built. Because these are taken for granted, it is often hard for executives working in the here and now to see the implications of change.

In the early stages of an inflection point, it is difficult to see the potential impact because the possible solutions are invariably incomplete — the change affects only certain parts of the system. The big mistake is to make a huge investment at this point.

There are three kinds of indicators in any business. Lagging indicators provide information about what has already happened and cannot be changed. Current indicators provide information about what is going on, based on assumptions about how the business currently operates (which can create blind spots). Leading indicators are the most critical for spotting impending inflection points, but they are the most difficult to make sense of — they are often qualitative and emergent.

The quality of the information you have to work with is inversely proportional to your ability to do anything to change the story. A way of increasing your decision-making confidence is to create a time zero event that represents something important that might happen in the future. Then you can work backward in time to see what could anticipate this kind of event.

By using a simple juxtaposition of key uncertainties, you can articulate very different time zero events, which can become points of inquiry among your management team. Allocating the time to do this work is crucial yet often overlooked, which can lead to strategic blind spots.

On the Lookout for Weak Signals: Defining Your Arena

[A company stalls] because the things they
believed the longest or the things that they
believe the most deeply are no longer valid.
Basically, what they know is no longer true.

—Matthew Olson, Derek van Bever, and Seth Verry

This quote, from a study of negative inflection points, which Olson, van Bever, and Verry came to call "growth stalls," identifies the single most significant reason that once-successful firms have sudden collapses in revenue. In other words, something in the environment has changed the assumptions that company leaders are making about the key elements of their strategy—their customers, the needs being met, the competitive set—and yet the organization hasn't responded.

TAKEN-FOR-GRANTED ASSUMPTIONS ABOUT SUCCESS CAN BE DANGEROUS

The growing mismatch between what once made an organization successful and the environment it finds itself in now eventually leads it to dramatically lower performance, if not to its demise. And Olson, van Bever, and Verry found that the revenue drops were not gradual.

Just as the theory we are exploring here suggests, a negative inflection point can lead to sudden and unfortunate declines in performance.

In my book *The End of Competitive Advantage,* I suggest several early-warning signs that an advantage is likely to be on the decline. How many of these do you think your organization's leaders would be likely to agree with?

- I don't buy my own company's products or services.
- We are investing at the same levels or even more but not getting margins or growth in return.
- Customers are finding cheaper or simpler solutions that are "good enough."
- Competition is emerging from places we didn't expect.
- Customers are no longer excited about what we have to offer.
- We are not considered a top place to work by the people we would like to hire.
- Some of our very best people are leaving.
- Our stock is perpetually undervalued.
- Our technical people (scientists and engineers, for instance) are predicting that a new technology will change our business.
- We are not being targeted by headhunters for talent.
- The growth trajectory has slowed or reversed.
- Very few innovations have made it successfully to market in the last two years.
- The company is cutting back on benefits or pushing more risk to employees.
- Management is denying the importance of potential bad news.

Finally, we come to the capabilities deployed by organizations to deliver the attributes present at each link. Think of capabilities as being translated into attributes that can be perceived as relevant by different actors in the situation. These capabilities can be thought of in terms of traditional ideas such as the value chain, or the "set of activities that a firm operating in a specific industry performs in order to deliver a valuable product or service for the market." Different value chains can produce very different attributes, and many traditional ideas in strategy come from that understanding.

	Basic—attribute is taken for granted by all players	Discriminating—attribute distinguishes between solutions	Energizing—attribute has a powerful emotional effect on stakeholder
Stakeholder sees as positive	Non-negotiable —stakeholder expects it from all providers (a clean bed in a hotel room)	Differentiating —stakeholder sees differences among providers (hip music in a W hotel as opposed to a Marriott)	Exciting— stakeholder has an overwhelmingly positive reaction (original formulation of Courtyard by Marriott for business travelers)
Stakeholder sees as negative	Tolerable— stakeholder will put up with it to get the benefits (price)	Dissatisfying —stakeholder would prefer to do without it, and there are differences among players (time-consuming check out process)	Enraging— stakeholder would prefer never to do business with this entity again (lack of free Wi-Fi)
Stakeholder is neutral	Neutral—not all stakeholders care about this (television in the room)	Parallel— stakeholder may see something in the experience other than the actual service (loyalty card program)	Doesn't exist

The goal of working through these elements is to open your eyes to the possibilities that might have a potentially important effect on your business, even if they are just out of sight. I also recommend that you take a page out of the design thinking handbook as you consider your strategy. Tim Brown and Roger Martin provide a really nice description of how you might do this in their article "Design for Action." In particular, the idea of throwing out multiple possible strategies and consciously debating them rather than incrementally working from strategies that are already in place is excellent.

The Arena Map

	Today's Assumptions	Potential Shifts	Future Possibilities
Resource pool			
Contestants			
Stakeholders and their most important jobs to be done			
The consumption chains that deliver these jobs			
The attributes stakeholders experience			
Organizational capabilities and assets			

The process is meant to be used iteratively, in conjunction with your strategy development process.

The shifts that potentially lead to an inflection point can be described as follows:

1. They can change the pool of resources that are being contested.
2. They can change the parties trying to grab some of that pool of resources.
3. They can change the situation in which the contest takes place.
4. They can cause one job to squeeze another out of an actor's consideration set or reduce the resources available to do that job.

5. They can meaningfully change the consumption experience.
6. They can lead to some attributes becoming more or less valued than others.
7. They can change the kinds of capabilities embedded in a value chain that are relevant.
8. They can change every element of the arena.

THE SHRINKING SHAVING BUSINESS: A NEGATIVE INFLECTION

Let's take a quick look at an example from the current state of the art with respect to men's shaving behavior, written from the perspective of Procter & Gamble's Gillette brand.

The basic story in the shaving business is that for years, P&G's Gillette brand had a dominant position in the market. The company poured resources into R&D to develop better, premium-priced products. Typically, they sold razors with multiple blades, claiming that this produced a better shave. Because razors are expensive (I call them catnip for shoplifters), many retail outlets keep them under lock and key, meaning that consumers have to find a retail worker to unlock the case (what I call the razor fortress). It's also easy to forget to buy razors.

In the 2010–2011 time frame, an explosion of new competition, informed by both digital possibilities (YouTube, Facebook, Amazon Web Services) and a changing attitude toward the necessity of being clean-shaven among a new generation of customers, sent shock waves through the Gillette business model. Upstarts such as the Dollar Shave Club and Harry's explored a direct-to-consumer model with less expensive blades offered on a subscription basis. Gillette's market share went from roughly 70 percent of the men's shaving market to around 54 percent. Stunningly, the entire category seems destined to shrink as attitudes toward hair removal and its importance decline.

How might an analysis of this arena look using the framework described in the previous section? Let's try it.

	Today's Assumptions	Potential Shifts	Future Possibilities
Resource pool	Men's spending on personal grooming, in particular on shaving.	Social shifts to make daily shaving less essential to younger generation; willingness to grow beards Greater price sensitivity	Resources devoted to entire category might be in decline
Contestants	Gillette 70% share Schick 20% share Others very small	Digital enables creation of direct-to-consumer market	Explosion of competition even in a shrinking market
Stakeholders and their most important jobs to be done	Three types of shavers: Ritualistic—get the job done at high quality Begrudging—get the job done quickly and cheaply Aesthetic—focus on the look and emotion	Shaving itself losing relevance to many men in favor of a different look—the job is shrinking in importance	Consider running a smaller business more efficiently Find ways to open the market to more demand
The consumption chains that deliver these jobs (awareness, search, selection, contracting payment, etc.)	Sales through retail channels	Digitally enabled platforms make other channels possible	Direct-to-consumer becomes popular
The attributes stakeholders experience	+ Decent shave – "Razor fortress" – Expense ? Differentiation ? More blades = better	Sources of differentiation have eroded for Gillette Men are finding other razors good enough Global supply made by few manufacturers	Adding more blades is not going to be differentiating; may require a really disruptive strategy
Organizational capabilities and assets	Huge spending on both R&D and marketing Relationships mediated by retail channels	Probably need to change the mix	Be a controlled cost player

Gillette has responded to the post–inflection point world partly by going on the defensive and partly by moving toward developing direct relationships with end users with its Gillette On Demand. Defensively, it's lowered the price of its razors to be more competitive with the upstarts'. Offensively, it's introduced the Razor Maker project, which allows users to personalize their shaving devices with 3-D printed handles. The company is also exploring ways of making the shaving consumption chain less irritating. For instance, you can now order blades by sending a text message, and the company will deliver them straight to your home. Notwithstanding all of this, it doesn't seem likely that the comfortable days of Gillette's dominance in the shaving business are likely to return.

WHEN ONE JOB IN AN ARENA SQUEEZES OUT ANOTHER: THE CASE OF APPAREL

Pity the purveyor of clothing for teenagers in this hypersocial and hyperconnected age. This population in particular is so keen to connect with one another digitally that virtually nothing else has a similar allure. Indeed, concerned psychologists, observers, and marketers have called the devotion to digital devices "addictive."

The pool of resources being contested is, in this case, discretionary household spending among teens in the United States. The situation generally involves those in charge of household budgets (a combination of teens and their parents) deciding what to spend money on over the course of a period of time. The job to be done is anything that might prompt a trip to the mall or a visit to a website — the need for clothing for work or play, the need to update a wardrobe, the need for an outfit for a special occasion, whatever. The consumption chains assembled to address these needs consist of both online and offline merchants who supply apparel to their customers in a variety of settings. The attributes most stakeholders care about are related to the products, represented in styles and trends, not customers' entire experience. And the capabilities required to participate in this marketplace are those that have been assembled over several decades by retailers of all kinds, often based on traditional constraints (such as how long it takes to redesign a style or supply a store).

So far, so good. Well, along comes the cell phone revolution of 2007 (with the introduction of the iPhone and the commercialization of Android), and the order of jobs to be done by household budgeters changes dramatically. By then, social media was firmly established, and the desire to be connected was well entrenched, giving teens not only a reason to want to connect but also the technology with which to do so. The job of being connected has displaced – to some extent – the job of buying clothing. Not that clothing isn't still being purchased, but if you were to think of jobs to be done in a hierarchy, the job of connection has significantly increased in importance.

Since that has happened, the resources that would have gone into the purchase of apparel perhaps are now being redirected. That in turn means that an entirely different consumption chain has become more relevant to buyers – which has then shifted the attributes they are anxious to obtain, which implies that the capabilities assembled to deliver traditional retail offerings are less relevant as well. The inflection point is rippling through the arena.

Anticipating a Change in the Arena

This is all very well in retrospect, but the question is, how might we have anticipated the coming inflection point?

As I have said, an arena is primed for an inflection when some kind of change takes place that shifts one of the key metrics important to an established business or creates a new category with entirely different key metrics.

Let's consider the case of American teenagers. In 2007, the year of the iPhone's introduction, market researchers found that teens themselves had spending power that amounted to about $80 billion, and that their parents kicked in another $110 billion for other items, including food, entertainment, clothing, and personal care. If that is the critical resource your organization depends on, you'd probably like to start understanding where such spending is likely to shift.

Among the key metrics retailers traditionally obsessed over for this population was the all-important "back to school" season. As one observer remarked, "The business models that stores were built on – and on which retail businesses still largely depend – were rooted in those key periods of profitable performance." And the assumptions that many retailers made were deeply embedded in traditional metrics, such as sales per square foot and same-store sales compared across time periods. Most retailers, glued to traditional metrics like those, would not even have seen the impending threats emerging from the Internet.

Had they been paying attention, however, back in 2007 researchers were already commenting that the Internet – and, more specifically, social media – had dramatically affected how teens were spending their time. Teens, they found, were transferring the kinds of friendship behavior that age group had engaged in forever (talking on the home phone, hanging out) to social websites and the Internet. A *Washington Post* story about teen shopping habits found that even then, and even when teens were shopping in a brick-and-mortar store, cell phones were frequently utilized to check in with friends or get approval on a purchase. One of the teens in the *Post* story described the job clothing did for her back then as introducing her to people around her. "I want them to know a little bit of who I am," she said. "And I'm proud of it." Eerily, the job that clothing was supposed to do for her then is today easily supplanted by technology.

By 2014, the weak signals that teenagers' relationship to clothing and their clothing purchasing experience was undergoing dramatic change were no longer weak. In fact, by the time of the *Wall Street Journal*'s analysis, it was pretty obvious that a major inflection had arrived. A 2014 *New York Times* article titled "More Plugged-In Than Preppy" describes attitudes that would strike fear into any teen-oriented retailer's heart.

> "Clothes aren't as important to me," said Olivia D'Amico, a 16-year-old from New York, as she shopped at Hollister with her sister and a friend. "Half the time I don't really buy any brands. I just bought a pair of fake Doc Martens because I don't really care." She probably spends more on technology because she likes to "stay connected," she said.

One frustrated retail analyst explained trying to get a conversation going with his teen audience about upcoming fashion trends. "You try to get them talking about what's the next look, what they're excited about purchasing in apparel, and the conversation always circles back to the iPhone 6. You get them talking about crop tops, you get a nice little debate about high-waist going, but the conversation keeps shifting back."

A surprise for researchers trying to understand teen spending patterns was an increase in the amount of money teens spend on food, again relative to apparel. It turns out that food (for example, at McDonald's) is merely purchased so that teenagers can access restaurants' free Wi-Fi systems (again, via their phones).

Perhaps most important from the point of view of a retailer selling to teens is what all that communicating is about. It turns out that platforms such as Instagram, Facebook, and even Twitter and its ilk are where teens post photos. And to be seen wearing the same clothing in picture after picture? Well, that's really lame.

This trend is even having an effect on such fashion events as fashion week and the traditional fashion show. With styles on the runway broadcast to a worldwide audience, potential purchasers find the looks "dated" by the time the clothes are actually available in stores. The name for this? "Product fatigue." Here's what it feels like:

> Ken Downing, the fashion director of Neiman Marcus, said recently that he was showing a client a hot-off-the-delivery-van $11,000 embroidered jacket, only to have her wrinkle her nose and say, "But don't you have anything new?" "It arrived the day before," he observed. But it had been online since last October.

So let's understand the impact of these interrelated developments on key metrics for retailers of teen merchandise. First, we have an increasingly mature e-business ecosystem in which potential customers expect to be able to buy just about anything they want not only online but on their phones. They also expect a consistent experience with brands whether online or in person. Second, we have devices that are now widespread enough that the majority of customers in the target audience have access to them. Third, with the rise of social media, there is an increased emphasis on cultivating an online presence, which makes too many repeat outfits less desirable than perhaps they previously were. In sum, the inflection point looks like very bad news for traditional retailers.

Thriving in Light of an Inflection Point

As with all inflection points, those who are well positioned to pass through the inflection in teen apparel could enjoy significant benefits. Inditex, the parent company of Zara and other brands, essentially invented fast fashion. Its business model presents massive challenges to the conventional assumptions in clothing retailing. Instead of designing clothing for seasons, Zara seeks to make creating and distributing designs an ongoing and continuous process deeply informed by customer inputs. Instead of spending a lot of money on advertising, Inditex spends on real estate — seeking to occupy sites on the same blocks with the much more expensive designer brands. And rather than hiring expensive designers, Zara more or less politely copies them, using its deep connection to customers to suggest alterations.

As early as 2015, analysts noted that purveyors of fast fashion were enjoying torrid growth, despite the doldrums of the conventional apparel industry.

Companies such as Inditex, H&M, and a more recent entry, Forever 21, thrived as traditional buying seasons disappeared, customary prediction and stocking practices were overturned, and customers became omnichannel consumers of all kinds of goods. Relatedly, shoe seller Zappos enjoyed remarkable growth throughout the first decade of the century, reaching $1 billion in revenue and being acquired by Amazon in 2009 for $1.2 billion. During the first two quarters of 2017, Amazon's growth in shoe sales outpaced the total US growth in 2016.

New key metrics, such as dollars acquired per customer, are likely to be important in this changed environment.

And, in another development sure to give even Zara pause, startups such as ASOS, Boohoo, and Missguided are making fashion even faster. They connect to customers via social media to pick up on new trends and use local sourcing to make clothes available within days or even hours.

AN ENERGY MAJOR PURSUES A NEW ARENA

Arena-based analysis can also apply to nonconsumer businesses. Statoil, Norway's government majority-owned oil and gas company, has been engaged in a major transformation to become something entirely different while also retaining its presence in the energy arena. The inflection point it is traversing includes the movement toward a low-carbon future – characterized by more-distributed energy systems and a general interest in greener sources – while still recognizing that the human population is likely to require more, not less, energy going forward. The transformation is so radical that the company even changed its name – it is now Equinor – completely dropping the "oil" designation, which had turned into a burden.

According to one news article, "The oil and gas company said the name change was a natural step after it decided last year to become a 'broad energy' firm, investing up to 15–20 percent of annual capital expenditure in 'new energy solutions' by 2030, mostly in offshore wind."

The article notes that in 2013, the company was ranked as the most desirable place to work among Norwegian students, based on a survey conducted by the Norwegian firm Evidente, using the website Karri ereStart.no. By 2018, it had dropped to fifteenth place, signaling unease among young people about the company's contribution to climate change and a desire to turn away from fossil fuels altogether.

Key Takeaways

Consider whether the assumptions you are making about your business might need a fresh look. Review the warning signs of fading advantage.

Start defining your arena by asking which pool of resources – typically revenues – your business currently relies on. What other players might be trying to grab those same resources, even if they don't make or offer products and services similar to yours?

What are the key jobs your customers are trying to get done that influence spending decisions?

What is the consumption chain your customers go through to get a job done? Does it involve spending on something you could sell them? Are there any places where the chain breaks down?

What about doing business with you do customers see as positive (they would buy more or be more loyal because of these features)? What do they see as negative?

Finally, how might the configuration of these things change given shifts in the environment and new possibilities? Are there issues you need to begin preparing for now?

4

Customers, Not Hostages

In Wyoming with 10 investors at a ranch/
retreat, I think I might need a food taster. I can
hardly blame them.

— Reed Hastings, CEO of Netflix, 2011

Reed Hastings, the founder of Netflix, was late in returning a video-cassette of the movie *Apollo 13* to his local Blockbuster video rental store, and was furious at being charged a significant late fee. He went looking for a better way to get movies to watch at home.

That is indeed a great story about how Netflix started. Regardless of whether it is true or not, the inflection point that created the opportunity for the company that became Netflix was the original commercialization of the DVD. DVDs were not only digital but also less expensive to manufacture than videocassettes, with the result being that movie studios offered them for sale (rather than their being rented) as a retail product.

Videocassettes were large and heavy. DVDs were light enough to mail in a greeting card envelope, which was the first proof of concept that Hastings and his cofounder, Marc Randolph, conducted. With the ambition of becoming the "Amazon of something," as one observer noted, they launched their company in 1997 and ignited a revolution in how people all over the world would consume content.

It is worth mentioning at this juncture that Hastings, like many who have seen pending inflection points coming, had a technological/ scientific background. With a degree in computer science from Stanford and the founding of his first company, Pure Software, in 1991, he was keenly aware of what digital technologies were capable of and where they were going. In August of 1996, Pure Software merged with Atria to form Pure Atria. One year later, in August of 1997, Rational Software acquired Pure Atria, freeing Hastings up to launch Netflix.

Hastings foresaw the advent of the streaming model early. What he didn't expect was how long it would take consumers to adopt it. As he put it, "In 1997, we said that 50% of the business would be from streaming by 2002. It was zero. In 2002, we said that 50% of the business would be from streaming by 2007. It was zero . . . Now streaming has exploded . . . We were waiting for all these years. Then we were in the right place at the right time."

THE JOURNEY TOWARD STREAMING

The idea for what would eventually become digital streaming, or video on demand, had its roots in the humble VHS, or Video Home System, developed by the Victor Company of Japan and commercialized in the late 1970s. It was introduced in the United States in 1977 (ending the prospects of an earlier videocassette technology invented by Philips), and immediately ignited a tug-of-war between content providers and their viewers. Content providers wanted customers to be hostages to their preferred way of doing things; viewers wanted to be free of those constraints.

Content providers wanted to tightly control when certain shows were on, show advertisements during them, and manage the cost of the content. Viewers, on the other hand, preferred to take control of when they could watch shows and potentially skip over annoying commercials. "Watch Whatever Whenever" was the rallying cry for one of Sony's early models.

The television people were not amused. In a 1976 case that eventually went all the way to the US Supreme Court, they lost their argument that because VHS recording devices could lead to copyright infringement, they should be illegal. The Court, in a ruling that seems almost quaint by today's standards, disagreed. It decided that as long as a product had substantial legitimate uses for which it could be sold, it could legally be offered, even if some users committed crimes while using it. By then, the idea that people could exert control over when they looked at content was firmly entrenched.

Cassette tapes as content repositories, however, had a lot of drawbacks. You had to rewind them to replay them. Returning to a given spot (for instance, if you wanted to pinpoint a particular section of an exercise tape) required carefully monitoring the tape machine's counter. This spurred inventors to see if there might not be another format that would be more convenient. One of the first attempts was the LaserDisc, an expensive vinyl-record-size storage medium that also required an expensive player and couldn't record — it could only play back content that was prerecorded. Clunky and incomplete (you had to flip it over mid-movie to watch the whole thing!), it never took off in the United States. (Although my parents, early adopters, were distraught when the format came to its last gasp.)

A breakthrough came along with the digitization of content. Digital DVDs as we know them were introduced in 1997, providing the inspiration for Hastings. The ill-fated peer-to-peer file-sharing network Napster further showed the power of being able to share digital content (albeit illegally, as it turned out) in 1999, providing evidence both of the ability of the technology to support this capability and of user demand for digital content. Moreover, pirates began to share video content illegally, forcing the hands of content producers who might have preferred to stick with the old system. It became common knowledge that streaming video content — in other words, video on demand — was likely to take hold as a popular medium.

Indeed, a Harvard Business School case study on Netflix in 2000 included this passage for students to ponder:

> With the widespread adoption of the internet, analysts believed that home video would eventually be delivered directly to consumers over high-speed internet connections. The eventual advent of video-on-demand meant that video retailers had a limited time frame in which to position themselves for this new environment. Although it was generally agreed that such a change would take place, there was less agreement on the length of time it would take.

BLOCKBUSTER BLOWS IT IN STREAMING

In a classic example of moving too early on a potential inflection point, Blockbuster took this streaming idea seriously and, in the year 2000, went into partnership with Enron (yes, *that* Enron) to explore the potential of streaming video. Enron Broadband Services (EBS) was a particularly innovative young organization. One observer noted that EBS "was not the inventor of concepts such as cloud computing, services embedded in the network, and apps on demand – however, by the time EBS began talking with Blockbuster in 1999, EBS already had working versions of those technologies, in use with customers, long before these now-dominant technologies were in wide commercial use by other firms."

While EBS was remarkably successful at building out a working video on demand platform, the venture stalled as complex negotiations with movie studios over content took place. At the time, there were no conventions for how revenue from streaming services would be divided (a dilemma that has still not been resolved). The Blockbuster people, who would have had far more clout with the studios, weren't particularly keen on the streaming idea, and the pricing strategies required to cut the deals meant that the movies that were available were expensive. Even more, given the state of broadband at the time, downloads still took a while, and you couldn't watch these movies on a television without buying a special adapter. The venture failed, the parties blamed each other, and both companies ended up in bankruptcy – albeit for very different reasons.

So, by 2000, there was widespread agreement about the eventual transition to streaming of video on demand. And yet, it took the better part of the following decade for companies like Netflix to make this a reality. This again illustrates the "gradually, then suddenly" principle of inflection points. As Jeff Bezos has observed, it isn't usually all that difficult to identify key trends. The hard part is knowing when to move and bringing the organization with you when you decide to take action.

Before we get into the streaming wars, however, let's have a look at how Netflix established its powerful position in people's homes by capitalizing on a different business model than the one Blockbuster had put forth.

CAPITALIZING ON NEGATIVE ATTRIBUTES OF AN INCUMBENT'S OFFERING

At the time Netflix was launched, its competitor Blockbuster occupied a strong position in the everyday lives of consumers. It had millions of customers and thousands of store locations, incredible brand recognition, and, at its peak in 2004, revenue of more than $6 billion. But the dirty little secret behind Blockbuster's business model was that customer-irritating late fees accounted for a significant percentage of its profits. According to one source, in 2000 the company earned $800 million in such fees, or 16 percent of its revenue.

In other words, the most significant factor contributing to the company's success was the penalties imposed on its customers. That is what I would call a "tolerable" attribute, a concept that was introduced in the previous chapter. This is a basic feature that customers view negatively. As the word implies, customers will tolerate negative features as long as they do not feel they have viable alternatives. Once something comes along that allows them to capture the benefits they seek but eliminates the "tolerable" feature, that attribute becomes a "dissatisfier" and eventually an "enrager." Netflix took advantage of this DVD inflection point to introduce an entirely different model for its customers, one that eliminated the enrager of excessive fees.

Now, the folks over at Blockbuster were not blind to this. Observers report that CEO John Antioco started to take action on the threat that Netflix (and other nascent streaming services) represented around 2004. (Recall, that was the peak for Blockbuster in revenue terms.) He led a move to discontinue late fees and launch a subscription service. On top of that, he had the idea of leveraging Blockbuster's considerable brick-and-mortar presence to offer something Netflix couldn't at the time — immediate gratification. Done watching your movie? Want to get another one right away? No problem — head over to your local Blockbuster, hand in the one that you're done with, and pick up a new one immediately. The new initiative was called Total Access.

At the time, it was widely hailed as a strategic breakthrough. One breathless observer noted, "All of a sudden, all of that expensive real-estate and infrastructure is no longer a liability for Blockbuster—it is an enormous advantage that Netflix simply can't match."

Antioco's initiatives, however, were going to cost the firm serious money, and also depress short-term profitability, as is often the case when a business needs to go through a strategic inflection point. Carl Icahn, an activist investor, entered the fray, putting members of his own preference on the board and eventually easing Antioco out. Under his successor, Jim Keyes, Antioco's changes were reversed, and Blockbuster stubbornly tried to hold off the inflection point. The company went bankrupt in 2010.

The Blockbuster versus Netflix story illustrates why inflection points can open up areas of real opportunity. Many incumbent providers of all kinds of services accumulate negatives in their offerings over time, as Blockbuster did with its late fees. When an inflection point opens up the possibility to escape the negative, customers often depart, transferring their resources and relationship to a more accommodating provider. In other words, customers "escape" the incumbent and start doing business with the new provider. It is hard work for an incumbent to apply that kind of reinvention to itself. This is why the story of how Netflix transitioned its business model is such an interesting one.

SEEING AN INFLECTION POINT COMING, BUT MOVING FASTER THAN ITS CUSTOMERS COULD ACCEPT

Consider a rare misstep by Netflix. Its original success stemmed from doing the job of providing customers with movie rentals in a convenient, affordable way. In its original model, customers paid a monthly subscription fee to receive mail-ordered DVDs of movies. They could create a "queue" of movies they wanted to see. When they returned a DVD to Netflix, the next one in the queue was sent to them.

As mentioned earlier, predictions that video on demand would shift to a streaming format had been made since the late 1990s. The real challenge for leaders is to identify the point at which it makes sense to take action with respect to such a pending inflection point. With the spreading availability of high-speed Internet connections, Reed Hastings and his team at Netflix began a modest experiment to see whether the time might be right for at least some of their users to try the new format. Given what was possible at the time, the quality of streamed movies was going to be far inferior to that of those seen on DVDs or Blu-ray discs, but the movies would be available immediately.

Netflix launched its Watch Now service in January of 2007. It offered about a thousand titles in that format, ranging from classics such as *Casablanca* to cult movies, foreign films, and miniseries. The goal at that point was to offer something for everyone from the Netflix archives. At the time, users paid $5.99 per month for the plan, which got them six hours of streaming per month.

When launching Watch Now, Hastings said, "We named our company Netflix in 1998 because we believed Internet-based movie rental represented the future, first as a means of improving service and selection, and then as a means of movie delivery. While mainstream consumer adoption of online movie watching will take a number of years due to content and technology hurdles, the time is right for Netflix to take the first step."

The streaming business was economically attractive for the company, eliminating the need for the cumbersome activities involved in mailing DVDs around. Netflix was so confident in the anticipated growth of the streaming service that they circulated a widely viewed chart in 2010 projecting that the DVD business would peak in 2013 and that streaming would almost entirely replace it in the subsequent years. As they said at the time in an investor presentation, "The goal is to have content so broad, engaging and affordable that everyone subscribes to Netflix."

The framework presented in the previous chapter can be used to evaluate the advent of economically viable streaming. As always, it's smart to begin with the limiting pot of resources for which an organization is contesting. In this case, that pot is household spending on entertainment. Given that, the situation (who, what, where) might well evolve from predominantly the living room at home to anywhere people would like to consume content, especially in light of the advent of greater mobility and faster cellular service.

The job to be done likewise might expand beyond just watching a movie on a weeknight to the popular distraction of binge-watching entire series. The consumption chain would change dramatically—from queues, mailboxes, and the iconic red envelope with a DVD inside, to simply and conveniently clicking on an app on a smart device and watching on demand.

And the capabilities also would change—from a business with heavy physical dimensions that creates, stores, and mails DVDs to one that offers an entirely digital experience. All the key metrics used to manage the DVD business would change should streaming become the platform of choice.

Hastings felt that it would be foolhardy to keep the two businesses together. Aside from the Netflix brand and its well-developed relationship with content providers, there were few commonalities, as the metrics, investments, and drivers of success would all be different. Even the attributes used to watch on a streaming platform would be different. Netflix envisioned a purely digital consumption experience *without* the negatives associated with DVDs (needing a separate player, having to physically insert the DVD, having a limited number of physical places where they could be viewed).

Given this belief, Hastings made a fateful choice in July of 2011. Since he felt strongly that the future was going to be streaming and the DVD business was going to decline, he decided to separate the streaming business from the DVD mail-order business. The DVD business would be transferred to a subsidiary called Qwikster. Customers would pay separately for the DVD service and the streaming service. Pricing would change from an all-inclusive subscription of $9.99 per month for both DVD mailing and streaming to $7.99 per month for either the instant streaming plan or the DVD plan alone. In effect, customers who wanted to retain *both* services would now have to pay $15.98 per month.

Customers mutinied. They perceived the price change not as an offering to provide them with greater choice, but rather as a massive price hike for a service they had been receiving for $9.99 per month. Plus, the content available via streaming was more limited than that available on DVDs, leading many customers to declare that they would drop the streaming part of their subscriptions. Even more infuriating for customers who subscribed to both services, they would have to establish two queues for the two services. The fallout was so severe that by October of that year, reports with headlines such as "Netflix Facing a Fight Against Obsolescence" began to appear. Some 800,000 customers defected from the service.

The Qwikster concept was quickly dropped, and Netflix returned to a bundled price.

You can think of this as a case of moving too quickly in anticipation of an inflection point. Yes, streaming was likely to be an important and essential way in which the job of accessing entertainment and content on demand would be met in the future. But trying to force customers to give up convenience, flexibility, and an affordable price to do it generated nothing but anger on their part.

WHAT TO DO ABOUT THE
LOOMING INFLECTION?

This nonetheless left Hastings and his team with an unsolved problem: the future might well be streaming, but the profits of today were delivered by DVD. The solution was to quietly implement what the original split was intended to accomplish: create a separate business with its own URL (DVD.com), its own business structure, and its own operations. The URL was purchased in March of 2012, and at that time Netflix said it was for "defensive" reasons.

The streaming side of the business would focus on growing its customer base around the world, while the DVD side would focus on increasing efficiency and maintaining profits even as subscriber numbers dwindled. The two groups have separate management teams, are located in headquarters some distance apart, use different metrics, and incentivize their people differently. By 2018, the streaming business reported 118 million subscribers worldwide. The DVD division reported 3.4 million subscribers, down from around 20 million at its peak in 2010. Hank Breeggemann, a longtime Netflix leader, was put in charge of the DVD business, freeing up Hastings to focus on the next big inflection point in the entertainment world — the creation of original content.

The move into original content reflected a change on the part of incumbent content owners. While for years they had been happy to license their reruns and past shows to Netflix, often for considerable amounts of cash, once the company began to show consumers how pleasant a streaming, ad-free environment could be, and for a very reasonable price, loyalty to the vaunted cable bundle began to erode. To preserve the status quo, content owners began to reverse course on letting Netflix show their programs. This was probably too little, too late for the incumbents because, as one reporter noted, "every minute, another six people will cut the cord."

Netflix was not the first to venture into the production of original content, but relative to others, it had one enormous advantage: fifteen years of incredibly rich data on what customers enjoyed watching. With the decision to enter the world of creating original content, Netflix managed to pull off an amazing feat — content so desirable that reportedly 75 percent of all US households now subscribe to the streaming service. The company's mission today reads as follows:

> We strive to win more of our members' "moments of truth." Those decision points are, say, at 7:15 pm when a member wants to relax, enjoy a shared experience with friends and family, or is bored. The member could choose Netflix, or a multitude of other options.

HOW EASING CUSTOMER FRUSTRATION CAN CHANGE AN ARENA

In the previous chapter, we reviewed some hypotheses about how an inflection point might change a business and potentially open up new opportunities. We examined how a change in decision-making around teen spending (the available resources in the arena's context) created an inflection point as spending on communications and the Internet squeezed out spending on apparel. As we saw, this shift hurt many traditional retailers, but it benefited others that were prepared — whether by fortune or by strategy — to respond to the advent of fast fashion.

So far in this chapter, we have studied how Netflix took advantage of an opportunity to do the job of providing rented entertainment better than Blockbuster, which had loaded this job with one big negative (late fees). We've also examined how challenging it was for Netflix to go through the next transition, from DVD to streaming, and from there to becoming a streaming-centered creator of original content, while still preserving its existing core business profitably.

Three analytical lenses intersect in this example. The first is the consumption chain, which reflects the journey customers go through as they interact with an organization. Reed Hastings famously ignored a friend's advice that he would not want to manage two queues for entertainment content, failing to understand that this was a less desirable customer experience than the one they already had. The second lens is the attribute map, which highlights how customers react to the features of an offering at various points in the chain. In this case, customers were enraged at what they perceived to be a price hike for a lower-quality service. The third is the job to be done, or what customers are trying to achieve, which motivates their behavior at any given link in the chain.

When you identify a barrier to achieving a job to be done, you have identified a vital point at which an inflection might change the arena. You need to understand the barriers, obstacles, and frictions that get in the way of customers and other key stakeholders getting what they want out of a given situation. And you can't rely on asking them. Even when a situation may be poorly designed or may frustrate them, they may not be aware of this. You may see them unconsciously engage in workarounds, simply put up with the inconvenience, or — worst case — do without an offering altogether because it doesn't do the job well.

THE NEXT INFLECTION FOR NETFLIX?

Despite its success, it is clear that the next round of competition for Netflix will be different from the last. Rather than simply being a conduit for content, it is now going directly into competition with original content providers by creating its own shows. And not just low-budget, cheap and cheerful shows either. In 2018, Netflix released three original movies directly into theaters — *before* offering them on its streaming platform. The company decided to do this so that the films would qualify for coveted Academy Awards, for work both in front of the camera and behind it. The team at Netflix clearly feels that original content is essential to maintaining subscriber loyalty and that top on-screen talent is key to the quality of that content.

This comes in the wake of some content providers, surprised perhaps at how effectively Netflix has grown its subscriber base (and reduced the attractiveness of bundled cable programming), parting ways with the company. Disney Studios has announced that it intends to remove its content from Netflix and introduce a competing streaming service, Disney+. AT&T, which now owns Warner Media, another major content producer, is also likely to part ways with Netflix and launch its own streaming service. Many of the large cable companies, such as Comcast, already offer streaming bundled in with their cable fees, On Demand movies and programming, and Pay-Per-View, for which they charge.

Interestingly, Hastings and his team seem prepared for the reactions of competitors. This is perhaps because they are thinking in terms of *arenas*, not in terms of the standard or conventional television industry. Netflix has very deliberately not defined its arena in terms of traditional television. Instead, it has framed its challenge in terms of increasing the percentage of their leisure time its members spend on the service. As their investor messaging says:

> We compete with all the activities that consumers have at their disposal in their leisure time. This includes watching content on other streaming services, linear TV, DVD or TVOD but also reading a book, surfing YouTube, playing video games, socializing on Facebook, going out to dinner with friends or enjoying a glass of wine with their partner, just to name a few. We earn a tiny fraction of consumers' time and money, and have lots of opportunity to win more share of leisure time, if we can keep improving.

Imagine — a network large enough to rival Facebook's, for which subscribers actually pay, without the data collection that could eventually run afoul of regulators and members themselves. This may well represent the next inflection point for the streaming entertainment business.

WHY CELL PHONES GET THE
JOB DONE BETTER THAN
TRADITIONAL CAMERAS

Remember, a useful way to think about potential customers is to consider the jobs they are trying to get done in their own lives and how a shift in constraints can have an effect on how those jobs get done. A powerful source of inspiration with respect to the next inflection point is to consider what gets in the way of customers achieving their goals. This means that paying attention to the situations potential customers are in, what they are trying to achieve, and what outcomes they seek is key.

An incredible example of a device that helps customers get jobs done more easily is the modern smartphone. It has replaced myriad single-function devices, from a flashlight to a digital recorder, a camera, a video camera, an email platform . . . I could go on and on. The smartphone has been brilliant in helping us get more and more jobs done, all without having to carry around specialized devices. Today, digitization means we create and interact with more content than ever before, while using traditional tools less. This in turn has created an inflection point in how we experience the world around us.

For instance, consider watching Tiger Woods play golf. In a tweet that has since gone viral, Ryder Cup Europe and European Tour content director Jamie Kennedy compared what the crowd watching Woods looked like in 2002 versus 2018. The 2002 crowd was, well, simply watching Woods play. But by 2018, Woods was playing amidst a veritable sea of cell phones, all trying to capture photos and videos of the famous player. In other words, during his 2018 comeback tour, the audience was not so much watching him as they were recording him, overwhelmingly via cell phone. Like the teenagers in the previous chapter, just being at an event isn't enough. You need to have photos and footage that *prove* you were there.

To put this situation in the context of jobs to be done, we might describe it this way:

When . . .	I want to . . .	So I can . . .
Situation	**Motivation**	**Outcome**
I am watching a live event of great interest to others I care about	Capture it in some way	Share the video and images with others who couldn't be there with me

When you think about it this way, it's clear that cell phones are far better for accomplishing this outcome than conventional cameras. Even today, dedicated video cameras are bulky. They are single-purpose. They run out of battery power quickly. They take up a lot of space on storage media. And then to share the video you've captured with others, there is usually a complicated process of pulling the content from some kind of storage media and transforming it into a format that others can see as well. With a smartphone, you simply fire up the camera app, set it to "video," and away you go!

This is an example of how shifting constraints — everything from the replacement of bulky videocassettes with slim DVDs to the ability to take videos on a device that is probably in your pocket anyway — can help a company identify opportunities to change the customer journey. To begin to anticipate the effects of a shift in constraints, it's important to experience the customer journey and customer frustrations at not being able to get their jobs done. This leads us to think through what customer pain points may be at different links in the consumption chain.

Let's consider how ride-hailing companies such as Uber and Lyft seemed to come out of nowhere to disrupt traditional taxi service, particularly in places like New York City. It's a classic example of how the assumptions in an existing business can blind its leadership to changes that will unravel them.

I'll take New York City as an example. During the Great Depression, many unemployed people turned to driving cabs in a desperate effort to support themselves. The consequences were too few customers being chased by too many drivers, intense traffic congestion, and unsafe conditions, including run-down vehicles and reckless driving. This situation eventually convinced New York City leaders that the taxi business could benefit from regulation that would ensure riders a safe trip, fewer drivers, and some guarantee of quality. In 1937, the Haas

Act put into place the "medallion system" for cabs that could be hailed on the street. Medallions had to be purchased from the City, and a market for them subsequently developed. The number of medallions was strictly limited (13,587 in 2013), which led to the price of a medallion skyrocketing to as much as $1.3 million by 2013.

The monopoly on supply that medallion restrictions created, while guaranteeing taxi drivers and fleet owners steady business, inadvertently created a large number of downsides for customers. As Megan McArdle, a writer for the *Atlantic*, explained in a 2012 article titled "Why You Can't Get a Taxi," the service offered was less than ideal from the customer's point of view.

> Like most urbanites, I've spent a lot of time voicing the standard complaints about taxis: They're dirty and uncomfortable and never there when you need them. Half the time, they don't show up for those six a.m. airport runs. They all seem to disappear when you most need them — on New Year's Eve or during a rainy rush hour. Most cabbies drive like PCP addicts. Women complain about scary drivers. Black men complain about drivers who won't stop to pick them up.

In her article, McArdle enthused about the new service offered by a company called Uber. At the time, Uber's business model was basically to match potential riders with existing limousine companies. The model in which ordinary people could become Uber drivers had not yet emerged. Taxi companies objected to Uber and tried to use regulations to prevent the company from expanding, but the reality that it was customers, not regulators, they would need to win over was not yet evident to them.

The situation was ripe for disruption.

When . . .	I want to . . .	So I can . . .
Situation	**Motivation**	**Outcome**
I need to get somewhere that is too far to walk and I don't have the use of a car	Successfully arrange a trip	Get from point A to point B with a minimum of expense, hassle, and complexity

That's when ride-hailing companies stepped in to change the job of getting from point A to point B.

Consumption Chain Link	Conventional Taxi Practices	Negative Attributes/ Customer Pain Points
Booking a ride	Call central dispatch Hail on a street corner Arrange limo beforehand Go to a taxi stand	Unreliable Not available where I am Long wait times Drivers discriminate
Taking a ride	Uneven experience Dirty cars Driver on cell phone Old vehicles No temperature control Wild driving	Unpleasant environment in general
Paying for the ride	Use cash Use credit card in cab Ask for receipt	Driver doesn't accept credit cards Driver doesn't carry change Long wait for receipt to process with expense account

This analysis throws up some important customer pain points—that is, factors that interfere with customers getting their job done as conveniently and affordably as possible. The next step is to ask why the pain points are the way they are.

Negative Attributes/ Customer Pain Points	Why Is It This Way?	How Might It Be Changed?
Unreliable Not available where I am Long wait times Drivers discriminate	Economies of central dispatch: it isn't economical to have a fleet of vehicles widely distributed	App to connect drivers and riders who are geographically dispersed
Unpleasant environment in general	No sanctions for an unpleasant experience—monopoly conditions	Ratings system in which riders rate their rides and drivers rate their riders
Driver doesn't accept credit cards Driver doesn't carry change Long wait for receipt to process with expense account	No investment in new technology—monopoly conditions	Credit card preregistered; no need to process card at end of trip; receipts automatically captured and available online

Ride-hailing companies' solution to the transportation problem has proved to be a major inflection point for the taxi business in places like New York City. Legislators and public officials were taken by surprise by the inflection point represented by the rise of these services. By 2017, Uber was making more trips than the city's yellow cabs.

This is frequently the case: institutions take a while to catch up to the changes wrought by inflection points. One institutional response to ride-hailing services has been for New York City to mandate that drivers earn a minimum wage from the company. With studies suggesting that the only way these companies make money is by banking on inadvertent subsidies from its drivers, the change represented by the ride-hailing revolution may already be on to its next phase.

And, of course, other on-demand alternatives to urban transportation are blossoming as well. Recently, competition has become extreme in the market for on-demand scooters. The e-scooter company Bird was valued in 2018 at over $2 billion. There are even rumors that ride-hailing companies are interested in moving into the bike-sharing programs operated by Motivate, which runs such offerings as Citi Bike in New York. While Uber seems intent on offering across-the-board access to urban mobility solutions, it isn't clear yet which ones will survive the inevitable shakeout.

Back to our analytical approach. The issue you need to focus on in your analysis of arenas is whether a change in the daily constraints that your business operates under might allow a competitor to address customer pain points differently or better than you do.

Think about that.

If that's a real possibility, then it's time to pay attention.

REDRAWING AN ARENA: THE TANGLE THAT IS HEALTHCARE IN THE UNITED STATES

Warren Buffett, CEO of Berkshire Hathaway, is ever brilliant at the turn of a phrase. In describing healthcare in the United States, he calls it a "hungry tapeworm" affecting the economy. Not only are healthcare costs in the United States higher than in the rest of the world, they've also been rising faster than elsewhere. According to *Consumer*

Reports, if you sliced out healthcare spending in the United States and made a country out of it, it would be the world's fifth-largest economy.

The negative consequences of one sector sucking up so much of the economy are indeed dire. Funds going into healthcare aren't available for other things — things like raises for workers, for instance, which contribute to flat wages and limited earning power for many. The 2018 agreement between Jeff Bezos, Warren Buffett, and Jamie Dimon (CEO of JPMorgan Chase) to enter into an as yet unnamed joint healthcare venture signals that the frustration with seemingly intractable momentum in rising costs has reached some kind of tipping point. In other words, they are going to try to spark an inflection point by changing just about every element of the healthcare arena.

The piecemeal delivery of most fee-for-service healthcare services in the United States creates incentives to do more, not less, even if the activity is not strictly speaking necessary. Unlike other industries, in which increased efficiency makes an organization more competitive, efficiency in healthcare delivery often means less revenue. Innovating to require one CT scan rather than three, for instance, means a provider only gets paid once, not three times.

To better align incentives with rewards, many players in the ecosystem have concluded that a payment system based on *value* — on patient outcomes, for instance — rather than activities makes more sense. If a group made less money, not more, by operating inefficiently, the incentive to do so would diminish. The unintended consequence is that with the incentives now heading in the opposite direction, there may well be rewards for withholding necessary or expensive care from patients. Or of rationing care, which is already common practice in countries with single-payer systems. The United States differs from most other countries where effectiveness calculations are used to determine who has access to care. The result in many places is rationing. The sad reality, of course, is that the United States is no different from any other place in the sense that only so much can be spent on healthcare and so some form of rationing is inevitable.

While dealing with the whole US healthcare system would be worthy of an entire book, for our purposes let's focus on the potential opportunities reflected by a shift in simply how pharmacy benefits are managed. This represents a potentially significant inflection point for an industry that has grown so complex and opaque that its inner workings are extremely difficult to figure out.

Pharmacy Benefit Managers: Middlemen Gone Rogue?

Pharmacy benefit managers (PBMs) are organizations that act as intermediaries between various players in the healthcare system. They were originally created to "reduce administrative costs for insurers, validate patient eligibility, administer plan benefits as well as negotiate costs between pharmacies and health plans."

In the years since this relatively straightforward service was created, PBMs have grown enormously and become involved in just about every aspect of the prescription drug business. Critics argue that their eye-popping profitability comes as they make money from every element of the pharmaceutical supply chain. Indeed, the *Wall Street Journal* found that "pharmacy-benefit managers are exceptionally profitable; 85% of their gross profit converted into Ebitda over the past two years."

The firms, such as Express Scripts, OptumRx (a unit of the insurer UnitedHealth Group), and CVS Health, processed 72 percent of the nation's prescriptions in 2017, according to Pembroke Consulting. A 2017 analysis showed that $15 of every $100 spent on brand-name pharmaceuticals goes to middlemen, as opposed to about $4 in other countries.

In a clear indication that standard PBM practices are not necessarily in their customers' best interests, the industry has strongly resisted being held to a fiduciary standard (in which they would have to keep the interests of their customers in mind as they made recommendations). As Bloomberg reported in 2018, "Some of the biggest players in the industry have warned that a fiduciary standard could be deeply damaging to their business. Express Scripts Holding Co., which agreed to be bought by health insurer Cigna Corp. this year, said in a 2015 filing that a fiduciary rule 'could have a material adverse effect upon our financial condition, results of operations and cash flows.'"

In a sign of what I anticipate will become an inflection point for these businesses, an increasing din of criticism of industry practices is rising.

Inconsistent and Opaque Pricing

Some consumers have found that they can purchase drugs for less by paying directly for medications rather than using their insurance. The negotiating tactics of PBMs have been blamed, as has the industry for making drug pricing so complex that nobody can understand it.

This situation led to the founding of GoodRx, a startup that offers customers an app that searches for different prices on the same drugs in their local area. A search for a thirty-pill prescription for Lipitor in my area found prices that ranged from $9 (cash, at Walmart) to $27.62 (with a coupon, at Duane Reade).

Clawback: List Prices That . . . Aren't

PBMs negotiate discounts from list prices with drug manufacturers. That doesn't help customers with respect to reimbursements, however. As one observer noted in an ABC News report, "List price does matter when it comes to co-pays, co-insurance and other out-of-pocket costs. These payments are often based on the list price of a drug, not the discounted price. So if you are paying 20 percent co-insurance on a $200 vial of insulin per month, but your insurer is paying a discounted $75 per vial, you pay the 20 percent on the list price, or $40, instead of the $15 you would pay if the co-insurance was 20 percent of the discounted price." The patient doesn't get the savings.

According to the same report, "Claw backs allow pharmacies to keep the full customer copay amounts, even if it's more than the reimbursement. For example, if a patient's copay is $10 and the PBM reimburses the pharmacy for the cost of the generic drug plus a dispensing fee for roughly $6, the PBM pockets the extra $4 paid by the patient."

There are even cases in which the co-pay for a prescription exceeds the actual cost of the prescription, with the difference in price going back to the PBM. Lawsuits have been filed with respect to this practice, and public anger is so intense that several state legislatures have started to evaluate banning it. In a particularly nasty twist on this, some pharmacists have reported being told by their employers that they are not allowed to let patients know that the drug might be available at a lower price. A court ruled against Cigna for doing this in a

2018 case, and the issue is getting a lot more attention from lawyers and legislators.

The Murky Practice of Rebates

PBMs and manufacturers negotiate so-called rebates on various drugs. The pharmaceutical company charges the PBM the list price of a drug, then pays a rebate back to the PBM. This allows that all-important list price to look higher than the real price that is actually paid for the drug. In an escalating interindustry battle over healthcare profits, pharmaceutical companies have been attempting to draw attention to the actions of PBMs (rather than their own price increases) as the reason for increased costs to consumers.

What's the bottom line? All these practices are now seeping out into the public's perception, creating real confusion and an overall distrust of the whole business. To see how that's playing out, let's take a look at how one major corporation has taken on the challenge of reducing prescription drug costs for its employees.

CATERPILLAR: PART OF THE FUTURE THAT ISN'T EVENLY DISTRIBUTED YET?

As mentioned in Chapter 1, science fiction author and artist William Ford Gibson is often cited as the first person who said, "The future is already here — it's just not very evenly distributed." That is an extremely useful perspective in terms of anticipating potential inflection points. The goal is to find situations where forward-thinking entities have overcome some of the constraints of the ways things are done today and are innovating to find a better solution. With that perspective, let's see how Caterpillar has circumvented the constraints of the PBM business as it is currently designed.

In 2004, fed up with prescription drug expenditures that rose an average of 14 percent annually between 1996 and 2004, managers at Caterpillar vowed that they would institute a new process because the current approach made them feel that they had "no leverage and are at the mercy of a confusing system. We wanted to challenge the system." According to their estimates, that system entailed 10 to 25 percent waste.

Using the analytical framework applied earlier in this chapter, we can see how the ways in which the PBM business had evolved represented an opportunity for Caterpillar to take action. The following table summarizes what Caterpillar did to free themselves from being "hostages" to the existing PBM arrangement.

Consumption Chain Link	Negative Attributes/ Customer Pain Points	How Did Caterpillar Address These?
Selecting a benefit manager	Conflicts of interest	Found a PBM committed to transparency in pricing
Understanding costs	Lack of transparency	Negotiated directly with major pharmacies
Deciding which drugs will be in the formulary	Little transparency, inflated costs	Brought the decision in-house
Pricing involving clawbacks	Higher prices	Pursued transparent pricing with suppliers

The results of Caterpillar's actions have been impressive. Although actual cost savings haven't been reported, experts estimate that they could be in the realm of $37.5 million each year, with the company agreeing that its 2015 costs were actually lower than those in 2004.

Todd Bisping, Caterpillar's healthcare benefits manager, who led the charge in the company's efforts, is also involved in the Health Transformation Alliance, a multiemployer membership group with the goal of helping other organizations to rein in their ever-rising medical costs, beginning with some of what Caterpillar learned. While the results of this initiative and others have been largely incremental to date, the commitment by CEOs such as Bezos, Buffett, and Dimon to accelerate businesses' role in changing the way healthcare is delivered seems well on its way to marking an inflection point for that sector of the economy.

Of course, Bezos's Amazon itself seems poised to enter the healthcare sector, which could produce the same kind of sweeping changes it has triggered in other parts of the economy.

Key Takeaways

Practices that displease or even enrage customers can create an opening for a disruptive player to come into your markets and cause customers to defect.

Even when you see an inflection point on the horizon, it can take a lot longer than you think for it to actually arrive.

Customers will only remain hostages for so long. Eventually, the model that imprisons them is bound to collapse.

It may make sense to separate the operating functions of a growing business from those of businesses in decline. The two require different metrics and operational considerations, and different points of value to customers.

Deeply understanding the situations customers are in, the jobs they are trying to get done in those situations, and the outcomes they are seeking is vital to anticipating how those situations might change.

Deeply understanding the structure of a system (such as the way prescription medicines are sold) can allow you to spark an inflection point, one pain point at a time.

5

What Must Be True?
Creating a Plan to Learn Fast

People who are right a lot work very hard to
do that unnatural thing of trying to disconfirm
their beliefs.

— Jeff Bezos

The discussion of seeing around corners has taken us first to the edges — to those places where the potential for inflection points first begins to make itself known. We've created some approaches to establishing early warnings — imagining very different future scenarios and working backward to see where they might be in their evolutionary stages. We've explored the idea of an arena, rather than an industry, as being a crucial level of analysis. We've looked at how irritants and blockers in key stakeholders' paths to getting jobs done can open the door to an inflection sparked by an organization that removes those attributes. We're now on the brink of considering what actions should be taken next.

But first, a few caveats. The techniques described here are not about making predictions and being right. They are about generating possibilities and opening your mind to what *might* happen, so that as evidence gets stronger, you are ready to take action. For any future state, there are many variables that can lead to one outcome or another. What is valuable in complex systems is to be able to keep multiple possible futures in mind so that if and when they unfold, the landscape is more recognizable.

Intel, for instance, has employed science fiction writers, futurists, and students to produce creative works about aspects of the future, with the purpose not of making predictions, but of opening people's minds to emerging possibilities. Seeing around corners is about broadening the range of possibilities you consider paying attention to. Your ability to look into the future is only as well developed as the set of possibilities you are prepared to entertain.

THE INFLECTION POINT GETS
JUST A LITTLE CLEARER

Having seen an inflection point coming, you are now at the moment of deciding what exactly to do about it. The real dilemma facing a decision-maker at this point is that uncertainty is still extremely high. In other words, the ratio of assumptions that must be made relative to the hard-core knowledge that one has is high in the extreme. As I have written about extensively elsewhere, the thought process that such precarious situations require is entirely different from the thought process that one follows when the direction is known.

To be blunt, getting through this tricky process begins with confusion, experimentation, and a touch of chaos, followed by a single-minded determination to make progress against an overarching goal. You must be able to passionately advocate for the vision to drive the outcome, while also being prepared to change the means. This approach is consistent with futurist Paul Saffo's recommendation to form as many forecasts as quickly as possible — and then prove them wrong as quickly as possible — as well as to "hold strong opinions weakly."

Discovery-driven planning, perhaps because more and more of us have been thrust into ever more uncertain circumstances, is gaining significant traction as a new generation of managers recognizes that the critical challenge is planning to learn. Briefly, discovery-driven planning asks you to set some parameters for a future state — and then to work backward to figure out what must be true to make that future state real. Similar to the weak signals exercise first discussed in Chapter 2, this process differs from the risk-averse, failure-avoidant nature of many corporate planning processes.

The idea is not to plan out in great detail what should be done. Rather, with an inflection point in mind, the idea is to make what Peter Sims has called "little bets" and which I call "planning to learn." Before making a large commitment, in other words, start by breaking the monolithic plan down into smaller pieces. These pieces are each punctuated by what I call a *checkpoint*.

A checkpoint is simply a point in time at which you will learn something. At each checkpoint, you want to be asking two questions. The first is whether what you are learning is worth the cost (or risk, or time) required to achieve it. Elsewhere, I've referred to an organization's "appetite," which is the determination, in advance, of what we think we will learn and how much that learning is worth to us. The second is whether, given what you are learning, it still makes sense to continue with the plan or whether a shift of some kind is warranted.

The catch you want to avoid is getting tangled up in the need to be right when you really don't have all the facts. Huge amounts of human breath have been wasted in meetings where people argue back and forth about being right. Instead, think of a low-cost, creative way to determine how you might find out what the right answer really is. In that case, even if your assumptions are not borne out, you've learned something. In fact, even if you've learned that you are at a dead end, that's actually progress because you can always shift course, or "pivot."

An entrepreneurial mindset is incredibly useful here. The key is being *discovery-driven*. Stop pretending you know all the answers. In a highly uncertain and fluid environment, neither you nor anybody else has answers. Arguing about being "right" or having a detailed plan going eighteen months out is just wasting your breath. Instead, articulate and pinpoint the major uncertainties and how you might gain some insight about them.

Nassim Nicholas Taleb offers a valuable perspective on this somewhat chaotic period in thinking about seeing around the next corner in his book *Antifragile: Things That Gain from Disorder:* "Anything that has more upside than downside from random events (or certain shocks) is antifragile; the reverse is fragile." What you are trying to do as you formulate a discovery-driven approach to the next inflection point is capitalize on the upside of your potential learning, while containing the cost and downside. This type of planning exactly reflects Taleb's point that the best way to approach change is to fail cheaply, demonstrate that your hypotheses are wrong quickly, and continue to see a big upside to your actions.

BUT IT ISN'T BASED ON FACTS YET!

As I mentioned earlier, when an inflection point first appears on the horizon, it is extremely easy for us to leap into action too early and to invest substantial resources before a real understanding has emerged as to what that point really means. Many an organization has learned this lesson to enormous regret, especially with the advent of what we call the digital revolution.

Making the wrong moves with respect to digital technologies often begins with misunderstanding the enormity of the change digital represents. The unique effects of digital were discussed in Chapter 1 in terms of combining bits of information that used to remain safely separate. If you think of digital's effect on a traditional organization's strategy and operating model, you can see why so many otherwise high-performing companies can easily make wrong strategic bets because they underestimated digital's impact on their future business, as my colleague Ryan McManus has so clearly explained.

THE MELTING SNOW OF DIGITIZATION

Digitization, simply enough, means replacing activity that used to be done in an unconnected, analog way with connected activity intermediated by a technology layer. For example, once upon a time if you wanted to understand how well a company treated its customers, you would look up its ranking with the Better Business Bureau or Consumer Reports. Today, while those sources of information still exist, consumers are also able to view ratings by other consumers on a wide variety of platforms such as Yelp and TripAdvisor. Rather than rely on a salesperson to explain the benefits or differences between products in a store, potential customers can now click on reviews posted by other users presumably like themselves.

Earlier, I used the idea that snow melts from the edges to suggest that if you want to be strategic about a potential inflection point, you need to be exposed to where it first turns up — usually at the edges of your organization. The digitization process takes us further with this idea, as it shows not just the early signals that something is changing (snow is melting) but how the change is progressing.

Starting with Marketing

Digitization began, sneakily enough, in realms that seem distant from the strategic core of a business, such as marketing. In the early dot-com gold rush, that meant securing the ".com" URL, capturing digital real estate for banner ads, and trying to get people to subscribe to blogs. The disruptive effects in this first phase were initially felt by organizations that were used to providing one-way flows of information to relatively powerless external players. The first wave of melting snow utterly changed the taken-for-granted assumptions about how organizations should present themselves to the world. But for many, this change didn't seem central to future organizational survival, since it seemed only to be affecting marketing.

Indeed, one of the more interesting effects of the early Internet wave was to increase the amount spent on — wait for it — analog marketing. Publications such as *Wired,* on the new-economy side, and even *Fortune,* on the more traditional side, were bursting with endless pages of advertisements. They could hardly fit in your mailbox. In 2000, advertising reached a walloping 2.5 percent of GDP in the United States, only to retreat back to historical norms of 2.2 to 2.3 percent with the ensuing dot-com crash.

This early stage might well have lulled those providing traditional advertising into a sense of security. And yet, in 2000 Google launched its AdWords advertising product, which offered advertisers the ability — with relatively little personal effort — to put their advertisements in front of people searching for terms that might indicate a proclivity to purchase. By the end of its first year, Google AdWords had reached $70 million in revenue. Using the product, advertisers could determine how much they were willing to pay to have their advertisements appear next to designated search content. When a user did a search, Google's algorithms scanned the database and generated a ranking based on willingness to pay. If a consumer clicked on the ad, Google would charge the advertiser a "cost per click" determined by the advertiser's willingness to pay, what others had bid to be shown next to the same search subjects, and a small surcharge. Other advertising models charged advertisers a "cost per thousand impressions" based on how many viewers were likely to have seen the ad.

This was the beginning of the transition from advertising that flowed through traditional analog channels to advertising that appeared on digital ones, a transition that has led newspapers, for instance, to suffer double-digit declines, from advertiser spending of close to $90 billion in 2005 to less than $50 billion in 2017. The shift decimated traditional media, but even as that inflection point rolled out, many traditional businesses still didn't see how it would affect them.

Creeping into Operations

The next phase of the inflection point represented by the digital revolution was to change how companies performed their basic business functions. Firms such as CEMEX, the Mexican cement supplier, found that digital enabled them to service customers in entirely new and very compelling ways. For instance, in its ready-mix concrete business, CEMEX realized that a just-in-time service solution would be far more valuable to construction customers than a solution that relied on being able to project needs and utilization in advance. Using insights from companies such as Dell, CEMEX created a just-in-time call center mode. When customers needed cement delivered, they would place an order and, within a relatively short period of time, receive a delivery.

This phase of the digital revolution rocked many of the taken-for-granted assumptions in the world of operations. Costly, high-friction transactions were replaced with relatively inexpensive, low-friction transactions, opening up vast possibilities.

Next, to Products and Services

In light of the new possibilities that digital enabled, it was only a matter of time until digital products and services became meaningful participants in a great many arenas. Entertainment and media were utterly changed as photos, books, movies, magazines, and other content "went digital" and created not only different products but also different consumption experiences. In effect, products came to consumers — consumers no longer had to go to them.

The attributes of even ordinary products and services in this phase were altered as well with the addition of a digital component. Automakers and their suppliers, for instance, started to consider how the addition of communicative technologies to automobiles could result in a change from cars that are essentially focused on transportation to cars that are nodes in a connected network. Profits are likely to shift as well, away from selling the cars themselves to offering all kinds of services, including auto repair, diagnosis, and insurance. In addition, all the data cars generate will have value of its own, in applications that are still to be invented.

And Then to Business Models

Digital is at its most disruptive when it changes the parameters that have held conventional business models in place. As discussed earlier in this book, it is extraordinarily difficult for incumbent decision-makers to "see" that the traditional rules they operate under have changed, often because they are simply not looking.

Take insurance. Digital technologies have the potential to completely change the way the different components of the traditional value chain are managed. Further, digital business models can often be delivered far less expensively than traditional models, creating enormous pricing pressure for incumbents.

1. **Distribution** — The traditional broker "selling" a customer on policies disappears, to be replaced by an interactive, on-demand experience, probably through a mobile device. Because this is now feasible and affordable, more and more insurance offerings can be provided "on demand" based on usage, more tightly fitting

the provision of insurance services to the actual activity being insured. Smart contracts facilitated by blockchain technology could even become self-executing, eliminating piles of paper and tedious record keeping.

2. **Underwriting and pricing** – The core competitive advantage of many large traditional insurers was that they had access to massive databases that other companies did not, upon which they could base smarter pricing decisions. But with the advent of massive, connected, and to some extent widely available databases, plus artificial intelligence, the need for manual underwriting and the deep expertise associated with that process has disappeared for all but the most unusual cases. And proxies for favorable insurability – such as having an advanced degree or working in a certain profession – also have disappeared as decisions are more and more based on real data, not approximations.

3. **Claims** – While companies such as Progressive have been inching toward real-time claims processing and settlement for years, widespread and inexpensive technology will accelerate this trend. Sensors, drones, and powerful smartphones will dramatically change what insurers call "first notice of loss." Smart algorithms can then figure out what the insurer should pay, and the insured's transactions progress seamlessly from that moment on.

Clearly, if you are in the insurance business, you want to begin taking action to prepare your organization for the massive business model changes to come. And this is where the trouble starts. In the early days of an inflection, even though the signals are extremely strong that things are about to change, it is easy for an organization (sometimes with the help of rather expensive consultants) to conclude that they know enough to proceed, and then begin to pour money and resources into a "damn the torpedoes, full speed ahead" digitization effort.

Unfortunately, this is almost always a mistake. Even with very strong signals, there is still a substantial amount of uncertainty about the nature and magnitude of changes to come. The task is indeed taking action and planning, but *planning to learn*, using a discovery-driven approach.

ILLUSORY CERTAINTY AND DIGITAL FLOPS

Big, ambitious digital initiatives bear a strong resemblance to big, ambitious innovation projects of other kinds. They are characterized by decision-makers having to make assumptions without the benefit of having facts to work with. Decisions seemingly need to be made — urgently — but the context is so uncertain that it would be nearly impossible to guarantee that they are correct. Instead, in this highly uncertain context, decisions are pretty much guesses. In an organizational system that is based on decision-making in highly predictable circumstances, this can lead to a vicious downward spiral.

Decision-makers establish projections based on assumptions. As information starts to come back about the consequences of those decisions, assumptions are sometimes shown to be incorrect. And yet, having invested personal capital and often organizational capital in promoting a given point of view, decision-makers escalate their commitment, becoming even more committed to the same ideas. This train wreck proceeds until it becomes obvious that the project is never going to work and someone finally has the courage to pull the plug on it.

Unfortunately, for those of us seeking to learn from these failed experiments, in most cases the topic instantly becomes undiscussable, the players who were involved in it disappear, and everybody remaining pretends that it never happened. This is, of course, rather frustrating for business book authors who would like to be able to derive some lessons from such failures. There are a few, however, that are sufficiently public that documentation about them survives. Let's consider one, the BBC Digital Media Initiative, which ended up costing the organization some £98 million with nothing to show for that expenditure.

THE BBC DIGITAL MEDIA INITIATIVE

The clear specter of on-demand news and entertainment in the late 1990s was discussed earlier in the context of Netflix. Indeed, as early as 2000, it was obvious even to Harvard Business School case writers that technologies such as video on demand were likely to change the way media was consumed.

At the BBC, the desire to do something about this looming inflection point crystallized in the form of a project called the Digital Media Initiative, or DMI, in 2008. The initial impetus for the project came from a desire to create "completely tapeless" production workflows. The BBC's director of technology, Ashley Highfield, was the public face of the initiative, which was approved by the organization's decision-making body, the BBC Trust, and funded to the tune of £81 million. Siemens, the BBC's traditional technology provider, was chosen as the contractor to work on the project, with consulting support from Deloitte. The original proposal projected a total benefit from the program of £99.6 million. As a technology partner described it at the time: "The DMI is a pan-BBC project designed to prepare the broadcaster for an on-demand, multiplatform digital environment and provide a reusable foundation for the cost-effective delivery of new and emerging services."

Failure to Realize the Organizational Significance of a Digital Inflection

One of the first untested assumptions that is very clear in retrospect was that this program was approached as though it were a relatively straightforward operational and efficiency-oriented project. In reality, however, such a dramatic shift in process workflows actually required a true business model overhaul, which, to be successful, would have to reach deep into the core workflows of the organization. It would, therefore, entail a significant change in the management component in addition to whatever changes the technology would demand, with substantial political battling likely.

The contract with Siemens was awarded on a fixed price for fixed deliverables basis. The assumption of contracts priced this way is that it is completely clear what work needs to be done and what a successful outcome should be. From a user perspective, this framework had the effect of causing the BBC not to question — too much — what Siemens was working on, since they perhaps felt that interfering would negate the intention of the fixed price. From the Siemens perspective, it set up the traditional argument for why big IT projects fail: the IT vendor doesn't deliver what the user wants, while the vendor accuses the user of changing its mind and not specifying clearly what its needs are. It is symptomatic of assuming certainty where there is none.

The sheer number of subprojects included in the initial BBC brief was breathtaking. There was to be a new "media ingest system," which would change the way content entered the BBC ecosystem. This would be complemented by a new media asset management system, which would be the way that future audio, video, stills, and other content would be managed. Storyboarding would be done online, rather than through preexisting manual processes. All these other systems would be accessible through a metadata sharing and storage system. The project team from the BBC awarded the contract for the work without requiring competitive bidding, and the relationship with Siemens (the primary vendor) and its other contractors was described by one observer as "distant."

Assuming the Whole System Must Be Built to Realize Any Value

This brings us to a second set of untested assumptions, namely that doing these digital projects all at once was necessary and digestible by the BBC. This was a particularly dangerous idea. In an organization with low levels of digital maturity, starting small and building capability over time makes much more sense. Launching aggressively into an approach with all the funding given up front is a recipe for disaster. Even if a project works out, the organization is unlikely to have developed the new workflows and practices that will allow it to benefit. It also illustrates the mistaken idea that an organization can apply a build/development model — usually called the "waterfall method" — from a previous era to an entirely new market context. Hiring outside firms that didn't appreciate the difference between the old and new models didn't help the BBC project much either.

A third set of assumptions has to do with the evident perspective of senior leadership that the BBC could safely delegate the design and implementation of such a complex system to contractors, with relatively little oversight. In a discovery-driven approach, the project would have been undertaken in such a way that it would provide proof of value all along the way. This would have involved creating quick checkpoints at which specific assumptions about the way the project would ultimately work would be tested, and implementing course corrections if they were thought to make sense. Instead, the DMI project didn't appear to have an effective governance process incorporating senior business leaders as well as technical staff, or to require regular project reviews that would have fed into this process.

Those with the Information to Sound the Alarm Had No Voice

In violation of the principle of people with direct experience being able to sound the alarm and be heard by senior leadership, those closest to the DMI had few mechanisms to be heard. As one observer noted, "There was a culture which apparently did not allow staff involved to be given a voice, so, unable to feed their concerns about projects into review processes, they were instead reduced to privately voicing them."

In September of 2009, the BBC and Siemens parted ways on the project, with the BBC electing to bring it back under in-house management.

The lessons learned from this project were bitter indeed. As a project review that ended up going all the way to the British Parliament makes clear, the assumption of knowledge where none existed could have been foreseen right from the beginning. Reviewers concluded that "the Programme had proved much more challenging than Siemens had first believed and that Siemens had lacked in-depth knowledge of the BBC's operations. The BBC itself had only limited knowledge of Siemens's design and development work."

The Right Approach – but Too Little, Too Late

After bringing the program back in-house, the BBC staff elected to pursue a different approach, using "agile" methodologies to create some near-term positive results via collaborations between users and technologists, just as a discovery-driven approach would suggest. This turned out to be too little, too late. Dominic Coles, the director of operations at the BBC, decided to pause the project in October of 2012 and to terminate it altogether the following year. As he observed, with respect to the progress of the project,

The pace of technological and digital change has been rapid; business and production requirements changed within the BBC; and the industry has developed standardised off-the-shelf digital production tools that did not exist five years ago. Developing such an ambitious and technically complex solution that was able to cope with the myriad demands BBC programmes would place upon it due to the variety and complexity of our content, proved far more challenging than expected, which led to delays . . . The decision has now been taken to stop the project at a total cost to the BBC of £98.4m. The cost is so great because much of the software and hardware which has been developed would only have a value if the project was completed and we cannot continue to sanction any additional spending on this initiative.

With a discovery-driven mindset, value is created all along the development cycle, not just realized at the end. As with other kinds of innovation projects, the assumption that the entire system must be built to realize any value at all is extremely dangerous.

Let's contrast the BBC case with an equally big, ambitious undertaking with a strong digital foundation — the effort to bring digital insight into the treatment of cancer. As I hope to demonstrate, the use of a discovery-driven approach can yield far more possibilities for success in a highly uncertain context.

DISCOVERING A WORKING BUSINESS MODEL IN MEDICAL DATA

Former vice president Joe Biden's son Beau died in 2015 from brain cancer. Biden tried to understand the medical system designed to treat his son. He was horrified. "It's frightening, it's complicated, it's serious, and it's neglected," he said in an address to the American Association for the Advancement of Science in 2018.

Different parts of the system were not connecting, data that could prove transformative was locked away in individual file drawers and unconnected systems, and information about what helped some patients wasn't available to doctors who were treating others. Despite astonishing gains against the disease, the system in place to treat it had grown up haphazardly and was deeply flawed.

In 2016, President Barack Obama tasked Biden with leading the National Cancer Moonshot, with the ambitious goal of ending cancer as we know it. This goal was deliberately intended to spark an inflection point. In particular, the Cancer Moonshot was to be the linchpin of activities that stretched across the federal government and the private sector, connecting actors throughout the system who might in earlier years never have even spoken with one another.

At around this time, the US Congress passed the 21st Century Cures Act, which directed the FDA to permit data other than clinical trial data to be used in support of drug approvals (earning it criticism from pharmaceutical industry skeptics).

All of that brings us to where we are in the journey of this book. The announcement of the Cancer Moonshot, new FDA regulations, and the expressed desire to create an inflection point – the messages of impending change are clear: The weak signals have become stronger. The entire arena is up for grabs. And a new way of collaborating across the whole system is clearly called for. So far, so good.

An unlikely player to emerge in light of this massive shift in how cancer was viewed was Flatiron Health, a data-sciences software company that undertook a discovery-driven journey to benefit from the inflection point. The two founders of Flatiron were entrepreneurs at an incredibly young age, embodying the principles of entrepreneurial thinking – looking for opportunities and capitalizing on them at the right time – which entails being able to see around corners. But first, a bit of background.

From Snake Breeding to Advertising Software

Nat Turner and his longtime business partner, Zach Weinberg, were not your ordinary twentysomethings when they cofounded Flatiron Health in 2012. Turner was twenty-four when he sold his first company, Invite Media, to Google for a reported $81 million in 2010. He was thirty-two when he sold his second, Flatiron Health, to Roche, for nearly $2 billion in 2018.

Although both Turner and Weinberg had been involved in the startup world prior to meeting at the Wharton School at the University of Pennsylvania, the entrepreneurship program there gave them a head start on the business that would eventually pay off in a major way. The discovery-driven growth methodology is part of the core entrepreneurship curriculum at Wharton (with credit to my coauthor and longtime entrepreneurship center director, Ian MacMillan).

In truth, neither Turner nor Weinberg had a particular interest in healthcare. In fact, Turner's previous businesses had begun as hobbies and morphed into cash-generating organizations in sectors as diverse as food delivery, web design, and, yes, reptile breeding. It was while Turner was running the snake-breeding business that he discovered a proclivity for the Internet. As he describes it, he made a website for himself, then other breeders liked it and asked to have something similar.

The evolution of Turner and Weinberg's company Invite Media is illustrative of the ideas of arena-based thinking and discovery-driven learning. The concept of doing something with advertising emerged as the two were working as interns under the sponsorship of one of the Wharton entrepreneurship adjuncts, at a company called Video Egg (now known as Say Media). While there, Turner later told the *Financial Post*, "we had noticed how screwed up the online advertising industry was in terms of technology complexity and adoption . . . Starting Invite Media at first was both an attempt to address that observation but also an attempt to build a big business."

Notice that they first defined a broad arena (online advertising) and then a problem people were having in that environment getting essential jobs done. This formed the genesis of a business that they anticipated could be very big indeed.

With discovery-driven planning, the starting point is to define what success *could* look like — not to predict that it will occur, but to outline what the upside could be. Just as I proposed in Chapter 3, Turner and Weinberg began by mapping out a potential arena for the firm, charting what they called "dollar flow" (which is very similar to my suggestion to start with the pot of resources for which you are contesting when thinking about an arena). They then examined how badly the solutions available to different industry players did the job of matching an advertiser to the desired audience. Turner describes how the business started:

We started as a video ad network in a way. We met the founders of YouTube before they launched and they had this idea to build this massive video destination site. We saw all this video inventory out there — all these people watching videos — and we thought, "There's no advertising against it." A company I'd worked at called VideoEgg had 500 million video views a day or something like that — or a month — that weren't being monetized. It was half a million dollars in server costs just to serve these videos. There wasn't a way to get advertisers on.

The name Invite actually comes from the fact that we wanted to build a unit, an ad unit that popped up — kind of like when you're watching basketball on TNT and you see the new TV show trailer pop up in the bottom left corner of the screen. That's what we called an "invite." It was inviting you to watch something, inviting you to do something.

He described the initial idea for their business as "frankly awful." They redirected the business to doing something with Facebook ads, which didn't work out either. Eventually, they realized that there was a gap in the market for advertisers to be able to identify relevant video content to advertise against, and set about creating a program that would facilitate the monetization of advertising space.

So the next idea was to create an electronically mediated advertising exchange. That seemed more promising, but the company "morphed," as Turner said, into an advertising agency–based model. He said it took a year and a half to go from "Let's explore this area" to "This is going to work, let's hire people and build something." As he recalled, his investors were very nervous during that year and a half, with one of them referring to the founders' willingness to adapt when new information came in as the "idea du jour."

A final pivot was to work with advertising agencies to place ads against relevant web content. The product Invite Media eventually sold to Google was called Bid Manager, and its main benefits were to allow agencies and media buyers to buy more efficiently across exchanges. Turner and Weinberg thus ended up launching the first universal buying platform for display media. That has subsequently become a critical part of the advertising-supported ecosystem that pays for the Internet as we know it today.

In a controversial decision, Google bought the three-year-old company in 2010 for $81 million and brought its two cofounders on board to integrate their technology with its DoubleClick offering. The two knew that this wasn't going to be a long-term gig, however, and they started scouting around for new business ideas that could be their next opportunity.

With the demonstrated success of Invite Media behind them, they had credibility, access to funding sources, and an attractive lure for future employees. For ideas, Turner and Weinberg engaged in angel investing. As Turner later said, "It was selfish, I admit. Zach and I learned by being involved with the entrepreneurs in these startups and we got a lot of insight into the health care industry." Notice again the behavior of making small investments to open up new perspectives — but not committing to a single point of view about the future. And that led to Flatiron.

From Advertising Software to . . . Healthcare?

Actually, the real impetus for the firm that became Flatiron Health was personal. Turner's younger cousin was diagnosed with leukemia. The boy's father said to Turner and Weinberg, "A few hundred kids get this every year — what drugs do they get, and do they work — I can't find any information." Misdiagnoses, lost time due to travel, and a host of other problems with his cousin's care convinced them that automating information flows in the cancer care system was a big, important problem that would be potentially worthwhile to address.

That simple question from his cousin's father caused the duo to drop all the other ideas they were flirting with in the healthcare space (insurance, medical malpractice, and others) and to focus on the idea of putting together a platform that could provide a unified view of all data flowing through the treatment system for cancer patients. As Turner said later, one of the characteristics that both he and Weinberg share is a relentless curiosity: "We ask a million questions and we want to know: why is it that way?"

The insight that sparked Flatiron was that by bringing together two worlds — digital capabilities and medical training — they could create a different perspective on the entire treatment experience. The two entrepreneurs went through a period of being "obsessed" with this idea, following doctors around, meeting with "20 people a day" and trying to learn as much as they possibly could. You can see the emphasis on learning in the guidance Turner offers to other would-be entrepreneurs:

> Turner recommends meeting with as many people in the industry as you can (Turner and Weinberg met at least 500 people before getting Flatiron off the ground). "Take notes and pitch ideas and prototypes and get your idea in front of a lot of people who know their stuff — physicians, hospital administrators, insurance companies and clinics — to get their feedback early."

As they discovered, you are unlikely to find a solution to a software problem by relying on people steeped in a medical background. What Flatiron has now created is the ability to take in both structured and unstructured data from community oncology offices. It can use that data to perform sophisticated analyses in order to better determine a course of treatment for a given patient, as well as to find larger patterns in the information.

Flatiron is one of the beneficiaries of regulatory changes on the part of the FDA that allow data extracted from electronic health records to be used in support of clinical trials. As FDA commissioner Dr. Scott Gottlieb said in a 2019 speech, "Digital technologies are one of the most promising tools we have for making health care more efficient and more patient-focused. This isn't an indictment of the randomized controlled trial. Far from it. It's a recognition that new approaches and new technologies can help expand the sources of evidence that we can use to make more reliable treatment decisions."

Another major issue that concerns the FDA is that clinical trials are often not representative of the population, potentially distorting the results that come from them. With Flatiron's technology, smaller and more tailored approaches using vastly more information than was typically available are now possible. The company, which was acquired by Roche in 2018, will be pursuing the analysis of what it calls "regulatory-grade" information. For example, in 2018 Pfizer and Flatiron presented evidence at a breast cancer conference that data from a cohort of Flatiron patients matched data from a group of patients in the control group — meaning those who had not received treatment — in an advanced study. The intriguing idea is that if reliable data reflecting what would happen to a group not treated with a promising therapy could be obtained from a database, perhaps it would be unnecessary to assign patients randomly to receive treatments or not. This would, for example, allow all trial participants to receive promising therapies and reduce the cost of conducting such trials.

HOW ENTREPRENEURS SEE AROUND CORNERS

Turner and Weinberg's story has many similarities with those of other successful entrepreneurs who are also able to "see around corners." In particular, over the years I've studied what are sometimes called "habitual" entrepreneurs — people who have started many businesses. The reason they are so valuable from a research point of view is that it is highly unlikely, if they've done it over and over again, that their success has been a result of mere good luck. Instead, what we find with this population is that they have a set of methodologies they use to gather lots of information, detect patterns, test assumptions, and bring together resources.

They have vast and nonredundant networks that they can turn to in order to generate ideas and solutions. My colleague Ian MacMillan calls this "webbing": habitual entrepreneurs are tireless in connecting with others, particularly those who do not overlap with their own knowledge. They are also incredibly curious. It is such an ingrained part of their personality that they may not even be conscious of it — they are simply really interested in why things work the way they do. They are also resourceful. As Mac is fond of saying, they "spend their imagination" to validate assumptions rather than buying their way into an answer. They also do things quickly and are unafraid to change direction when new information comes in. They look for patterns in what they see. Are there underserved segments? Unmet needs? Places in which key stakeholders are working around a process because it doesn't work? Are there areas of surplus? Scarcity?

Consider serial entrepreneur Steve Blank, a colleague of mine at Columbia and a legend in the startup world. He's guided four companies to IPO status and mentored many more. To find opportunities, Steve says, an entrepreneur has to be endlessly curious and to recognize patterns that no one else does, by, as he puts it, "showing up." To validate ideas, he advocates "getting out of the building" and learning how a potential innovation might change a customer's life. He calls this "customer development." After taking an idea to market, in what Steve calls the "build" stage, he recognizes that new information always requires adaptive behavior. And finally, he realizes that what a serial entrepreneur enjoys is starting businesses, not necessarily running them once a scalable, repeatable model has been discovered. But such entrepreneurs can leave behind immense amounts of value once they have moved on. As Steve put it in 2012:

> I loved everything until it got big. My job was great from search to the beginning of build. When it started to feel like I became the HR department, then it was time to go. In my second to last company I first lost $35 million, then raised $12 million and eventually returned over a billion to each investor. Only in entrepreneurial clusters is there a special word for failure like this: It's called "experienced."

Creating a plan for fast learning is something successful serial entrepreneurs do almost by instinct. The rest of us can learn to do the same. It does, however, require a different mindset than we bring to the planning situations of business as usual.

"FALL IN LOVE WITH THE PROBLEM . . . NOT WITH A PARTICULAR SOLUTION"

I first heard this saying, which has popped up in any number of stories, from Kaaren Hanson, who at the time was vice president of design innovation at Intuit, when she was speaking at a Columbia Business School BRITE Conference. Although many seem to recognize its wisdom, it is very hard to remember it or implement it in an organization that is focused on planning in the conventional or traditional way.

To that end, a mistake I often see people in organizations make is to link, in their minds, the outcome they are seeking with a particular solution. It is entirely possible to have appropriately identified a desirable outcome, but to be completely wrong about the best way to get there.

For example, Procter & Gamble initially attempted to commercialize PuR, a chemical that allows users to create safe drinking water from dirty water. The chemical worked as advertised, but it failed as a commercial product because the target customer was not conditioned to trade off scarce resources for cleaner water. It also required behavioral change, which meant commercial uptake of the product was painfully slow. The company considered canceling the product altogether in 2004.

Greg Allgood, a senior P&G executive at the time, was a huge believer in PuR and sought a different path to making it available to the people who needed it. Coincidentally, right around this time, a devastating tsunami hit Southeast Asia, and P&G donated over $3 million in aid, including 13 million packets of PuR. This experience, according to Allgood, was a turning point in the business model for the product. Instead of trying to make it a commercial consumer offering, the company made it a social venture.

P&G partnered with international aid organizations that paid for the product on a cost-recovery basis and distributed it for free. With this model, P&G also realized that the program was a public relations bonanza, that it could help them understand consumers in emerging markets, and that it gave them a position of strength in discussions with governments, NGOs, and other strategic partners. P&G eventually sold off its other water purification initiatives but kept hold of (and branded) PuR. This illustrates the idea that you can get the basic "job to be done" part of the arena right without first figuring out what the best solution might be. This is a classic case of seeing around the corner, and doing so due to unusual and unexpected circumstances.

DEFINE WHAT SUCCESS LOOKS LIKE

To begin a discovery-driven planning exercise, articulate what would make a particular initiative worthwhile. This could be couched in terms of finances and numbers. It could also be couched in terms of opening opportunities or expanding the reach of an organization. As we saw with the Flatiron Health founders, they were looking for a large problem that had not yet been adequately solved, essentially following Nassim Nicholas Taleb's guidance that when uncertainty increases the upside of an opportunity, it can create valuable opportunities.

The next step is to specify the benchmarks that suggest whether the initiative is realistic or not in terms of key comparisons. Then spell out how, operationally, things would need to be done to make it a reality. As you do this, you're going to find yourself making a great many assumptions. Write them down and then think of how you might validate or, even better, invalidate the assumptions.

The practice that brings this all together — and that differentiates a discovery-driven plan from a conventional one — is planning around critical learning moments, which I call "checkpoints." A checkpoint can be a naturally occurring event (the regulation passes or it doesn't). It can be part of an experiment. Whatever the case, quickly moving through these checkpoints is the key to mobilizing an organization that is facing potential strategic inflection points.

Discovery-driven planning is well suited for those situations in which the change (potentially ushered in by an inflection point) increases the uncertainty that decision-makers face. It can provide structure, discipline, and thoughtful resource utilization.

DISCOVERY-DRIVEN THINKING IN AN
ENTIRELY DIFFERENT SETTING

Lest you think that the methodology applies only to high-tech start-ups and other big business initiatives, let's examine the thought process by considering the evolution of a real project that I encountered on Kickstarter.

The toy industry has been through its share of inflection points, with hundreds of retailers closing their doors as toys increasingly were sold by Target, Walmart, and other large retailers; children aged out of toys earlier; and screen-based entertainment began squeezing out traditional toys. Despite strong growth fueled by a number of blockbuster movies and tie-ins to toys, Toys "R" Us, the largest dedicated retailer in the sector, shut down its US operations in 2018.

Further, the digital revolution has not bypassed toys. Many innovative startups (and some incumbents, such as Mattel) are adding a digital component to their toys.

So let us consider one product (it's real, and on Kickstarter) whose team is trying to benefit from the collision of physical toy properties and advanced digital intelligence. It is called Octobo, produced by Thinker-Tinker. Octobo is a physical plush toy crammed full of sensors that allow it to respond to touch and movement. Its intelligence comes from a tablet inserted inside the toy.

The vision of its creators was that it would provide an educational and interactive experience for kids (and parents), and because the intelligence behind the device is tablet-based, the toy can "grow and develop" with children, bringing about essentially an upgradable object.

The project won an OpenIDEO award, and its evolution is outlined by Thinker-Tinker's founder, Yuting Su, in the documentation submitted for the prize. Calling Octobo a "plush companion robot," Su says she was inspired to start the business when she was pregnant with her own child and initially developed the plan as part of her master's thesis for her degree in game and interactive media design from the University of Southern California in 2015.

She describes the problem she was trying to solve as follows:

> Toys and learning tools today fail to engage young children to learn in a safe and enticing way. Although children develop rapidly, many times toys cannot keep up with a child's learning curve and have only limited replayable value. Most toys that integrate technology today are actually detrimental to the amount of time a child spends with their family, with other children, or even reading a physical book. This and the ability of Octobo to grow with the child are examples of digital's ability to fix these problems.

What Su intuited, and the corner she was seeing around, was a gap. Conventional toys are used for one or two things only, and children can quickly tire or grow out of them. Digital interfaces, on the other hand, aren't suitable for very young children, aren't interactive, and just encourage more passive entertainment. She recognized that parents could become enthusiastic about a toy that promoted interaction and learning rather than the addictive game playing of conventional digital apps. Her eureka moment was the inspiration to conceive of a way to create a toy that had all the cuddliness of a plush stuffed animal, but with the engaging interactivity of a tablet computer.

Su observed that as digital devices become unavoidable, children aren't being given enough opportunities to play in the physical world, which is essential for motor development and other skills. "Physical play trains us and helps us grow," she said in a 2018 interview. "Our hand-eye coordination. The training of our littlest muscles. The different textures actually educate our bodies by helping us sense surfaces. We learn not just on an intellectual level but our bodies learn through tactile objects." While it is still early days for Octobo and Thinker-Tinker (Su described it in the interview as a "roller-coaster"), the combination of digital and physical play is likely to create a significant inflection point for the conventional toy business.

Among the checkpoints the Octobo venture went through were:

- A Facebook ad campaign to collect data about potential users and customers
- Identifying potential manufacturers for the scaling of the project
- Realizing that content development could proceed faster by going beyond in-house production to connect with communities of content creators
- Identifying educators to both provide content expertise and evaluate the design of the product
- Identifying key metrics for success and how they might be measured
- Lots of interactions with the prototype product

Each of these checkpoints represents a moment in time at which critical assumptions made by the project team could be tested, with the learning being used to inform subsequent choices. As of this writing in early 2019, the Kickstarter campaign has nearly reached its goal, with the next major uncertainty for the team being how they will scale up production capacity while maintaining the level of quality the product requires. The toy itself has received many enthusiastic reviews and is in prelaunch.

BEYOND INNOVATION THEATER

To benefit from the upside of an inflection point that opens real opportunities, organizational leaders need to develop a continuous flow of innovations to replace advantages that have faded away or to respond to challenges that mean that old business constraints have changed in meaningful ways. Unfortunately, many organizations are still dealing with "innovation theater," in which a lot of lip service is paid but the process itself suffers from a lack of rigor, corporate-level practices, metrics, and other essential elements that would make innovation a proficiency.

Perhaps the biggest myth that gets in the way of innovation is that it is all about the big idea. Get a good enough idea, people say, and the rest will magically fall into place. Nothing could be further from the truth!

Good ideas are, of course, important, but the initial ideas that innovators pursue are seldom the ones that make it to market. Instead, innovators need to go from an idea through a process of incubation, in which the idea is made more concrete and market-ready, and then eventually through a process that I call "acceleration," in which the idea is scaled up so that it can become part of the parent organization as an operating business. Discovery-driven planning provides the road map for navigating this process.

Key Takeaways

As the weak signals of an impending inflection point become stronger, there will come a time when it makes sense to explore what to do about them. However, you will still be grappling with a very high ratio of assumptions you'll be making to knowledge based on facts. The best path forward, therefore, is to deploy a discovery-driven approach in which you plan to convert assumptions into knowledge, rather than simply try to prove that you were right.

Your goal at this stage should be to generate as many possibilities as you can and to see if you can invalidate them quickly.

Don't worry about being "right." Instead, think about whether it is worth it to learn about the next step.

Start with your arena: where are the funds going to come from, and is there enough there to make this effort worthwhile?

Habitual entrepreneurs use a set of practices that help them see around corners, such as building varied, nonredundant networks of connections for advice, resources, and insight. You can learn these practices as well.

6

Galvanizing the Organization

> Big trends are not that hard to spot (they get talked and written about a lot), but they can be strangely hard for large organizations to embrace.
>
> — Jeff Bezos

Imagine a Microsoft senior leadership meeting kicking off with "EMPATHY" in all capital letters projected on a screen. For those with any historical experience working with the company, this would be a bit of a surprise, to say the least. And yet, that's what Satya Nadella, Microsoft's third CEO, passionately believes will transform the company — having empathy with customers, empathy with one another, and creating psychologically safe, growth-mindset-oriented working environments.

This is a far cry from the internally competitive, rather hostile culture lampooned in a cartoon featuring the firm's organizational chart in 2011.

Nadella was determined to wipe out this impression and galvanize the organization to share a common point of view about the future. While he has been given a lot of credit in the media for making this change happen in his current role, the real magic of his approach began long before he rose to the top job in the company. Throughout his career at Microsoft, he has leveraged the power of the people around

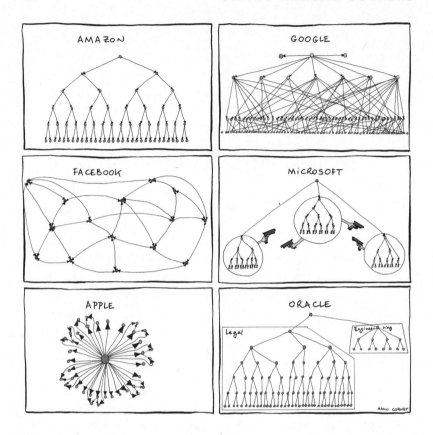

him to create alignment regarding the company's perspective on the future.

That is the core message of this chapter. We tend to imbue CEOs and senior leaders with supernatural powers when they succeed and with damning deficiencies when they fail. But the real heroes of galvanizing the organization are typically elsewhere in the hierarchy. In fact, you might be one of them.

These are the people close to the coal face of the organization (the edges discussed in Chapter 1), who often have the flashes of real insight into what is going on. The senior leadership role is often more about providing a space for those insights to be heard, recognizing the ones that are significant, and empowering those with the most knowledge to do something about them.

In organizations that navigate inflection points well, these people are listened to, their ideas are acted on, and the people themselves are often promoted into more influential roles. In organizations that fail to handle inflection points effectively, the bearers of news (whether good or bad) are not "heard," and subsequently their ideas are not acted on. The underlying concept is that we need to transition from a view of organizations as merely complicated to a view that recognizes them as fundamentally complex. The big difference here is that in a complicated operation, you can predict what is going to happen by simply knowing the initial conditions. In a complex one, because the outcome results from unpredictable interactions *among* components, no such predictability applies.

Flying a plane is a good example. A Boeing 747 is a massively complicated machine, but we have figured out how to make its operations relatively predictable. The air traffic control system, however, is complex — its parts are interdependent, which means things can change at any moment, creating outcomes that are surprising or unexpected.

In much the same way, before an organization can do something about an emerging inflection point, a critical mass of people need to believe that they are indeed at a turning point. That is, if no action is taken now, the future will be dim. Although senior leadership has a role to play in the process of capturing all employees' hearts and minds toward this purpose, the actions of *many* people, up and down the hierarchy, are what truly lead to a desirable outcome.

Leaving this critical set of activities in the hands of those at the very top of an organization is an almost certain recipe for failure. The role of leadership — rather than trying to control a complex environment — is much more about orchestrating individual inputs so that people feel empowered, whatever their formal positions, to take fast, confident action when new information is revealed.

THE PROMISING RISE AND TRAGIC FALL OF MICROSOFT'S KIN PHONE

A tale that illustrates the downside of treating a complex environment as if it were a complicated one is the story of Microsoft's disastrous introduction of its Kin mobile phone back in 2010 (long before Nadella took the reins). What makes it a tragedy to me is that I have long thought the strategy was really smart, the product itself had a lot of interesting elements to it, and the team working on it was exceptionally talented. Its failure offers a number of lessons to be learned about how *not* to take action in the face of a looming inflection point.

A Bit of History

J Allard joined Microsoft in 1991, shortly after graduating from Boston University. He started as a networking programmer. On January 25, 1994, he famously saw around one of the biggest corners of our time, the rise of the Internet.

First, some background. Allard had been one of those people on the edges, perceiving looming threats and possible inflection points early on and bringing that message to senior leadership to prompt organization-wide action.

After joining Microsoft in 1991, he was one of the first to see the impending inflection point that the Internet represented for a company that made most of its living selling boxed software for personal computers. Before the Internet inflection point was obvious to everyone, in January of 1994 Allard composed a memo titled "Windows: The Next Killer Application for the Internet." He wrote, "The Internet provides an incredible opportunity for Microsoft to effectively explore large-scale networks from many levels: customer needs, technical challenges, quality-of-service issues, electronic commerce and information-browsing technologies." He was all of twenty-five years old at the time.

Allard's view of the world to come was vivid enough that Bill Gates convened a high-profile, all-day meeting bringing together senior executives and a group of the younger folks, Allard among them. Allard, described by the *New York Times* as an "evangelist," made a passionate case that the Internet was going to change their world entirely. As one attendee later recalled, Gates concluded, "We're going to make a big bet on the Internet." The release of Windows 95 following the meeting incorporated the Internet-friendly TCP/IP protocols in the operating system (later getting the company in hot water for supposedly undermining the competitive chances of Netscape, a standalone Internet browser). Eventually, Allard's message inspired a major redirection of the company.

Weak signals of another inflection point that threatened Microsoft were also picked up along the edges. In this case, it was Sony's talk of its PlayStation 2 becoming the center for entertainment, information sharing, and other digital activities in the home, posing a threat to traditional personal computers. A group of Allard's peers began mobilizing to push Microsoft to meet the looming challenge by entering the gaming business. After some arm-twisting, Allard joined what would become the Xbox team, and he was widely credited with having a critical leadership role in that product's design and subsequent success. He then led Microsoft's ultimately unsuccessful effort to enter the MP3 business with the Zune music player, although his reputation within the company (and strong relationship with Bill Gates) remained intact.

Enter the Mobile Computing Inflection Point

What happened next has its roots in the turn of the millennium. At that time, mobile phones were all the rage, with reports that over a billion people were carrying them around. Their main uses, however, were for making calls and engaging in various forms of messaging (remember the "BlackBerry prayer"?). Three former Apple engineers — Andy Rubin, Matt Hershenson, and Joe Britt — formed a new company called Danger in 2000. Their vision was to create an "end-to-end wireless Internet solution focused on affordability and great user experience."

What they came up with was a tiny computer that could sit on your hip, hence its initial name, the Hiptop. Originally, the device — which later became known as the T-Mobile Sidekick — was referred to as "the Peanut." Its designers wanted to make the Internet available to the average person on the go. At the time, the big Internet portals really only interacted with users at their desks, often only at work. In contrast, the Peanut was an inexpensive key fob–friendly device that would allow an ordinary person to download and carry around information, such as to-do lists, recent emails, and addresses, that was stored on the big portals. It used only one-way information transfer. The business model called for selling end users the device for $1, then charging the portals a monthly fee for every user.

What we now recognize as having been a big breakthrough, at the time seemed only incremental. The goal envisioned for the Peanut was that users would sync the device to their computer (and to their preferred portal) each day, which would download the most critical data (remember, this was a one-way sync to the device). The development team thought that more-minor updates would be sent to the device during the day over an FM radio subcarrier. The idea was that if you could receive FM radio, you could receive a signal, and the company intended to lease spectrum in major metropolitan markets to accomplish this outcome. The FM signal concept "turned out to be a really bad idea," according to Chris DeSalvo, a senior Danger engineer at the time.

Abandoning the doomed FM idea, the team then turned to exploring the two-way communication potential of a technology hosted on GSM networks called GPRS. One of the firm's investors even found a carrier interested in showcasing the technology, which was looking for devices that could take advantage of the new capability. That carrier was a company called VoiceStream Wireless, a spin-off from Western Wireless. (I was one of the original VoiceStream subscribers with an Ericsson phone I owned back in the day!) VoiceStream was eventually purchased by Deutsche Telekom in 2001 and renamed T-Mobile USA in 2002.

With the tantalizing prospect of real-time two-way communication before them, the team dropped the Peanut idea and built a new-to-the-world device they hoped other people would want to use as well. That led to the Hiptop, which DeSalvo described as "the first always-on, internet-connected smartphone." Among its many innovative features was what we would recognize today as real-time storage of your data in the cloud and even an app store of sorts called "download fun."

In October of 2002, T-Mobile rebranded the device, releasing it under the name Sidekick. It became enormously popular, the go-to device for celebrities and teens, and it even starred in a celebrity scandal involving the theft of nude photos of Paris Hilton, who carried one.

Conceiving of the Kin: A Disruptive Idea

Back to J Allard. Sometime, ironically, around the same time that Apple was inching toward releasing the first iPhone, Allard had a vision that there was space in the market for a phone along the lines of the Sidekick. It was to be a "platform agnostic, cloud-centric featurephone. A featurephone that could be had at a relatively low cost, and sold to a burgeoning market of teens and young adults who had little need for a BlackBerry-level device (or pricing)."

Allard believed that the market for such a phone could be huge — for people who wanted some of the functionality offered by smartphones without the huge price tag or expensive data plans. It would be sold to the kind of individuals (typically young) who lived on social media and wanted technology to support sending photos and texts to one another. The first step toward making this a reality was Microsoft's acquisition of Danger, which took place in September of 2008 and reportedly cost $500 million.

I'll editorialize a bit here. I actually think that strategy could have worked well. Making a phone that could appeal to the low end of the market but with some of the features found at the high end — if it were inexpensive enough — could have been quite disruptive and done for Microsoft what the advent of inexpensive personal computers did. To do that, however, they would have had to come quickly into the market and have the full weight of the company behind the product.

Allard is a persuasive evangelist, and others believed it was a good idea, too. Initially, a host of potential partners eagerly sought to be part of the project. Microsoft eventually went with Sharp to manufacture the phones and with Verizon to be the exclusive carrier for them. Allard (with the backing of Steve Ballmer, Microsoft's CEO) kept his organization completely separate from the efforts of the higher-end Windows phone group. He sought to pull resources from across the company (for instance, from Zune).

The two operations were located in two different divisions at Microsoft — Project Pink (as the Kin project was called) was in the Entertainment and Devices Division, headed up by Robbie Bach, a very highly regarded senior executive who was also credited with the success of the Xbox. The Windows products were being developed in their own division, led by Andy Lees.

Meanwhile, Apple was already causing a stir with its iPhone. Android, purchased by Google (with Andy Rubin, the original founder of Danger), was revealed in 2007 as well and started shipping in 2008. And Microsoft? They were nowhere in particular. The mobile effort at Microsoft, according to one observer, was "withering."

That is where the trouble started. According to Engadget, "To put it bluntly, he [Lees] didn't like that Pink existed. To quote our sources, Lees was 'jealous,' and he was likely concerned that Kin was pulling mindshare (and presumably resources) from Windows Mobile's roadmap. With enough pressure, Lees ended up getting his way; Pink fell under his charge and Allard was forced into the background."

The rest of the Kin story is rather sad. Lees made a number of decisions (such as making the operating system more like that of Windows 7) that delayed the project. He also didn't support much investment in critical features that users were expecting. Verizon, which had initially agreed to offer entry-level pricing for the data plans, ended up offering a far more expensive monthly plan than the intended customer segment could afford. The phone suffered an ignominious end, remaining on the market for only six weeks. The price tag? North of $1 billion, according to many observers. The product's failure was cited as one reason Steve Ballmer's bonus was cut in half that year. Another of Allard's projects (an early version of something like an iPad, called Courier) was canceled, some said because powerful people at Microsoft felt it wasn't consistent with the road map for Windows Mobile. Allard eventually left the company.

The Kin issues are emblematic of the difficulty Microsoft's leadership had in galvanizing its troops around a common vision. Even as the world was moving toward tighter, more integrated customer experiences, Microsoft struggled to have people working together.

What the company historically got right was listening to people on the edges, particularly in the Bill Gates era. But what it historically was frustrated by was not being able to take those messages and transform them into a galvanizing common purpose.

Microsoft began the millennium with a market capitalization of $642 billion. Over the next ten years, it continued to reap the rewards of its dominant position in desktop computers, generating enormous cash flows. From 1996 to 2005, the so-called Wintel (Windows + Intel–designed microprocessors) enjoyed a dominant share of the market for personal computing operating systems. By 2012, however, Wintel's market share was down to 35 percent, with Apple and Google devices edging it out.

Under Steve Ballmer, Microsoft released the Vista operating system, an ambitious overhaul of the core Windows platform that took a long time to design and was roundly criticized by customers. Some felt that the Vista episode distracted Microsoft from the growing shift in utilization posed by smartphones and mobile applications. Indeed, Ballmer laughed at the iPhone after its imminent arrival was announced. He reasoned, quite sensibly, that a phone without a keyboard would not appeal to businesspeople. He felt the expense of the product and its lack of a keyboard would confine it to the consumer market. "I like our strategy," he said at the time.

Essentially, although Microsoft realized that mobile was going to be important, the company wasn't able to capitalize on that insight to create a compelling offering. As Derek Thompson of the *Atlantic* noted in 2013, "Microsoft still isn't a place that builds things people really like. It's a place that builds things people – and, particularly, business people – think they have to use." Around the same time, after Ballmer announced his intention to retire, a writer for *The New Yorker* wrote, "Microsoft needs someone who can attract brilliant developers as well as she anticipates trends. They need someone very different from Ballmer."

Empathy as a Galvanizing Force

The Kin story, and Microsoft's immense failure to make much headway at all in the world of mobile phones (clearly an inflection point for tech), exemplify the lack of a key component of being able to drive through an inflection and emerge in better shape at the other end. This is when seeing the inflection coming is not enough. To mobilize the organization around the messages being sent by weak signals, it is essential to create a company-wide shared point of view about the future. In contrast, the story of Microsoft today is a textbook example of how to do this, beginning with, yes, the word "empathy."

Satya Nadella took over as CEO in February of 2014, ending a bruising six-month search that looked at people external to the company. In his very first public commentary, the themes that Nadella had been using to mobilize the organization were evident. The first was a promise to create "people-centric" IT, centered on the user, whether at work or at home, overcoming the traditional distinction many have made between consumer-focused versus enterprise-focused business.

He mentioned creating great experiences (rather than great products). He talked about partnerships and ecosystems and cooperating with others.

Most significantly, Nadella placed a huge emphasis on culture. As he later said, "There is something only a CEO uniquely can do, which is set that tone, which can then capture the soul of the collective. And its culture." One of the biggest changes he made was to focus explicitly on leading indicators, which is entirely consistent with the theory I've been describing in this book. He explained, "We no longer talk about the lagging indicators of success, right, which is revenue, profit. What are the leading indicators of success? Customer love." His challenge, as he described it, was the challenge of "getting an entire organization to fall in love with these leading indicators of success."

That, in essence, is what this chapter is all about: how do you create the conditions in which a critical mass of people all share a common point of view of the indicators that will presage future success?

ARCHITECTING A RESILIENT CULTURE

A classic tension in any successful organization is the tension between exploiting a repeatable business model and identifying a new one. When a business model is repeatable, the emphasis is to become efficiency-oriented. After all, if things don't change very much, you can optimize the system by breaking down all the activities into their constituent parts and maximizing the efficiency of each part. This idea has informed the practice of management since the days of Adam Smith and became part of the unquestioned fabric of how organizations should be run with the work of Frederick Winslow Taylor. Today, we are turning to algorithms that optimize workers' behavior.

The dilemma is that when the challenges facing an organization are not about repeatable execution, but about innovation or responding to complexity, the idea of breaking things down into well-understood parts is not only unhelpful, it can also be a dangerous trap. As noted earlier, leaders need practices such as continuous reconfiguration rather than a reliance on stability. They need to be able to fluidly enter (and exit) new situations. They need to be able to allocate resources across the entire enterprise, rather than having them trapped in silos. They need to be able to obtain and respond to new information, without being concerned that they will be perceived as flip-flopping. And they need to remember that every voice might matter. Such practices are associated with a culture that is built for resilience in the face of complexity, not for execution.

Nadella recognized the urgent need for a major shift in emphasis from shipping great products to building and inspiring new capabilities. This required a structural change at Microsoft, in which business units were de-emphasized in favor of other capabilities. As he said in 2018, "I want a silicon capability. I want a cloud-computing capability. I want an AI capability. I want great product aesthetics in devices. Then we want to be able to take these capabilities and apply them to different markets at different times . . . Digital recognizes no business unit. You need to be able to bring things together."

As he visits different stakeholders on a bruising travel schedule, Nadella articulates a broad purpose for his foreign missions. "What does a CEO get to do?" he asked in 2016. "You've got to pass judgment on an uncertain future and curate culture. For both, I feel, I learn a lot from these trips."

Early on, Nadella's emphasis was like an arrow aimed right at the heart of the classically competitive Microsoft culture. In the old culture, "smart talk" and knowing a lot of things were highly prized. Discussions were often spirited, but with the goal of being right and winning. According to Nadella's 2017 book, *Hit Refresh*, he realized how much of this attitude was consistent with what Carol Dweck has come to call a "fixed mindset." People in the grasp of a fixed mindset spend a lot of time being excellent, proving how good they are, and seeking to be right. People who approach problems with a "growth mindset," in contrast, are focused on learning, on keeping an open mind toward new information, and are less concerned with being good than with getting better. Nadella set about figuring out how to build a growth mindset into the culture at Microsoft.

Dweck herself has consulted to the company, calling Nadella's hunger for new knowledge and willingness to learn from mistakes "spectacular."

This extends to a new focus on who gets to be part of the leadership team. As Nadella has said, "I've optimized for people who want to work as part of a team." For years, Microsoft "cultivated leaders who wanted to run their own show." No longer. "To run the show you have to work as a team. That's a very different Microsoft. That's at a premium for me." In his chosen leaders, Nadella prizes the abilities to bring clarity, to create energy, and to suppress the urge to whine. "I say, 'Hey, look, you're in a field of shit, and your job is to be able to find the rose petals,' as opposed to saying, 'Oh, I'm in a field of shit.' C'mon! You're a leader. That's what it is. You can't complain about constraints. We live in a constrained world."

Hence that session about empathy at the management meeting.

CLARITY OF PURPOSE . . . DARE I SAY "STRATEGY"?

A question I often get as someone who writes about strategy is whether the concept of strategy, and the long-range implications associated with it, are of any use at all. After all, when competitive advantages are transient and the next big thing is impossible to predict, why put all that effort into defining a point of view about the future?

That couldn't be more wrong. In a complex situation, when you want to empower the entire organization to be able to act *without* direction from the top, having a shared view of what the purpose is and how each participant fits into it is absolutely critical. It is only with a basis of a shared understanding of what we're *all* trying to achieve here that distributed action is possible.

In organizations that don't have a clarity of strategy and alignment, decisions get made and unmade, resources are spent on things that are not really relevant, people end up confused, and the stage is set for the kind of infighting that contributed to the demise of the Kin. When there is clarity, broad agreement, and even enthusiasm, people can pull together in a common direction.

In 2014, Nadella said of his overall goal, "For us to be a 100-year-old company where people find deep meaning at work, there's the quest." In fairly short order, he completely overhauled the strategy that had been in place at Microsoft. He focused the company on the cloud, as opposed to desktop software. He wrote off the ill-fated attempt to get into smartphones with the acquisition of Nokia's handset assets (a disengagement move that some have said cost the company over $8.6 billion). He invested heavily in data centers to realize the company's global cloud ambitions. He spent $26 billion to buy the networking site LinkedIn. He articulated a new company mission statement: "Our mission is to empower every person and every organization on the planet to achieve more." And, in a change of direction that was stunning to many who knew this Windows-based company, he de-emphasized Windows in a number of subtle ways.

EMPOWERING EVERY PERSON TO SPOT INFLECTION POINTS AND TO DO SOMETHING ABOUT THEM

As seen throughout this book, a key to navigating successfully through inflection points is the ability for *everyone* in an organization – not just the leadership – to spot inflection points and to mobilize action to take advantage of them. Nadella embraces this philosophy. As he says in his book, *Hit Refresh*, "We sometimes underestimate what we each can do to make things happen, and overestimate what others need to do for us. I became irritated once during an employee Q&A when someone asked me, 'Why can't I print a document from my mobile phone?' I politely told him, 'Make it happen. You have full authority.'"

Nadella has implemented mechanisms, both formal and informal, to make sure that employees' voices are heard and their insights are taken seriously. For example, his regular senior leadership team meetings begin with a segment called "researcher of the amazing," in which teams working on something interesting from across the company present to the entire executive team. In a *Fast Company* story, Harry McCracken describes how a team based in Istanbul beamed in to show off an app they'd developed that could read books for the blind. Unlike during previous regimes, Nadella makes a point of running his leadership meetings like a team sport. The free flow of information helps ideas percolate through the organization and provides pathways to decision-making.

Nadella also makes sure that he is exposed to experiences that can challenge his worldview and potentially offer fresh insights. Spurred on in part by his son Zain's severe cerebral palsy, he takes an active interest in Microsoft's community group for people with disabilities. He meets with them regularly – again, an opportunity for groups with experiences that are different from the norm to communicate up and down the organization.

Another experience Nadella credits with giving him something of a different perspective is his participation in the Netflix Insider program, which gave him the chance to shadow Reed Hastings, the CEO of Netflix, who at the time was a Microsoft board member. Having never been exposed to any company other than Microsoft, where proving how right you were was the characteristic behavior, Nadella found the Netflix environment eye-opening. As he pointed out to ValueAct Capital CEO G. Mason Morfit, "Netflix pivots very quickly based on new data." Morfit recalled Nadella telling him that "he thought that was very interesting compared to the bureaucracy Microsoft had built up."

Upon hiring Peggy Johnson as vice president of business development in 2014, Nadella told her, "I want you to be outside of Redmond [the home of Microsoft's headquarters in Washington State] as much as you are inside of Redmond." His instructions were clearly aimed at picking up new information from external sources and in building ties to Silicon Valley. He himself visits the Valley regularly (a new behavior for a Microsoft CEO), and his outreach to startups in the Valley has started to pay off. Some of them are building up their own businesses using Microsoft's Azure cloud platform rather than simply defaulting to Amazon Web Services.

Nadella also makes sure that his teams know that if he thinks their efforts are promising, that he will be an enthusiastic backer. Upon first being shown the company's then secret mixed reality system, HoloLens (before becoming CEO), he was blown away. Alex Kipman, who drives that technology at Microsoft, said that "the mean time from 'I don't understand this' to 'this is the future of computing' was the fastest I've ever seen . . . and he's been a strong supporter ever since."

Microsoft's $26 billion acquisition of LinkedIn has also been hailed as a way to gather data from its 500 million users – with far less risk of the bad behavior that we see on more personal platforms such as Facebook and Twitter, because LinkedIn is a professional network. Combined with the more than a billion users worldwide who use some version of an Office product, that's a lot of users to help the company train its artificial intelligence software and to promote machine learning. Having access to LinkedIn's treasure trove of data also helps Microsoft "see" trends and discussions that travel across that platform.

Part of seeing around corners is making the determination of what is *not* going to be relevant in the future. Nadella has disengaged from projects with limited promise — for instance, the Microsoft Band, a Fitbit-style fitness tracker. He made the difficult decision to write off $7 billion and to shutter the phone business the company had acquired from Nokia, laying off over 20,000 people and acknowledging that the inflection in mobile phones had passed Microsoft by. At the same time, he has encouraged the company to build software that can be used across technologies, even joining the Linux Foundation — which Steve Ballmer once called "a cancer" — to participate in the development of software. Ballmer, however, later warmed to the value of the Linux ecosystem, maintaining in 2016 that "now I love it."

It's easy for leaders to preach that people learn from their disappointments. It's much harder to live by that philosophy when something goes really wrong. In March of 2016, Microsoft revealed an AI chatbot named Tay on Twitter. Coming from its Future Social Experiences (FUSE) Labs, the idea was to learn how such technologies could interact with real people.

Unfortunately for Microsoft, Twitter proved to be an extraordinarily inhospitable environment for the bot. Trolls quickly learned that if they sent racist, sexist, or other negative messages, Tay would spew some of them back. In just one day, the bot was basically brainwashed, sending messages that were more and more offensive as the day went on. Critics had a field day, and the experiment became a massive humiliation. The bot was taken down.

Nadella's response? He sent a note to the team: "Keep pushing, and know that I am with you." As he often says, sometimes his role is to provide "air cover" when things go wrong. This further encourages employees up and down the organization to take risks.

Nadella has replaced the annual all-hands meeting with an event called One Week, which now includes 18,000 participants in the United States, China, India, Israel, and other countries. Participants can choose "passion projects" to work on. Many of them end up as new offerings in what Microsoft calls its "garage," a place for people to experiment with new ideas. Dozens of apps are on offer there in the "workbench," featuring a huge variety of tasks — from drawing in 3-D to translating presentation subtitles. Some are whimsical, but all are the results of encouraging experimentation at the edges of the organization.

ADAPTING INCENTIVES

So we now know that culture and strategy are important. So far so good. But too often, earnest efforts to create a more resilient organization hinge on the need to overhaul the incentives and rewards that act to drive behavior. It is all too common for a shiny new strategy to be rolled out without anything being done to make sure that the work people are being rewarded for — which, after all, does have a role to play in steering hearts and minds — is in alignment with the rest of the organization.

At Microsoft, a seismic shift in incentives has involved going from a system in which rewards depended on selling so many units of something to one in which compensation is based on how much users consume of it. The company has moved to shared metrics for its leadership (to reinforce collaboration) and to making a distinction between what he calls performance metrics versus power metrics. Performance metrics assess how well people have done in a particular year on things like revenues and profits. Power metrics are about future year performance. Leading indicators include customer satisfaction and measures of "customer love."

As Nadella has said, "We track metrics such as monthly actives, monthly active versus daily active ratios, consumption and consumption growth. These are all the things that we measure as much as we measure any end-quarter revenue or profit by segment."

FINAL THOUGHTS

This chapter has focused on the importance of galvanizing coopera-
tion among a large group of people, as illustrated by the dramatic example of Microsoft's turn toward the cloud, AI, and a different business model. A similar story could be told about any organization that
is moving through an inflection point. Command and control, Tay-
lorist thinking, and individuals maximizing their own goals are all potentially lethal in an environment of complexity.

For now, be thinking of the power of having dozens, hundreds, or
even thousands of your employees acting as ambassadors for a shared
sense of purpose. That's a key component of seeing around corners.

Key Takeaways

It isn't enough to see an inflection point coming. Many people in the
organization need to align around a common point of view in order to
respond effectively.

Internal friction and competition can undermine even a correct
response to changing times. Managing politics is a key task for any
would-be change agent.

Big changes are often signaled by seemingly small and incremental
shifts that nonetheless release a constraint in an existing model, opening it up to an inflection point.

Sometimes companies are their own worst enemy when it comes to
the big changes an inflection point brings.

Bringing a growth mindset, rather than a fixed one, to the problem
of detecting and responding to inflection points is crucial.

Empowering individuals to take action broadens the amount of experimentation an organization can undertake, increasing its odds of
seeing the early warnings of an inflection point in a timely way.

If you want experimentation, people who try things that don't work
out need to know that they will be supported.

Building leading indicators into your organization's incentives en-
sures that people will pay attention to them and increases the likelihood that they will be acted upon.

7

How Innovation Proficiency Defangs the Organizational Antibodies

> Entrepreneurship is not "natural"; it is not "creative." It is work . . . Entrepreneurship and innovation can be achieved by any business . . . They can be learned, but it requires effort. Entrepreneurial businesses treat entrepreneurship as a duty. They are disciplined about it . . . they work at it . . . they practice it.
>
> — Peter Drucker

Gisbert Rühl doesn't look like a revolutionary. He looks more like the combination of the engineering and accounting type that his background would suggest. And yet, his aspirations are nothing short of revolutionary—disrupting the way business is traditionally done in the venerable global steel trade.

But first, a word about the somewhat arcane way in which steel finds its way from producer to steel customer to, eventually, you. I knew nothing about this process when I was invited to give a keynote address at the Metals Service Center Institute in 2014. (Who knew this was a thing?) There I learned that there is a vast network of what are called "metals service centers." They exist as intermediaries between the big steel suppliers and smaller consumers. The big suppliers think about selling tons of the stuff. The smaller buyers don't want or need that much, nor do they want to hold inventory to make the actual items they use.

Enter the metals service center players. They buy in bulk from the large manufacturers, alter the steel to better suit customers' needs, and then resell it to their accounts. They also carry inventory — a lot of inventory — to make sure they can meet customers' expectation of virtually just-in-time delivery. Klöckner, which is based in Germany, is one of the larger players in the metals service center business.

TAKING THE REINS IN THE TEETH OF THE GREAT RECESSION

Gisbert Rühl became chairman of the management board and CEO of Klöckner in 2009. It was a terrible time for the world steel industry. Demand was down, and capacity had not shrunk enough to keep prices from plummeting. Chinese manufacturers were putting more product into the system, creating even more overcapacity. The Organisation for Economic Co-operation and Development published worried tomes on the "crisis" in the steel business worldwide.

Job #1 for Rühl was the unpleasant one of (as corporate types like to call it) "restructuring." Klöckner's cost reduction efforts went on for years and included cutting administrative and sales overhead, selling and consolidating locations, and implementing an unprecedented workforce reduction of over two thousand employees. The company, nonetheless, was still showing losses. It even stopped offering its normal dividend. Rühl was not happy, and he knew it wasn't going to get any better in a hurry. In 2013, he was quoted as saying, "While we are anything but happy with the earnings situation, the numbers plainly show that thanks to the restructuring measures, we are making headway under our own power against the pressure on earnings from the ongoing negative market trend."

And yet . . .

Even as the core business was being massively reduced and transformed to be competitive in the old regime, Rühl was thinking about what a new regime might hold in store.

That same year, 2013, Rühl attended a World Economic Forum private session at a meeting in Dalian, China. The title of the session was "Fostering Innovation-Driven Entrepreneurship: A Global Perspective."

One of the key points made during that session was that increasingly, innovation was a collaborative endeavor requiring organizations to reach across boundaries to source ideas and create value. If the attendance at that conference was any indication, even traditional players were starting to rethink their customary competitive activity.

Outside the steel industry, by 2013 digital platforms had gone mainstream. Airbnb (founded in 2008) convinced people by the thousands, and eventually by the millions, to utilize excess capacity by renting out spare bedrooms and vacant homes. YouTube (founded in 2005) showed that you could build a global media presence on the basis of user-provided cat videos (among other things) without needing a television network or content creation network. Facebook (founded in 2004) allowed users to send messages and original content to thousands, even millions, of people in the blink of an eye. And, of course, Amazon Web Services (launched in 2006) made it possible for anyone with an idea and an unsolved market problem to create a platform that could potentially solve that problem without the need for fixed assets or much in the way of computer hardware.

At the core of these platforms' success was that they all freed up and leveraged trapped capacity and then very efficiently matched supply to demand. In the language used in Chapters 3 and 4, they opened entirely new resource pools and created new arenas.

Each of these companies radically redefined the arena they entered. None of them competed head-on with any existing player. Instead, they found a way to gain traction (and to drive exponential growth) by solving customer issues with jobs to be done better than they could be solved with the incumbent system design.

It was this scenario that troubled Rühl. As he surveyed the arenas within which Klöckner competed, he saw massive inefficiency and considerable frustration among customers all along the value chain in trying to get jobs done. He described his thought process in a 2015 presentation.

Our traditional core business in the value chain of steel is stock-holding. So we are buying steel from the big producers, here in Europe and in North America, and then we are stocking the steel and then we are selling the steel to all kinds of different industries — construction industries, machinery, mechanical engineering industry, to the automotive industry — to all industries which are using steel. We have to stock the steel because we don't really know what our customer is buying the next day, especially in the spot business, such as construction. The construction companies typically order the steel today, and then we have to deliver tomorrow. We are providing availability through stock holding, which is of course inefficient. But not only are we stocking steel, also the producers are stocking steel, because they don't know what the distribution channel needs because we are giving them no information about what steel we need to be supplied with going forward. The supply chain is several times interrupted, very inefficient, and on top of that our customers are ordering pretty typically by fax or by phone. The only innovation I would say in the last ten to twenty years is that we are getting more and more orders by email.

That was the trigger to think about, about two years ago, about the value chain and to think about what will happen when the world is changing. When the world is changing toward a digital world, is a company like Kloeckner still needed, or partially needed, and how could the value chain look like five years from now. That's where we started.

One of the insights Rühl had at that time was that if the steel industry didn't begin to digitize, a new player could enter the industry and push them out — disrupting the business entirely just as the other platform players had disrupted industries they had touched.

This prompted a vision for a cross-industry platform that could reduce friction in fragmented industries such as steel (but for others as well). The thought was that it would be not a proprietary Klöckner platform (although the company was developing that, too), but a more or less neutral digital space in which suppliers, customers, and third parties would be able to trade. In short, Klöckner would be leading the charge in going from a linear process with lots of inefficiencies to an integrated ecosystem that could operate transparently.

WE'RE GOING TO DIGITIZE THE SUPPLY CHAIN . . . OR SOMEONE ELSE WILL DO IT FOR US

This was the beginning of Klöckner's journey to do something about disrupting and digitizing the arcane steel supply chain. Prompted in part, no doubt, by the painful years of the old system failing, the company had the ambition to discover a brighter future. But where to start?

A Fragmented Industry Offers an Opportunity for First-Mover Advantage

The opportunity for a digital platform existed in the steel industry because the industry structure was a mess. While the supplier space was concentrated (over the years, mergers and acquisitions and the need for scale economies had led to consolidation), the producer/distribution space had become highly fragmented. End customers had no way of doing what most of us take for granted when we buy things — compare prices, check for availability, and place online orders, for instance.

Klöckner is one of the larger players in steel. Most of the other companies run relatively small shops offering simple products and services. Without the scale to digitize themselves, these smaller players were likely to join the first platform that promised to offer them exposure to more opportunities while not imposing the cost of platform development on them.

The existing setup was not very helpful to customers who were trying to get a complete job done. It did not offer third-party or complementary products such as insurance. It didn't make price or service comparison easy. And it assumed that the steel players would handle everything, rather than let more specialized actors do pieces of the work (such as logistics). Further, if a customer needed, say, plastic pipes to complement the steel ones, they would be out of luck in trying to buy from an existing metals service center.

A Future-Focused Starting Point

Klöckner's first attempt to figure out potential disruption was to create an internal "innovations" group within the company. Located near company headquarters and moderated by a professor, the group struggled. As one might have predicted, the conversations about new possibilities were shot down by naysayers who couldn't get past the customary "we don't do it that way in the steel business" orthodoxies. After months of frustration, the executives at Klöckner decided that an entirely new approach was necessary.

Rühl, therefore, determined to use a separate entity to get things rolling. He studied how startups work and concluded that his transformation would need to begin with a dose of real entrepreneurial energy, using people who had different skills and backgrounds than the traditional employees who were toiling away at the headquarters in Duisburg. The goal was to quickly get to the "minimum viable product" (to use Eric Ries's term), which would first demonstrate the capability to address specific customers' jobs to be done as a proof of concept.

Rühl began by asking two people to open a small office in Berlin in order to be close to the startup scene there and to pave the way for subsequent recruitment. The group went under the name Klöckner.i to differentiate its activities from those of the parent company.

Hiring New People

A digital transformation requires people with different skill sets than those possessed by workers in the core business. Klöckner set out very deliberately to build a team with members from many different kinds of newcomers. Instead of hiring from the steel industry, they hired from the likes of Amazon, eBay, and other online startups near their Berlin location.

Decoupling the New Unit's Technology
Platform from That of the Mother Ship

You know the old joke: "God created the world in seven days," someone says as a challenge to the IT department. The reply: "Well, yes, but He didn't have a legacy system!" The instinct of an incumbent IT department will be to force the innovator to operate with its technology stack and its controls. The problem with that is that it slows things to a crawl and forces the newcomer to work in much the same way as the old established business, even as it is trying to accomplish something entirely different. Klöckner saw the need for a separation and allowed the new digital teams to create their own technology platform.

The first phase of the digital work was to create more or less stand-alone tools that were customer-centric and dealt with specific pain points that existing systems did not touch. In the second phase, Klöckner planned to expose its own customers to the digital tools, allowing them to choose how they wanted to connect on the digital platform. The third phase Klöckner envisioned was to open the platform to its competitors, allowing the experience of doing business on the platform to be as integrated for customers as possible.

Building In Connectors to the Core Business

Rühl realized that corporate Klöckner had the answer to a pressing problem that bedevils many would-be platform companies. In short, to be a profitable platform, you have to match would-be buyers with would-be sellers. It is often a chicken-and-egg problem of the first order, and failing to establish sufficient interest on both sides is a major reason platforms collapse or are stillborn.

For example, General Electric's efforts at a similar digital platform for manufacturing businesses focused too much on GE business unit needs to be of much interest to external parties. The company ended up facing a reboot after disappointing results. In Klöckner's case, Rühl realized that its position in the value chain meant that it could populate its platform with both buyers and sellers.

This addresses a point that often confuses leaders in established businesses, which is that setting up a startup unit to do great things is pretty easy, but without strong ties and translation mechanisms back to the parent firm, it's also fairly useless. It's the connection to parent capabilities that leads to corporate revitalization, and that is often not thought through very well.

Rühl in particular understood this point. "Our salespeople have to be convinced that this is our future," he said in his 2015 presentation. He recognized, however, that this was likely to be a difficult undertaking, as the new tools and approaches would disrupt the ways in which they had earned a living for so many years. Among the programs Klöckner invested in to make this buy-in a reality was its "digital experience" program, in which sales employees from different branches of the traditional company could take three- to four-month assignments in the digital division, Klöckner.i.

One of the things I find most compelling about Rühl is his respect for and sensitivity to the issues that the people in the incumbent business are likely to face. As a modest example, he explained to me in November 2018 that during the initial phases of the transformation, he was careful to dress as he conventionally had, with a conservative suit and tie. While this was seemingly a small thing, he clearly meant it to signal that he was not abandoning the core business for the shiny new objects of the digital system. Rather, he strongly believed that the two had to work together to realize the benefits of their association.

The company also implemented what Rühl calls "non-hierarchical communication" using the collaboration tool Yammer. Rühl can communicate with people all across the company he doesn't normally come into contact with. Anyone has the right to post a question or an observation and to get a discussion started. For a traditional company, this was a big, big departure from the norm.

Another innovative feature was the company's "Fuck-up nights" (honest, that's what they call them), where they invited startup founders who failed to come in and talk about why they failed. The program was then extended to allow employees to talk about things that had gone wrong and what they learned. Such gatherings are invaluable in trying to break down the fear of failure that often accompanies barriers to innovation.

Klöckner also made a big investment in digital training for employees in the traditional business. Employees were encouraged to pursue this opportunity during their working hours.

Among the side benefits of creating bridges between the startup parts of the business and the existing core was that the initiative began to gradually change the culture of the core. "Through in-depth communication with many of our employees, we have managed to bring them into the digital age," Rühl said in 2017. "As a result, they understand our digitization strategy and know how to contribute to making

digitization a reality. They also adopt increasingly agile working methods from the start-up scene and act in a less persnickety manner than
they did in the past. We as an organization have thereby become much
faster and more agile overall."

Four years into its digitization journey, in 2017, Klöckner reportedly earned 17 percent of its revenue from its digital channels, which
it attributed to a return to profitability and growth. Its goal is to make
that number more like 60 percent by 2022.

INFLECTION POINTS CHALLENGE
THE ASSUMPTIONS OF HOW
YOU RUN YOUR BUSINESS

We now come to the heart of why inflection points wreak havoc on the
management practices of once successful incumbents. I've defined an
inflection point as something that fundamentally changes the envelope of constraints in the arena within which an established organization operates. Back in Chapter 3, I broke these constraints down into
the following categories:

1. They can change the pool of resources that are being contested.
2. They can change the parties trying to grab some of that pool of
   resources.
3. They can change the situation in which the contest takes place.
4. They can cause one job to squeeze another out of an actor's
   consideration set or reduce the resources available to do that job.
5. They can meaningfully change the consumption experience.
6. They can lead to some attributes becoming more or less valued
   than others.
7. They can change the kinds of capabilities embedded in a value
   chain that are relevant.
8. They can change every element of the arena.

Over time, all the elements of an arena are baked into the fabric
of how an organization operates, as incumbents learn to optimize for

competing within that arena. The organization's measurement and reporting structures, reward systems, patterns of communication, informal networks, brand, assumptions, and so on, are all informed by the cause-and-effect relationships that its members believe operate in the arena as it is.

These relationships fundamentally shape what members of the organization pay attention to. They shape what members think is the "right" thing to do. They shape how members expect to be rewarded, how relationships among team members are defined, and who gets ahead. In short, questioning what you have inherited from a pre–inflection point system is nothing short of heresy.

When an inflection point changes the critical constraints that an organization operates within, those painstakingly built-up systems of relationships that kept the organization running smoothly also need to change. This is an enormously challenging organizational reality. The question is how an inflection *inside* the organization can be orchestrated to create a better fit with the inflections happening *outside* it. The process of making this happen is what I call "managing the mother ship."

That process can entail orchestrating a major shift in the core business (as Netflix had to do when it moved from selling DVDs to selling streaming subscriptions). It often involves shifting resources to support the next-generation core business even as formerly important businesses are downsized (as Apple has done in its move from desktop devices to tablet and mobile devices). And, in many cases, it can mean discovering an entirely new growth vector (as Netflix and others are doing with creating original content). Scott Anthony, Clark Gilbert, and Mark Johnson have described the challenges of shifting your core business even as you build a future business in their book *Dual Transformation*, which offers a wealth of useful tools and perspectives.

As we saw with Klöckner, imminent failure, or actual failure, can coax an otherwise unwilling organization to make the changes needed for its own self-preservation. For example, Walmart engaged in a ten-year struggle to become relevant in e-commerce. Despite hundreds of millions of dollars and a lot of executive exhortation, the incumbent organization pretty much hated the idea that some of its sales might go through that channel. It wasn't until a new CEO determined that the company probably had one last chance to get this right that they finally discovered a workable e-commerce model.

Building it required some highly controversial decisions. The first, in 2016, was to spend $3.3 billion on Jet.com, an unproven startup with little to validate its business model. The second was to take the CEO of that startup, Marc Lore, and put him in charge of all of Walmart's digital efforts. The third was to give that operation the resources needed to acquire companies serving upscale customers — the kind who would never set foot in a Walmart store. The men's clothier Bonobos is an example. Today, Walmart's e-commerce initiatives are picking up steam, and the company's assessment in the public markets is more as a growth player than simply an operating entity.

Building innovation proficiency can help your company overcome the resistant forces that can bring it to ruin in the wake of an inflection point.

KLÖCKNER IN CONTEXT: BUILDING INNOVATION PROFICIENCY

What Klöckner faced — and what an endless number of companies I've worked with over the years have faced — are organizational barriers to innovation-fueled growth. Just last week, I was leading a seminar with a group of senior executives at a major multinational. I asked them to list the blockers to innovation in their organization. Here's what they said:

- A lack of incentives.
- The existing business is too powerful.
- Management wants near-term success.
- Too many silos.
- Lack of customer focus.
- Fear of failure.
- It's "no one's job."
- Innovations are small, relative to the "mother ship."

- Innovations don't get big enough fast enough for us.
- We are focused on our quarterly earnings.
- We are afraid of cannibalizing our successful businesses.
- We have no tolerance for unpredictable results.
- There is no career incentive to work on innovation/growth projects.

"What," I asked them, "does every single one of these barriers to innovation have in common?" After a few halting remarks, the penny dropped. Every one is an *internally imposed* constraint. They are all there to protect and defend the orderly operation of the existing business and to keep it from being disrupted. More precisely, they are there to stop the kind of disruption that innovations can represent. And yet, if we collectively and consciously decide that these constraints can be addressed, we can move them out of the way. After all, God did not come down from heaven and declare, "There shalt be silos!"

As we saw in the case of Klöckner, there was little appetite for change among the old-timers, despite the reality that the existing business model was clearly eroding and the company's future was looking grim. Even though reinvention was the only positive path forward, even though the signals of being past an inflection point were so loud as to sound like sirens, the organizational "antibodies" swarmed. This is one reason that the initial effort to do something new—with the same people working at headquarters—failed. That effort was trying to tackle innovation challenges with people totally imbued with innovation blockers. It wasn't until the organization started to recruit and hire new employees with new skill sets working in a new location that new possibilities could even be seen.

The Klöckner case study illustrates one of the most profound journeys an organization can undertake: moving up what I call the *innovation proficiency scale*.

Innovation proficiency is a metric that I've developed (together with some colleagues) that can help identify where an organization is with respect to being able to innovate—in other words, to change—in pursuit of, or in response to, an emergent inflection point. The point is that just seeing an inflection point and getting the organization moving is, as has been discussed earlier, not enough. The organization has to be able to change. Recall that the reason inflection points can be so difficult to cope with is that they change something about the taken-for-granted assumptions in the business. The metrics and operations that used to work well to deliver performance no longer do. As the inflection washes over the organization, these metrics and operations need to change, typically through some kind of innovation process.

My scale has eight levels, corresponding to an organization's ability to make innovation an ongoing proficiency, not an on-again, off-again process that depends on key champions or senior people taking an interest.

THE INNOVATION PROFICIENCY SCALE

Level 1: Extreme Bias Toward Exploitation

Level 1 organizations are those in which the status quo is taken for granted as being the right (even the only) way to do things. There is a strong emphasis on sustaining and exploiting existing advantages. These companies often enjoy a long history of success and are usually in very stable markets. There may well be a high level of asset intensity and long competitive cycles, which makes innovation appear risky and unattractive. Companies in highly regulated markets, many NGOs and government agencies, and other bureaucracies are routinely found in this situation — but not for long.

Level 2: Innovation Theater

This stage represents the very earliest efforts to introduce some innovative thinking to an otherwise conservative organization. There is usually a desire to improve and innovate that exists in islands, but there is little general support across the organization. There may be some initial workshops, boot camps, and visits to Silicon Valley, but there is no sustained effort. The symptoms of this level are that there is a lot of talk and some activity, but things snap back to business as usual very quickly.

Level 3: Localized Innovation

What we see at this level is more – and more sustained – innovative activity, typically in fits and starts in various places in the organization. There is little organization-wide recognition of innovation as a discipline. One or two groups within the company will initiate local efforts to innovate. At this stage, innovation efforts are typically dependent on a key sponsor and are often episodic. They are also fragile: a change of a key executive, a setback, a challenge in the core business, and they simply disappear.

Level 4: Opportunistic Innovation

As some of the innovation efforts launched by the level 3 processes start to show some preliminary results, senior leaders start to recognize that building innovative capability is important. While innovative practices are still not a central part of the corporate agenda, they are used to go after ideas for growth that present themselves in an opportunistic way. Then more attention is paid to the process, and some resources are allocated, sometimes across business units. But the bulk of the organization still prioritizes the "day job."

Level 5: Emergent Proficiency

Here, sustained executive sponsorship includes dedicated resources of both time and money. We begin to see the first signs of innovation-related metrics being used (though they may not be regularly tracked). There is some early-stage governance, with funding and processes for innovation as separate activities from business as usual.

Level 6: Maturing Proficiency

Now we start to see strong, multi-executive commitment and resourcing. Teams have a set of repeatable, scaled best practices to guide their activities. Innovation becomes an important part of executive compensation and promotion discussion. Upper management monitors innovation metrics. Increased utilization of tools and connections across organizational silos, even extending to external sources of ideas, begins to sprout.

Level 7: Strategic Innovation

At this stage, the CEO and executive team articulate publicly that innovation is being integrated into the company's central defining mission. Each step in the product development life cycle benefits from innovation practices. These efforts are supported by and connected to robust governance, measurement, funding, and cultural practices. A critical mass of employees recognize their role in supporting the innovation process and feel empowered to innovate.

Level 8: Innovation Mastery

Corporate commitment to innovation at all levels creates a portfolio of wins, as well as cadres of highly skilled practitioners. The organization is heralded as an example for others and is often cited as a "best practices" entity. Shareholders (for public companies) reward the potential for growth represented by institutionalized innovation practices.

MOVING LEVEL TO LEVEL IN COPING WITH INFLECTION POINTS

Although in my experience every organization approaches its innovation challenges slightly differently, there is a pattern of factors that need to be in place in order for it to move up through the levels of innovation proficiency. As with other forms of organizational maturity, it is unusual for an organization to leap suddenly from, say, level 1 to level 6 or 7; it is usually a cumulative process that takes time. Of course, the more resources that are available and the higher the sense of urgency, the faster a transformation can proceed.

Each of the practices in this section can apply at any stage. However, I've tried to locate them roughly where I usually see them come up.

It is a good idea to start training people in innovation methodologies so that they can become comfortable with the ideas. At the very least, you might start a book club in which people from across the organization learn from thinkers like Steve Blank and Bob Dorf, Alexander Osterwalder and Yves Pigneur, Ian MacMillan and Zenas Block,

Clay Christensen and the Innosight folks, Cindy Alvarez, Curtis Carlson, and me. This would also be a good opportunity to start building a simple community of practice — perhaps organizing "lunch and learns" or similar events with people across the hierarchy, not confined within organizational silos.

Level 1 Challenge: Creating an Appetite for Innovation

Organizations at level 1 are either genuinely absent the need for innovation (relatively rare) or, more typically, just in denial about inflection points that are about to substantially change the context in which they do business. The challenge for an innovation champion in a level 1 organization is getting people to acknowledge that there may be real value and importance in becoming more proficient.

The emphasis at this stage is likely to be highly diagnostic, because the key here is for a critical mass of decision-makers to come to the conclusion that things cannot stay as they are. Finding out that your strategy is not going to be delivered by your current portfolio of efforts (something I call "growth gap analysis") can be a call to action. So, too, can investor enthusiasm for your future. By calculating your *Imagination Premium,* you can get a sense of how well investors think you are doing at seeing around corners.

The Imagination Premium is a metric that allows you to calculate how much of a public company's value stems from cash flow from operations (today's business) versus expectations for future growth (tomorrow's business). You start the calculation by obtaining your company's beta, which is a measure of the volatility of your stock relative to the market. The more volatile it is, the higher the beta will be. Based on the capital asset pricing model, a more volatile stock is riskier and thus should have a higher cost of capital. You then create a cost of capital estimate. By comparing that number with the organization's cash flow from operations, you can effectively price how much of its market capitalization comes from operations. If the market cap exceeds that value, we call it the value of growth. Dividing the value of growth by the value of operations (the percentage of market capitalization attributable to the existing business) yields the Imagination Premium. A low Imagination Premium indicates that investors don't believe you are going to be on the right side of an inflection point.

Take Buffalo Wild Wings, for example, a food franchise that lost its luster in 2017. Its Imagination Premium was a really depressing −.66, meaning investors not only didn't expect growth, they expected shrinkage! What happened next, however, happens with regularity to low–Imagination Premium companies: an activist investor swooped in, demanded seats on the board, pushed the CEO to step down, and eventually ushered the company into the arms of an acquirer. So, a low Imagination Premium can also create an incentive for action.

Another analysis we often do is to look at investments across a portfolio of opportunities arrayed by level of uncertainty. This is called an *opportunity portfolio analysis*. Most relevant to seeing around corners is the presence of multiple options that are far less certain than the core business, such as Microsoft's apps in its software "garage" (see Chapter 6).

We also consider the arena in which the firm is competing in what is called a *context analysis*. Just as Rühl did for Klöckner, the question we ask is how well the existing arena is doing in addressing the jobs to be done for relevant stakeholders. If the answer is "not well" and there are potential profits to be made by another firm entering that space, the context analysis should begin to trigger alarm bells, just as it did for Rühl. "Disrupt rather than be disrupted" then becomes the mantra.

All of these analyses are useful, no matter where on the innovation proficiency scale an organization stands. But we have found them to be especially helpful for creating a sense of urgency to move forward on an innovation agenda in firms that have not previously had to think about this much.

Level 2 Challenge: Getting Started and Clearing the Way

The movement from level 1 to level 2 is often prompted by some kind of actual or imagined crisis. In the case of Klöckner, the crisis was the combination of terrible business conditions that went on for years and the imminent threat of new digital platforms knocking incumbents off their perches without their ever having seen the threat coming. At Whirlpool, it was CEO David Whitwam's despair in 2000 when looking at the state of the sector the company was competing in and seeing only a "sea of white" — row after row of virtually indistinguishable, commoditized appliances that no consumer found exciting.

As a company moves into level 2, there is actually something to be said for "innovation theater" in the sense that it has to start somewhere. And if it takes sending the senior people to Silicon Valley, bringing in consultants to run boot camps, having an idea day, or doing something else to get people excited and on board with the innovation agenda, so be it.

At Klöckner, for instance, the initial attempt to create innovative ideas among people from the existing business didn't work out. That failure, however, created the impetus for the decision-makers to find a different way, which turned out to be setting up a brand-new operation on a small scale in Berlin, right in the heart of Germany's startup scene.

As we saw in Chapter 1, the Adobe Kickbox program has been a smart approach to getting a broad group of people involved in the innovation process without requiring big, heavy corporate processes.

Level 3 Challenge: Local Proof of Concept

Level 3 can be tricky. People are convinced that innovation is important. They've had enough exposure now to think that they understand something about how it works. The temptation is to declare wildly ambitious goals to "own" some space or another. The problem is that at low levels of innovation proficiency, such efforts often end up as big, expensive disasters. Some examples include Revlon's Vital Radiance line of cosmetics; the Quirky manufacturing platform, which was supposed to be an open source platform for building other people's products but failed; and Google's misadventures into radio.

When you look at such disasters, you'll find a classic pattern: untested assumptions taken as facts, few opportunities for low-cost testing and learning, leaders personally committed to the project's every detail, generous up-front funding, and a "damn the torpedoes, full steam ahead" operating model. To avoid the same result, try to be humble about what you know (and don't know) about how to innovate. Identify a few people and a few projects that deserve modest resources in order to develop a proof of concept.

This is also the level at which many organizations authorize "skunk works" — small, often secretive operations given air cover by senior executives that are tasked with working on some great new thing without attracting unwelcome attention from the larger organization. According to a 2005 article in *General Aviation News,* the concept stems from a Lockheed Martin initiative called Skunk Works, launched during World War II to develop a new aircraft. The tent that housed the project was located near a plastic factory that created a terrible odor. One of the team borrowed the nickname "Skonk Works" from the popular comic strip *Li'l Abner* and raffishly answered the phone "Skonk Works" one day. The idea caught on, "Skonk" was changed to "Skunk," and the rest is history.

Skunk works, or whatever your organization calls them, can lead to wonderful things. (Who can forget the brilliance of the new computer created in Tracy Kidder's book *The Soul of a New Machine?*) All too often, however, a project created without the endorsement or support of the parent organization meets a grim end — either killed off in political infighting when it gets too big to ignore, or left to wither on the vine without the resources needed to realize its ambitions. As Steve Blank has pointed out, the very presence of a skunk works indicates that the organization has not yet mastered continuous innovation.

Level 4 Challenge: Launch a Few Opportunistic Wins

Having begun to work on projects in the level 3 phase, an organization with level 4 capabilities understands enough to take an idea all the way through to the potential scale-up and launch. Ideation is, of course, important. But the first version of an idea is hardly ever the one that eventually makes it to market. Instead, ideation needs to be followed by incubation, in which the idea is prototyped, tested, shown to customers, retested, validated, and moved forward. Steve Blank calls this the "customer discovery" process.

Following incubation is acceleration. I use the metaphor quite deliberately. Think of your main business as a number of vehicles rolling along an eight-lane highway at top speed. Your new, about-to-be-launched venture needs to be brought up to a pace at which it can join the flow of traffic without being mowed down. That is often an unexpectedly painful process for innovation teams.

Technical and organizational debts both need to be taken care of. On the technical side, code that was "good enough" now needs to be brought to industrial scale. A similar issue arises with organizational debts. In the hurry of starting and launching a new venture, all kinds of shortcuts are likely to be made on the people side: *Let's not worry about formal job titles, pay grades, or evaluations — let's build something great!* That's nifty in the early stages, but now you need people with real titles who are looking for a career path. Your venture, which has probably been protected from too much interference from support functions, now has to play nice with Legal, HR, Compliance, and the office of the CFO. It needs to connect to corporate rhythms, such as the budgeting cycle. Organizations with level 4 proficiency are often just beginning to figure this out and are still designing their acceleration programs in isolation.

Level 5 (Emergent) and Level 6 (Maturing) Challenge: Systems, Structures, and Routines

One of the biggest shifts from the earlier levels to these two is that a budget for innovation-related activities is now specifically set aside, across the organization. It no longer depends on the business cycle or the preferences of senior leaders, but is rather a routine line item, much the same as for other key organizational processes.

With levels 5 and 6 come increasingly routinized and repeatable practices for generating an ongoing stream of innovations. There is an identifiable innovation system that most members of the organization can talk about. There is a governance mechanism regulating decisions about which innovations should be supported, redirected, or stopped. There is a dedicated stream of resources that are focused on innovation rather than supporting the existing business. Innovation practices are measured, and it matters when the measures don't show progress.

The majority of employees have received some kind of training on innovation topics and are provided with well-understood mechanisms to present ideas. The criteria that determine whether a particular innovation is suitable to move forward are clear to most people. Resource reallocation across different projects happens more quickly and smoothly. The barriers that prevent business unit leaders from enthusiastically embracing innovation (such as being held accountable for unpredictable results) are removed.

We also start to see a reallocation of talent, in which the best people focus their attention and energy on potential growth projects rather than on problem solving for today's current business. There is also an increased flexibility about organizational structure, with innovations going into structures that are most likely to support them successfully. Attention is given to making sure that innovation teams are diverse in terms of thought processes, skills, and background.

Level 7 Challenge: Institutionalization

At level 7, innovation is associated with the organization's brand in a meaningful way, and senior leaders see fostering innovation as a key agenda item. Executives are expected to support the innovation agenda, and it becomes a critical element of their compensation. Employees know how to access small pools of resources to experiment and test ideas and what to do if those ideas look promising. Technology is used to supplement human communication and accelerate decision-making.

The company begins to tell the innovation story in internal and external communications. It creates a technology platform that underpins the effort (an innovation operating system). It continues core transformation while adding new resources.

At this stage, the organization should have a pipeline of innovations, solid governance and funding processes, employees trained and knowledgeable about these processes, and customers delighted with how well the company is serving them!

Level 8 Challenge: Continuous Renewal

Achieving a high level of innovation mastery doesn't imply that an organization will stay there. The big challenge for this level is preserving what is working and fending off the forces that might drag the organization back down the innovation proficiency scale. I have spent hundreds of hours (and my clients many, many more) helping to build wondrous innovation systems, only to have a subsequent regime dismantle them. This often leads, a few years later, to newspaper articles commenting on the organization's fall from grace, with headlines along the lines of "What the Hell Happened to X?"

It is extraordinarily tempting for leaders, especially if they were not part of the innovation journey in the first place, to slip back to prioritizing near-term results in the existing business. The structure of our public markets at present rewards such leaders with outsize benefits. Among the mechanisms that have been identified as undermining organizations' innovation processes are stock buybacks, which have become a vehicle for rewarding executives and investors. Buybacks boost stock prices, and therefore executives' compensation when they are awarded on the basis of stock price appreciation. Unfortunately, resources flowing into buybacks are not available for investment in the future (or in people, or in other assets). The challenge of creating a level 8 organization is keeping it a level 8 organization through the selection of leaders who have its long-term best interests at heart.

BUILDING PROFICIENCY STEP BY STEP

As we saw with Klöckner, tempting as it might be to try to leap from a lower level to a higher one on the innovation proficiency scale, such a move is almost always a recipe for disappointment. Building innovation proficiency is an organizational learning endeavor, and learning and mastering do not happen instantly. Recall how Klöckner moved through the stages in its years-long journey.

When Rühl took over Klöckner in 2009, my guess was that the entire steel industry was pretty much working at level 1. It was slow, conservative, and traditional. The trauma of the Great Recession of 2008, coupled with the aggressive globalization of the Chinese steel industry, convinced at least Rühl and his board that the current business model was not viable. In effect, they knew that the time had come to see around the corner.

The inflection point around digital technologies that attracted Rühl's attention sparked his movement into level 2 activity — first with a disappointing internal effort and next with a separate but liberated small group with different skill sets and assumptions. As the company moved through what I would call levels 3 and 4, work began taking place not only at the Berlin digital outpost but also back at the "mother ship." There was an effort to "horizontalize" and to broaden communications without regard for hierarchy. There was training. There were

processes whereby people who were not central to the innovation effort nonetheless benefited from its liberating effect on the corporate
entity.

As the digitization effort continues at Klöckner, it can be assumed
that the company will move methodically into ever higher levels of
proficiency, with digital providing the impetus for a major corporate
transformation and a return to inflection-driven growth.

Key Takeaways

Navigating through an inflection point often means working on two
massive challenges at once — bringing the core business forward in its
competitive capability and creating new capabilities that will be relevant to the future.

Digitally enabled business models are often collaborative. There
is a need to rethink where organizational boundaries lie. Incumbents
cannot depend on traditional barriers to entry.

When an existing solution set does a poor job of responding to customers' "jobs to be done," it creates an opportunity for a new entrant
to get a toehold.

Recognizing that both the existing business and the new business
have contributions to make and designing incentives accordingly are
key.

Simple techniques — such as a hierarchy-free communication system and widespread availability of training and upskilling — can help
break down hierarchical barriers.

Moving up the innovation proficiency scale often involves sweeping change in company practices and procedures. It is a challenge to
long-held assumptions, incentives, and organizational arrangements
and needs to be well orchestrated with significant senior level support.

8

How Leadership Can and Must Learn to See Around Corners

People will put up with awful, terrible, incompetent leadership, as long as things are going well. But when the inevitable crisis occurs, rank and file perspective changes, the focus turns to competence, and the pressure skyrockets.

— Brigadier General Thomas Kolditz, retired

I never intended to go to an all-women's university for my undergrad years. In fact, when I was admitted to Barnard College, one of the "Seven Sisters" at the time, it took a lot of convincing to persuade me that being in New York, being part of Columbia University, and being at a place with a huge commitment to teaching and learning would be worth living in some kind of nunnery for four years.

Of course, I couldn't have been more wrong. Barnard was transformative for me. When it came my daughter's turn to attend college and she, too, chose Barnard, I could not have been more proud. But while I'm more than happy to chat with you at length about the pros and cons of women's colleges, women's education, and relatedly of a liberal arts education, that's really not what this chapter is about.

Instead, it explores the kind of leadership models we should be thinking about in organizations that are prone to frequent and more destabilizing inflection points. So, back to Barnard (sort of). I'm now teaching at Barnard's sister (brother?) institution, Columbia Business School, often in our Executive Education classrooms.

ENTER THE WOMEN IN LEADERSHIP COURSE

A couple of years ago, I was approached by a small but passionate delegation from Columbia Business School's program development team. It seems that they had been meeting for quite some time with a group from Barnard's Athena Center for Leadership Studies.

The creation of the Athena Center was an initiative strongly sponsored by Barnard president Debora Spar, who had come to Barnard from Harvard Business School. She wanted to create a place that would focus on leadership in addition to the liberal arts curriculum for which Barnard was already well-known. The staff would use their knowledge of women's leadership to develop programs specifically to guide organizations in helping women advance. The center had elegant diagnostics and a small but very well-run set of sessions they were using with a few companies attracted by Barnard's brand name and clear legitimacy on the female-facing side of things.

The development team thought there was a great opportunity for these programs to be expanded into the open-enrollment sector (meaning that people from all different types of organizations could attend them). They wanted to create a working model in which the Executive Education group would manage the logistics, joint marketing, and promotion, and the Barnard folks would provide subject-matter expertise, their cool brand, and perhaps use of the gorgeous Barnard facilities. You have to love a place where all the oil paintings of the "fearless leaders" from the past are of commanding-looking women!

But I digress. It seems the whole idea had just one little glitch: they needed someone on the Executive Education faculty to agree to become the faculty director of the joint program. That person would be the face of the program and be responsible for selecting faculty, directing overall curriculum design, and creating a coherent experience for participants. That person also typically would be an expert on some element of the topic. Even though we have a fair number of faculty members who work in areas focusing on gender and women's issues, no one wanted to take on the responsibility of creating, launching, and running a brand-new program. As a result, the team worried that the plan was going nowhere.

Then one member of the team happened to be reading my bio and —bingo!—noticed that I was a Barnard graduate and a fairly loyal alumna. When the team approached me, I said that women's advancement and gender issues were not my thing, and besides, it was 2016, and why on earth would the world still need such a program?

In good academic fashion, the team proceeded to bury me in research. As I went through study after study on the myriad ways in which talented women (and the organizations that, in most cases, really do want to do well by them) fall out of the executive ranks, I was persuaded. Also a little enraged, to be completely honest.

"OK," I said. "Let's do this." The resulting course was called Women in Leadership: Expanding Influence and Leading Change.

We had a great launch, with star appearances by Nancy McKinstry, CEO of the global publisher Wolters Kluwer, and Sharon Price John, CEO of the Build-A-Bear Workshop. Glenn Hubbard, dean of Columbia Business School, and Debora Spar jointly kicked off the program, and the participants themselves were amazing. And then, of course, the "me too" movement erupted, making my skepticism about why such a program was still necessary seem more than a tad naïve.

WOMEN'S WAYS OF LEADING?

For our purposes here, what matters about my role in that program was a major "Aha!" moment—for me, anyway. We had invited Sally Helgesen, who together with world famous executive coach Marshall Goldsmith had just published a book called *How Women Rise,* to address the class. Helgesen made an observation that to her was probably a throwaway but that struck me profoundly. Back in 1990, she'd written a book that attempted to do for female leaders what Henry Mintzberg had done for male ones in the 1970s—namely, figure out what they actually did at work all day.

"What we've realized since then," Helgesen said to the class, "is that the qualities that I found were exhibited by the female leaders in my research were exactly the same qualities that we are now realizing are essential for leaders of all kinds in faster-moving, more uncertain environments." That got me thinking. Had those women in fact been at the forefront of a sea change in how we lead organizations – and were forced, perhaps, to come up with a new model because they didn't fit into the old one?

The broad outlines of that model, which were surprising then, are much less so now. The women in Helgesen's study focused "on the doing of various tasks rather than on the completion." They created "webs of inclusion" rather than hierarchies. Information flows were widely distributed, and the role of the most senior leader was as a connector and guide rather than a command issuer. Leaders did retain decision rights and authority, but they granted enormous autonomy to those closest to the situation.

This all started to sound very familiar to me.

When I look at the outstanding corporate leaders of today, male and female, I see these same patterns. Alan Mulally, legendary for turnarounds at both Boeing and Ford, refers to his role among his executive teams as a "facilitator." General Stanley McChrystal, the leader in the United States' fight against Al Qaeda, talks of creating what he calls "shared consciousness" and trust among team members, so that decisions can be made by those closest to the problem, regardless of their seniority. Mark Bertolini of Aetna took a personal interest in the lives of his employees and was shocked at the economic and thus personal toll they labored under. His controversial decision to raise Aetna's minimum wage and improve its medical benefits was the result. And in dozens of other examples I found in the research for this book, a new leadership model seems to be becoming more of a reality, and not just for women.

WHAT DOES THIS STYLE OF
LEADERSHIP HAVE TO DO WITH
SEEING AROUND CORNERS?

Throughout this book, I've emphasized that spotting and acting on emergent inflection points can't be done by one person in a lofty corner office. As Jeff Bezos has said, seeing inflection points coming is typically not the biggest challenge. It's seeing their implications for the taken-for-granted ways we do business, deciding which vector your organization will pursue, and then bringing the organization along that allows it to navigate through an inflection point and come out stronger on the other end. It's also thinking through the long-term benefits for the organization, even if the short-term transitions are somewhat painful.

In other words, you first have to see the potential for an inflection point as an organization. Then you need to decide what to do about it, collectively, as it isn't always clear what to do just because you've seen a change coming. Then you have to mobilize the organization, which is often difficult, as people will have grown used to the typical way things are done. Most people in the organization have never been through a major inflection point. Most people have been rewarded for, well, doing what is in the interest of the current way of doing business and business model. Expecting them to leave all that behind and embark on a journey that seems highly uncertain is a tall order.

If snow melts from the edges, then the ability to get to the edges and hear their messages is absolutely key. Being able to detect weak signals that things are changing requires more eyes and ears throughout the organization. The critical information that informs decision-making is often locked in individual brains. Somehow leaders need to be able to access that information and make it available, with the right level of accuracy, to everyone.

People have to be willing to bring you, as a leader, disconfirming evidence — indicators that your assumptions were wrong and challenges to the taken-for-granted ways of doing business. Genuinely relating to customers, their pain points, and their jobs to be done requires being motivated and incentivized to get into the field and empathize with them.

Providing people with the courage — and the methodologies — to engage in fast learning even when things are uncertain is something that can have an impact at scale only if the senior team is behind it. Mobilizing the organization around a common set of goals is, again, a core task of the senior team, as we saw with the experience of Satya Nadella and Microsoft's transformation. Bringing both the core business and the new business along together requires a deep respect for what both bring: sensitivity to the human side of things and a willingness to break the mold a bit, as we saw with the Klöckner story in Chapter 7.

Let's dig into what this looks like at a granular level. *What must one actually do to create an organization that can see around corners collectively?*

Let's consider one remarkable leadership story, that of a founding CEO who took a startup from just barely surviving to an IPO and then to a massively profitable acquisition over a grueling nearly seventeen-year stretch. Her name is Gail Goodman.

"THE LONG, SLOW, SAAS RAMP OF DEATH"

The email-marketing company Constant Contact provides a perfect inflection point story. The company made incremental progress for years before it finally achieved success.

In 1999, Gail Goodman joined the startup company Roving Software, a seven-person firm founded by Randy Parker and working out of an attic in Brookline, Massachusetts. She was, in reality, the startup's CEO. At the time, the company had an idea about creating software that would help small and medium-size enterprises, but it hadn't yet entered the market. As Goodman said in 2013, "I joined pre-product, pre-revenue, and pre-funding."

When it launched, the company offered email marketing support to small businesses and not-for-profits to help them build their audiences. Given their target customer base, a monthly subscription price of something like $30 was about all they could hope to get for their services. Goodman later said, "The VCs puked all over it. You cannot make the math in this business work." That was in 1999, before the business model for recurring revenue, software as a service (SaaS) was recognized as potentially attractive. She admitted, "They kind of had a point—to get to scale was going to take a long time, hence the long, slow, SaaS ramp of death."

Roving Software launched its cloud computing solution in October of 2000. Customer uptake was slow — starting with a hundred customers, then a thousand. The idea the company had at the time was that scaling would take place in inflection point fashion — that there would eventually be a tipping point and growth would then explode.

Unfortunately for them, the promised tipping point turned out to be so many "mirages." As Goodman would recount later, the early stages were a lot more like a flywheel than a hockey stick — find something, repeat it, find something else, repeat that, and so on. This went on for years.

Discovering an Arena in Which the Company Could Win

Finally, the company, which changed its name to Constant Contact in 2004, did reach an inflection point. What made that possible was figuring out the dynamics of its arena — as Goodman later put it, a "combination of understanding our channels at the top of the funnel, our funnel conversation, and our lifetime business value." When those all came together, the company invested strongly in growth. At last, a desirable inflection point — and the business took off! As Goodman somewhat triumphantly said in 2012, "So this year we will do over $250 million in revenue . . . and we will do it thirty-nine dollars at a time."

Clearly, results like this do not happen by accident. I was intrigued by the leadership lessons one might glean from this company's seventeen-year journey up to that point.

Leadership as Relentless Alignment and Collaboration

Goodman came to the company after she'd had a number of experiences at other firms that bugged her. As she told me in September 2018, "An interesting thing that I went through as a first-time CEO was that I had not seen an executive team collaboration role model. I hadn't been on a single executive team where everybody worked together. I set out to do that differently. I saw what a tremendous waste of resources it was to have all that infighting on the executive team. By getting on the same page, you can use your resources more effectively."

The Key Role of the CEO: Keeping Executives
on the Same Page and Working Together

One universal aspect of leadership of all kinds is that where the leader focuses attention is where the organization tends to focus it. "As a leader, where you are spending your time is one of the most important investment decisions you can make," Goodman has said.

The first distinction between the way Goodman approached her role and what we might think of as more traditional top-down leadership is how she defined the unique task that only the CEO can perform — acting as the essential glue that keeps a diverse set of employees working consistently toward a well-understood set of priorities. As she put it,

> The quality of the leadership team you can bring together is going to be a major swing vote in how successful your business is. But the point I would make is that it is not just about the individuals but about the quality of the teaming of the individuals as well. At Constant Contact, we invested a ridiculous amount of time in being a great team, at the executive team level, the next level down, and the next level down. Why? I had had several experiences before Constant Contact where the executives were not aligned, and were fighting. And what that did to the organization was just horrible. It was chaotic, it was wasteful . . . We all know these stories, but if you let it happen, it will waste resources in a dramatic manner . . . You will also find that the antidote to complexity is team alignment and prioritization.

In a 2013 talk, she described the process of taking a two-day off-site twice a year for the team, with a one-day off-site at other points. During that time, she said, "we got ourselves aligned." First issue: *strategy*. Strategy, she said, is pretty straightforward, defining "who are we serving, what problem are we solving, and what is our unique competitive advantage." While that seems right to the point, she cited the problems that can arise when the overall strategy is not clear to all the team members. If you're sloppy on the direction of the company's strategy, lots of things get built that aren't needed, and lots of people get confused about the "why."

The second thing on the table for alignment is what she referred to as *"the culture stuff."* This includes mission, vision, and values. She could recite each of these when she was at Constant Contact and made sure that everyone else on the team could as well.

Next is *alignment on key priorities*. Gaining clarity about what is really important in the business and in what priority order is a critical topic. These are called "rallying cries" in Patrick Lencioni's book *The Advantage*. "We would come out of these off-sites with rallying cries and priorities," Goodman explained, then added, "It's always better to do two or three things completely right than do a half-assed job at eight." As she pointed out, the executive team needs to exercise the discipline of making choices — and being aligned on the right choices takes time.

From Command and Control to Leading Through Feedback

Another aspect of Goodman's leadership that I find distinctly different from the traditional command-and-control model is the extent to which she emphasizes the importance of feedback in shaping her own behavior. In other words, she recognizes that only through feedback can she remain effective. As she said in 2013, you have to be willing to look in the mirror.

She described how, relatively early in her tenure at Constant Contact, she enlisted the help of a facilitator to obtain feedback from her colleagues. Her initial reaction was one of shock at how much she was doing that others perceived as not being very helpful.

She told a great anecdote about how we all tend to see our weaknesses as strengths (in our own minds). She said that one of hers is being impatient. "But it was also harming my team in some pretty profound ways. One of the things I invented along the way was my own little internal signal to presenters — it kind of went like this [a circular motion with her hands]. You know what it meant: 'I got it, I got it, go faster.' And again, I had a little rationalization to go with it — it's affirming to them that I'm with them [to much audience laughter].

"As is obvious to you in the audience, that is not a pleasant thing to be on the receiver side of. The first problem is that it was stunting discussion. Second, it was sending an immensely disrespectful signal to the presenter . . . But then, the really bad part started to sink in. I found that people were not bringing their up-and-coming new talent to present to me, because they didn't want them to get demoralized. These were the very people I wanted to meet and nurture. They were the future of the company, and I wasn't meeting them. And so I had to change."

Among the new practices she put in place for obtaining feedback was spending time with a peer mentoring group comprising people outside Constant Contact (and thereby outside her control). The group members would provide one another with feedback on a regular basis, such as asking, "Where did you spend your time last quarter and where do you hope to spend it this quarter?"

Within the Constant Contact management team, she went to great lengths to prompt the entire team to give serious feedback in terms of individual performance, team performance, and how well the team members related to one another. As she put it, "I had to be willing to constantly look at myself, as the CEO, as the leader, and recognize that I was screwing up the team." If the team is dysfunctional, she said, as the CEO, "it's you! It's you because either you're not creating an environment where the team is forced to resolve their conflicts or you are not listening, or one of your team is not listening and you're not telling them that that's not OK. One of your key responsibilities is making sure your team is a team. They don't tell you that in the CEO handbook, but it is, and it takes time to do that."

In addition to feedback loops, Goodman insists, engagement with strategy requires a huge investment of communication. Communicate, communicate, communicate — mission, vision, values, priorities, rallying cries, key themes. Communication has to go all the way down, not just one way but both ways. People have to engage with the material and the content to internalize it. As she has said, "People don't sit at an all-hands and get strategy."

Feedback is a gift, she notes, but it's a gift leaders would much rather give than receive. The more senior you get, the less unfiltered feedback you receive. And the more you need to structure leadership processes to guard against that.

Relentless External Focus and Leading Indicators

Consistent with the other great leaders featured in this book, Goodman kept her team at Constant Contact focused relentlessly on leading indicators and external data. Because their strategy was to attract large numbers of small businesses and to keep them as clients, the key leading indicator for them was managing the sales funnel. As she has put it, "Everybody in the company knew about funnel management." This brings to mind Satya Nadella of Microsoft urging his leaders to focus on leading indicators of customer utilization, including "customer love."

In conjunction with her focus on leading indicators, Goodman has said that she gets asked a lot why the company kept going during the long, slow ramp phase. She reiterates the fundamental passion that Constant Contact leaders had for their customers. "It was our customers, and their affirmation of our value. The number one thing that holds us together is our passion for helping small businesses. We just kept seeing that when they used our product, they got real revenue, and it lit us up. We told a customer story every week, and we still do. Because what we do matters to the small businesses."

Waking Slumbering Strategic Change Muscles

Goodman makes a distinction between the kind of leadership that is necessary in a changing, discovery-oriented situation and the kind in which you can just execute. As she told me in 2018, "If your model stays static, you can have a leadership team that isn't engaging their strategic change muscles. They are just executing — turn the crank and do it again mode. But if you are in an industry that is under change, you either have to change in advance or in response. You need your leaders to be in discovery mode, with you as the CEO. You cannot be in discovery mode alone. It does take a different leadership style — as a leader, you need them to understand the 'why.' What are we trying to figure out? The goal isn't to prove something is wrong, rather it's to get it right."

"CRESCIVE" LEADERSHIP: DID FEMALE LEADERS DISCOVER A NEW MODEL BEFORE ITS TIME HAD COME?

Back in 1984 (before Sally Helgesen had even done her research), Jay Bourgeois and David Brodwin set out to catalog different approaches to leadership. They duly cataloged a number of different, traditional leadership styles. They found, however, that they couldn't account for some of the leadership behaviors they had observed without including a category they dubbed "crescive" leadership.

In the crescive approach, as they described it, "the role of the CEO has moved from designer to that of premise-setter and judge. Here, the strategic problem revolves around the CEO's ability to define organization purposes (i.e., set decision premises) broadly enough to encourage innovation, and to select judiciously from among those projects or strategy alternatives that reach his attention."

Among the most significant departures from the other leadership roles they examined was that crescive leaders actually yield strategic control. As they put it, "The CEO in the crescive model must be willing to risk loss of control over strategy initiatives in order to capitalize on the new business opportunities impossible for him to apprehend from his perch at headquarters."

Follow the Talent

Michael Sikorsky, a serial entrepreneur originally from Canada, has been named a "CEO to Watch" by CNN Money, "Canada's Internet Revolutionary" by *Profit* magazine, one of Alberta's 50 Most Influential People by *Alberta Venture*, and the 2013 Technology and Communication EY Entrepreneur of the Year. His company, Robots & Pencils, is as good an example as I can find of an organization that embodies the notion of crescive leadership. Full disclosure: I am one of the company's founding fellows and an adviser, which is how I got to know about its fairly unique perspective.

Robots & Pencils has articulated what it calls a "follow the talent" strategy. Its strategic positioning is to help its clients "discover what's next" in the world of technology so that they can, as company leadership says, become "future proof." This is very much a company that has bet its success on helping clients navigate through inflection points. As its website says, "Our approach has been to create a company designed to follow the talent, allowing us to amass an unfair share of hyperskilled people who call Robots & Pencils home. A team of people who not only develop innovative solutions to transform businesses, but also create products that have been previously inconceivable."

Have Fun

One program Robots & Pencils invests in is called FunLabs. This is a direct expression of the idea of crescive leadership. As the company says, in FunLabs "internal teams work on self-directed hypotheses focused on new and frontier technologies." It is a cohort-based model, in which employees are deeply engaged in identifying technological inflection point possibilities they might work on. It is one way Robots & Pencils tries to stay on the cutting edge of what is coming next for their clients.

The process begins with a "considerations report." Every person at Robots & Pencils has the opportunity to provide input to the report on "frontier technologies and trends that look to be game-changers, what our talent is interested in diving into, and what we think will benefit our clients." The considerations report next goes to a FunLabs committee, a group that is freshly composed for each FunLabs cycle. The committee's task is to come up with three potential technologies or themes that they believe FunLabs should focus on for the next cycle. This is called the "outcomes menu."

Every employee has four weeks to put forward specific ideas for experiments that could be carried out based on the outcomes menu. The proposals are narrowed down to the top three ideas. The finalists then pitch their ideas in short, peppy presentations. The pitches are subject to a vote by the entire company. Rather than the vote being a beauty contest, there is a fairly nuanced voting structure. People who have been with the company longer get votes that carry more weight. Voting also takes into account whether the employees believe in the idea sufficiently strongly that they would leave current projects for the chance to work on it.

Once the selection process is complete, a team of three is located in the lab for sixteen weeks to conduct the experiment. After that, the team is expected to share what they have learned through blogs, demonstrations, and a quarterly "learnings report."

Notice how this process reaches right out to the edges of the firm to gain insight, engagement, and inspiration, and how little of it is driven from the top down. Senior leadership does set the general goals, but key individuals and the voting process define what the actual projects will be.

The first FunLabs venture was a product called Missions, which allows ordinary people to program workflows in Slack, the team collaboration tool that is increasingly used to provide what Gisbert Rühl has called "non-hierarchical communication" (see Chapter 7). Missions proved so compelling that Slack eventually acquired the product from Robots & Pencils, together with the team that built it.

Here's another interesting twist on conventional management practice: the employees who left Robots & Pencils to join Slack were offered an open door should they ever decide to return. No interviews, no application process, just the chance to come back to the company if and when that might make sense for them. In the meantime, the team is considered to be on "venture leave."

Moving on from the original articulation of what crescive leaders do, we can begin to define the practices that such individuals use to help their organizations navigate strategic inflection points.

Articulate a General Strategic Direction to Guide the Firm Through Inflection Points

Given the amount of change and disruption in the business environment, some have concluded that the entire enterprise of formulating strategy is to some extent futile. But my research suggests that a core strategy is more important now than ever before, as without real clarity on strategy and priorities, the crescive approach will disintegrate into rudderless activity.

Let's consider a potential inflection point that is gathering significant interest at the moment. Larry Fink, founder and CEO of Black-Rock and the manager of over $6.3 trillion in assets, sent a much-talked-about letter to numerous CEOs in January of 2018. In it, he said that companies must "make a positive difference" to society and that he intended to hold their leaders accountable. Andrew Ross Sorkin of the *New York Times* termed the letter "an inflection point in the long-simmering argument over the state of global capitalism."

Fink announced that going forward, BlackRock would be investing in such a way that would take into account the long-range impact on society created by the companies they invest in. Fink is among a growing group of observers who decry economic short-termism by public companies. One idea in particular is being criticized as particularly unhealthy for capitalism in its current form, and that is the notion that companies should be run only in the interest of generating financial returns to their investors. I mentioned the practice of stock buybacks utilizing resources that are then not available for innovation in Chapter 7. The larger issue — the idea that investors are the only stakeholders that matter — is coming under increasing fire. It is being blamed for thwarting investment not only in innovation but also in people development and community creation. It has been blamed for the potential "end of the modern political order" by no less an expert than Martin Wolf of the *Financial Times*. The instruments used to implement the "shareholder-first" perspective, such as share repurchases, lavish stock-related executive compensation, and extracting as much profitability from existing assets as possible, have also been widely criticized for distorting market pricing and rewarding executives and investors to the detriment of others, such as long-term employees, who have a stake in what happens to companies.

While the exact policies BlackRock is proposing are not spelled out in Fink's letter, it is clear that investors are now paying attention. As guidance, the firm posted on its website a document that lays out the questions it may well be asking in meetings with management teams and boards. Note that BlackRock is not telling companies to take a specific action. Rather, it is attempting to put this issue on the agenda of its conversations with CEOs and other investors. Strategically, in other words, firms that desire BlackRock's support need to have topics such as human capital management up front and center in terms of what they are paying attention to.

Note the way in which the strategy has been executed. Yes, BlackRock has said that social purpose is important, but it has not dictated what ways it should show up in company strategies. That is up to the individual CEOs with whom the company wants to have strategic conversations.

Interestingly, given the earlier discussion about women's ways of leading and the importance of diverse perspectives in strategic thinking, one of BlackRock's ambitions is to see that the companies it invests in put in place rigorous policies and practices to genuinely promote a diverse agenda.

Maintain the Openness of the Organization to New and Discrepant Information

Andy Grove articulated this point in his original work on strategic inflection points. Before the pattern is clear, he said, you have to let a certain amount of chaos reign. Lots of inputs, lots of ideas, and lots of arguments are essential. Only after you have sufficient information (the weak signals have become strong enough) should you coalesce the organization around a selected strategic path.

Absolute candor – and the willingness to confront unpleasant information – is crucial here. Wishing things were different is a recipe for corporate disaster. A colleague of mine calls this "nostalgia as business strategy." Skillful leaders recognize, as Alan Mulally of Ford is fond of saying, that "you can't manage a secret."

Experts such as Ram Charan, Don Sull, and Nassim Nicholas Taleb have proposed similar reasons why candor is essential to anticipating a change that could be significant. Charan and Sull agree that leaders should search for the presence of anomalies – events that occur outside the expected range. Taking in lots of information is seen as critical to seeing emergent patterns. Taleb points out an interesting approach to getting high-quality information: "Don't take advice from those who are not at risk" for the consequences of a possible inflection point.

High-performing CEOs are unanimously alike in this one thing: they insist on total candor and brutal truth, even if it challenges their previously held assumptions. No, make that *especially* if it challenges their previously held assumptions. Andy Grove (Intel), Lou Gerstner (IBM), and Alan Mulally (Ford) have all stressed in their management writings just how important this is.

Crescive leaders listen to alarmists – those people who occasionally are dismissed as Cassandras for conveying bad news. Instead of immediately dismissing them, we should think of them instead as "helpful Cassandras," who broaden the range of outcomes we are considering or who are exposed to subtle or key inputs that are different from those we normally see. The furor surrounding Facebook's sale of users' private data to advertisers and those who want to target individuals was not only anticipated but widely discussed by people like Danah Boyd years before it became public knowledge — as far back as 2006!

Push Decision-Making as Close to the Edges as Possible

General Stanley McChrystal is widely credited with having transformed the way US intelligence forces do their work. In his book *Team of Teams*, he describes how in the fight against Al Qaeda, even the military had to discover a different way of leading than the usual "command-and-control" that was their historical norm. He writes, "The wisest decisions are made by those closest to the problem — regardless of their seniority."

McChrystal has found that the answer to how senior leaders can become comfortable with the loss of control is by helping their teams develop shared consciousness. As he has said, "This means getting to a point where you trust almost anyone to make decisions on their own because you believe they have the same information and objectives you do."

Note how consistently this echoes Gail Goodman's observations about how having an aligned team allows progress to move faster.

Use Your Own Agenda and Networks to Make Lasting Changes

Brian Murray, CEO of the publisher HarperCollins, recalls a flash of insight he had at the Frankfurt Book Fair in the 2002 time frame. He suddenly realized that once data and products could be digitized, the economics of the publishing business would be forever changed. As he put it in 2017,

> All of a sudden I realized that there was a sea change that was going to happen. I didn't know how it was going to unfold, but that was one crystal clear memory . . . Digitization is still misunderstood.

I don't think our economy, our country, and corporations understand the impact of digital economics. Once you go to zero vari-
able costs, everything changes. And so books, of all the media, being the smallest file that exists and the easiest to transmit, even at
the time back then, you could see that there was going to be a fundamental shift in the business for book publishers . . . How can we
survive and thrive as those ecosystems were being built up around
us? There wasn't an off-site, we didn't get everybody in the room
and groupthink it together, it was incremental over many years of
trying to figure out how do you position the company and protect
the company's core business for an unknown future that was going
to have a heavy digital component.

Notice the language here: "it was incremental over many years."
Even though the insight that sparked the strategic activity arrived in a
flash, the organizational transition to respond to it was an incremental, adaptive activity.

Build Aligned and Trusting Teams
That Can Move Quickly

Alan Mulally's management system has been meticulously documented, so I won't spend much time on it here. The core of the system,
though, was Mulally's famous practice of having weekly review meetings at which team members were expected to reveal and work out
problems they might be encountering in the business. As Mulally has
said, the magic of this approach lies not in the weekly meeting, but in
the cultural norms he insisted on.

At a conference coordinated by the well-known executive coach
Marshall Goldsmith in 2015, Mulally distributed a handout listing the
guiding principles of a framework he calls "working together":

- People first
- Everyone is included
- Compelling vision, comprehensive strategy, relentless imple-
  mentation
- Clear performance goals
- One plan

- Facts and data
- Everyone knows the plan, the status and areas that need special attention
- Propose a plan, "find-a-way" attitude
- Respect, listen, help and appreciate each other
- Emotional resilience – trust the process
- Have fun . . . enjoy the journey and each other

Note how similar these ideas are to the leadership principles mentioned throughout this book. Gail Goodman's insistence that how executives "team," rather than who they are, is important and Satya Nadella's insight that Microsoft's internally competitive norms required an overhaul are two examples.

Simplify and Create a Rallying Cry

As mentioned earlier, Sharon Price John stepped into the CEO role at Build-A-Bear Workshop at a pivotal time for the firm. For those not familiar with Build-A-Bear, it was a brilliant entrepreneurial startup. Founded by Maxine Clark in 1997, it was one of the first companies to create the concept of experiential retail. Clark had risen to the rank of president of Payless ShoeSource and, like many leaders who go through personal inflection points, over time realized that the "spark" was no longer there. So she left Payless and began to look for a new idea. The inspiration came, suitably enough, from a shopping trip with a child of a friend of hers. As she described it in a 2012 interview,

> One day, I was shopping with Katie Burkhardt, the daughter of one of my good friends, and her brother Jack, who collected Ty Beanie Babies. When we couldn't find anything new, Katie picked up a Beanie Baby and said we could make one. She meant we could go home and make the small bears, but I heard something different. Her words gave me the idea to create a company that would allow people to create their own customized stuffed animals. I did some research and began putting together a plan.

Build-A-Bear Workshop was incredibly successful in an era when conventional toy stores (KB Toys, FAO Schwarz, Child World, Zany Brainy, and so on) were closing and sales of toys were becoming concentrated in the Walmarts, Targets, and, yes, Toys "R" Uses of the world. But the Great Recession hurt it badly, and the company was at an inflection point. In 2013, Clark announced her intention to retire from her position as "Chief Executive Bear," while remaining on the board of directors to provide continuity. Sharon Price John was hired as CEO in 2013.

As John described at our Women in Leadership class in 2016, she framed the journey of being a turnaround CEO with the acronym SPARK:

S: See it. Envisioning.
P: Plan it.
A: Action it.
R: Repeat it.
K: Keep the faith.

Throughout this book, I have shown how seeing around corners, envisioning what could be, is where navigating inflection points begins. For John, the "seeing" has to become an "authentic and inspiring vision . . . You have to be able to tell the story about this business and why it exists," she told the class. Build-A-Bear, she concluded, was in the business of selling memories—but it could also be more. The "more" was key to the company looking into a bigger presence in tourist locations, leveraging popular children's attractions like the movie *Frozen*, extending the brand beyond its stores, and doing more to appeal to boys (and even grown-ups).

In terms of "planning," she used the upcoming twentieth anniversary of the brand in 2017 as a pivot point to attract the attention of the rest of the organization. She said of her team, "They believe they change kids' lives. At the twenty-year mark, we're going to be prepared for the next twenty years. In our twentieth year, our goal is to have our best year ever. I don't know what that is yet, but we will make it happen."

The "action it" part of her acronym is difficult. As I have acknowledged throughout this book, it's not enough to see the problems or inflection points; the critical ingredient of powering through them is to get the organization to do something about them, when most of the time people would prefer not to. To address this issue, John created a short mantra, which she called SDSS, short for "Stop doing stupid stuff." If something doesn't have value, in other words, stop doing it so that you can free up time for more important activities.

Her lever to get the organization focused was a goal she announced when she first arrived. The company was losing something like $380 million a year. She said, "We are going to make a dollar" this year. The effect, she told the Women in Leadership class in 2016, was "magical. Everyone thought to themselves, 'Well, I'm not going to be the person who spends that last dollar.' We did it. We climbed back out, we broke even, and we were able to provide bonuses to people for their hard work."

Having achieved this first success, however, the organization could have lost momentum. The low-hanging and easy-to-understand things had been accomplished, and the path ahead was going to be much more difficult. At an all-hands meeting, John had one of the finance guys dress head to toe in a Gumby costume, symbolizing the need to be flexible, adaptive, and able to mold the situation.

And, of course, there was endless "repetition" of these common themes. As John says, it isn't so much that people resist what you're trying to do, it's that it is difficult to implement new behaviors that challenge longtime, taken-for-granted assumptions.

Finally, John always "kept the faith" that it would be both possible and worthwhile to make these changes.

WARTIME VERSUS PEACETIME CEOS

As someone who is not so much a leadership expert as a strategy and innovation scholar, I have found the proliferation of leadership models in classic management texts to be rather frustrating. There is certainly no one best way of leading, no one personality that works best under all circumstances, no one leadership style that makes the most sense. And, of course, all our thoughts on leadership are colored by the "Halo Effect"—drawing conclusions about what works by seeing what has succeeded in the past, without remembering that it is entirely possible to follow the wrong practices and succeed anyway, or to do everything right and nonetheless fail. Exhibit A at the moment is the unexpected downfall of Carlos Ghosn, former CEO of Nissan, a leader who was lionized for years, but who suffered a stunning and sudden fall from grace in 2018 under allegations of financial misconduct.

What a blessing, then, to recall Ben Horowitz's distinction between "wartime" CEOs and "peacetime" leaders. In his book *The Hard Thing About Hard Things*, Horowitz points out that when someone is handed the job of navigating through an inflection point, the time and space that one has in "peacetime" are entirely different from those that are available in "wartime." He writes, "In wartime, a company is fending off an imminent existential threat. Such a threat can come from a wide range of sources including competition, dramatic macroeconomic change, market change, supply chain change, and so forth. The great wartime CEO Andy Grove marvelously describes the forces that can take a company from peacetime to wartime in his book *Only the Paranoid Survive*."

The dilemma is that there is a tendency for an organization in crisis to turn to a command-and-control type of leader to right the ship. And yet, the research on the best leadership activities to take an organization through an inflection point suggests the dangers of this idea.

I thought, therefore, that it would be helpful to turn to the wisdom of a real wartime leader, my colleague and friend Thomas Kolditz, a retired brigadier general who built much of the leadership curriculum at West Point. Kolditz wrote his 2007 book, *In Extremis Leadership*, with a different goal in mind than that of most case studies about leadership in crisis. As he has said, most of the time as a leadership expert, "you're studying people in ordinary companies who never really wanted to be in a crisis but found themselves there and either fixed it or didn't. The problem with that is you're essentially studying crisis amateurs, and what I wanted to do was study crisis professionals—people who are in dangerous places all the time, and look at their techniques, their approaches to leadership, how they were different."

Kolditz's research among leaders in dangerous situations revealed patterns similar to those outlined in this chapter. The first requirement in a precarious situation, he found, is that leaders need to be able to keep people calm. They need someone "who can establish the vision for the way ahead—even if there is no detail to it." Hugely important here is the creation of trust and a sense of purpose. And trust can't be manufactured in the moment; it requires many interactions over time that build a sense of mutual interdependence. As Kolditz says, the job is to "literally deny the possibility of failure." Contrary to many of our misconceptions about command-and-control leaders, he points out, in a dangerous situation leaders don't need to create more emotion; instead, they need to be able to temper people's feelings in order to create focus.

The second requirement is to keep people focused on tasks and the environment, not on themselves. As noted throughout this book, inflection point leaders often use such an environmental focus as a rallying point. They keep it simple: *Think about X; just focus on X for the time being, and I'll let you know when that changes* would be a typical articulation.

Another element of successful wartime leadership is a sense of shared risk. Not setting yourself apart, being vulnerable when things go wrong, and being prepared to take some of the heat yourself are all critical. Think about Satya Nadella's communication with his team after the dramatically embarrassing failure of Tay, Microsoft's foray into AI. "I believe in you," he said, "and I've got your back." That doesn't mean he would tolerate sloppy execution in the future, but it does mean that he wanted them to have the confidence to try again.

Then there is common lifestyle. People are more likely to be led by those whom they can relate to on a personal level—those who share common experiences, who don't keep themselves apart or insist on special perks, and who can communicate about similar things.

And, of course, we can't overlook competence. In a dangerous situation, people have to make a judgment as to whether the leader is good enough to get them through this mess.

As Kolditz pointed out in an email to me, "The problem is, it is nearly impossible to suddenly become a successful 'wartime' leader, unless you've put money in the bank. It's too late to play catch-up. So the only solution, really, is to lead like a wartime leader all the time, as a matter of personality, of who one IS." He explained that simple leadership practices can make a big difference. "I used to visit new moms from our department at West Point when they were in the hospital the day following delivery," he wrote. "No real crisis, I'd just ask if they were getting proper care, etc. But more than one of them, later, said that the simple visits made them aware that if anything were *really* amiss, that I would *definitely* be there. That's money in the bank—and you have to invest well before any crisis." In terms of the transition to wartime, Kolditz stresses that some people who function well enough during peacetime have to go when a crisis hits. He wrote, "Step one of the crisis—fire those incapable of making the transition to the demands of wartime."

This leads me to conclude that the best leaders are continuously poised for wartime. Failing to put the practices in place to build trust, shared risk, and willingness to follow your lead during peacetime can lead to people being desperately ill-prepared in wartime. And as inflection points come at us more quickly and with greater consequences, falling into a purely peacetime pattern is dangerous.

Key Takeaways

Leaders who successfully take an organization through inflection points increasingly facilitate the energy, connections, and talents of the organization, while at the same time providing clear direction.

Simply seeing an inflection point on the horizon is the first step toward successfully navigating it. You next need to decide what direction you will take and then mobilize the organization.

Invest the time in keeping key executives on the same page and working together—a lack of alignment will diffuse your efforts. It isn't so much about the individuals' talents as about how they work together.

Clarity about strategy, the "why" of what you are doing and key priorities, is not optional.

Absent candid feedback, it is very easy to get off track. You don't have time to waste on anything other than total candor and brutal truth.

The role of the leader moves from designer and commander to premise-setter and judge.

Push decisions as close to the edge as possible.

Simplify complexity—create a common rallying cry that resonates with everybody.

As a leader, you may increasingly need to be prepared to act in wartime.

9

Seeing Around Corners in Your Own Life

> Very few people see inflection points as the
> opportunities they often are: catalysts for
> changing their lives; moments when a person
> can modify the trajectory he or she is on and
> redirect it in a more desirable direction.
>
> — Howard Stevenson, Harvard Business School

Most of this book has examined how organizations can do a better job of seeing around corners to anticipate what might happen in the event of an inflection point. But the truth is, many of the same principles that help organizations do this can also apply on a personal level.

Three overarching themes apply personally. The first is how you prepare yourself to "see" an unfolding inflection point and what it might mean for you. The second is how you prepare yourself to navigate it. And the third is to create a personal point of view of where you want to be heading.

As we have seen throughout this book, weak signals of an impending shift — *when recognized early enough* — can give you an important head start to prepare to take advantage of it. Let's briefly consider what some of the main lessons are on a personal level.

LOOKING FOR SNOW

Andy Grove's wisdom about traveling to the edges of your own experience to see what might be happening next is as valid personally as it is for organizations. Often, the experiences and insights that make the biggest difference in our lives come from unexpected places. So, in anticipating inflection points that could touch you personally, give some serious thought to how often you explore the edges of what is comfortable and routine to see what might be coming around the bend.

Where to Look

At the organizational level, we examined the context of an arena — that pot of resources available to us to help our customers get jobs done in their lives — and those outside players contesting for it. We further examined those conditions, in the form of an organizational arena, that can lead to an inflection point.

The shifts that potentially lead to an inflection point can be described as follows:

1. They can change the pool of resources that are being contested.
2. They can change the parties trying to grab some of that pool of resources.
3. They can change the situation in which the contest takes place.
4. They can cause one job to squeeze another out of an actor's consideration set or reduce the resources available to do that job.
5. They can meaningfully change the consumption experience.
6. They can lead to some attributes becoming more or less valued than others.
7. They can change the kinds of capabilities embedded in a value chain that are relevant.
8. They can change every element of the arena.

There are corollary implications of all of these shifts that is worth considering on a personal level. If an environmental inflection point is making some set of activities or capabilities more or less valuable, what does that mean for you? Failing to pay attention to the ramifications of change in the larger world around you can lead to a lot of grief.

Think of it this way: in much the same way that on a professional level you are trying to get a sense of what's coming around the bend for your company or organization, you would be well-advised to have the same kind of antennae in play regarding your personal development and career. The good news is that there are indeed real parallels between the way you see around corners for your business and the way you see around corners for your own career. The key is to be open to new ideas and to be wary of becoming too comfortable or too set in your ways.

Beyond Your Buddies

Just as organizations can benefit from having employees with diverse points of view weigh in on critical decisions, you should strive for diversity in the circles that surround you personally. We've seen how individuals who surround themselves with people just like themselves can get blindsided by something they didn't see coming but that would have been obvious to someone observing that activity on an ongoing basis.

Entrepreneurs like Nat Turner and Zach Weinberg, whom we met in Chapter 5, are brilliant in going beyond their own circles to find opportunities and validate their assumptions. Along those same lines, one of my favorite stories is that of Pähr Lövgren, a serial entrepreneur whom I worked with at Wharton when I was studying there. He has perfected the art of using his networks to find new opportunities. One of his companies, Megaron, specialized in CAD/CAM technologies — computer-aided design and manufacturing capabilities. He's started literally dozens of businesses that he has sold to larger organizations that can't figure out how to start them for themselves. His way of searching for inflection points in the environment offers a great lesson in how he finds the next inflection point in his career.

Lövgren makes it a part of his regular routine to have dinner (best place in town) with a network of consultants who work with companies facing technical challenges. All of the companies would be potential clients for his business. At these dinners, he asks the consultants to describe to him an emerging problem their clients face that might be suitable for a solution that his company could provide.

Let me give you an example of such a problem. It turned out that foundries in Nordic countries were having increasing difficulty getting workers. One of them, a client of Lövgren's consulting colleague, wondered if Lövgren might know of a solution — perhaps a robot that could take over some of the tasks the company couldn't get people to do. Armed with this idea, Lövgren went to a second network — of engineering professors he had worked with over many years — to assess whether such a solution might be feasible.

Yes, one said, he could build a prototype with a modest investment of $50,000. Now, most of us, particularly if we were as wealthy as Lövgren, would have simply reached into our back pockets and authorized the prototype. Not so. What he did was go back to his network of consultants. His goal this time was to see if the problem was widespread. The consultants made more inquiries and discovered that it was a widely shared dilemma. Lövgren asked the foundry managers who'd said they had the problem to invest their cash in the prototype. I confess I was a little nonplussed by this approach: "What would you have done if you couldn't raise the funding?" I asked when I saw him at a conference we were attending. Lövgren looked at me, rolled his eyes, and said, "Then I would have known it wasn't a big enough problem for them to solve, and I'd have moved on to another business." Eventually, the business of making "robust robots" specifically for foundries and other technically challenging environments took off.

Peter Sims, of *Little Bets* fame, has taken this idea of bringing together diverse perspectives to see into the future to an extraordinary level with an organization he started called Parliament. As he describes it on the organization's website, "Parliament became the first platform for a diverse group of people to access and harness horizontal power. Modeled after influences such as the open source software movement, Parliament being able to plug into the highest quality ecosystems is what increasingly drives faster learning, innovations, collaborations, and joint ventures." The participants in Parliament events are incredibly diverse, including authors, screenwriters, scientists, corporate leaders, and many others. They come together regularly to share insights and not only to see into the future but also to shape it. I'm delighted to say that I have been invited to a number of their events, and they have been incredibly worthwhile.

Negative or Unexpected Feedback Can Be a Gift

As we heard from Gail Goodman in describing her leadership journey, getting feedback – especially if it is uncomfortable or if it tells you something you didn't know about yourself – can be hugely valuable in seeing ahead. Most of us, however, don't use a structured process for going about getting the feedback that can help us to improve or to identify things that will hold us back. The corner you want to see around here is those personal habits, practices, behaviors, or assumptions that *other* people can see are getting in your way but that you can't.

Marshall Goldsmith, a world famous executive coach who works intensively with CEOs and soon-to-be CEOs, uses a feedback-rich technique called "Stakeholder Centered Coaching," which can be adapted to your own needs. It is one way to constructively go about getting useful feedback. It requires finding someone to help you – ideally someone without an agenda who is interested in seeing you improve. Let's call this person your coach, even if they aren't a formal, trained coach.

Essentially, you put together a list of your personal stakeholders (somewhere around twelve, let's say) – these are the people who are important to your own success and effectiveness. They can be people related to your work or personal life – for this purpose it doesn't matter. Your coach then interviews these people and asks for open feedback on what they think could be holding you back or could become an obstacle to your success. For instance, as Goodman learned with respect to her own leadership, cutting people off in their presentations was inhibiting the free flow of information and, even worse, preventing her from hearing from her own high-potential employees.

Your coach then synthesizes this information for you. As Goldsmith's clients will tell you, that initial, honest conversation can be tough, as it often challenges your own perceptions, and not necessarily in a pleasant way. Together, you and your coach decide what actions you would like to take to start working on the implications of the feedback and what evidence would suggest that you have been successful in addressing them.

One of Goldsmith's well-known clients is former Boeing executive and Ford CEO Alan Mulally, whom we met in the previous chapter. Feedback from one of Mulally's stakeholders when he engaged in this process as a rising executive at Boeing was that he wasn't sufficiently engaged in what was going on across the organization. That is, he knew his own area, but he didn't have a full grasp of the company's big picture. To address that problem, he instituted a regular communication process with his peers in other parts of Boeing. When Goldsmith checked back with the same stakeholders several months later, that issue had vanished.

Goldsmith also brings his clients together to share experiences and insights, again expanding their networks.

A couple of caveats: Your job is to be open to hearing the feedback, even if it isn't pleasant. Your job is not to argue, to explain, to justify, or to otherwise undermine the message. Goldsmith even fines people if they engage in any of these behaviors (with the money collected going to charity). Remember, these are *your* stakeholders — you picked them because you value what they might tell you! And if you're in a coaching session with Goldsmith, bring twenty-dollar bills.

Many people invest in other kinds of assessments to get a sense of how they might better prepare themselves for the future. Among the more popular are 360-degree assessments, so called because they gather input from people whom you directly report to, those who are your peers, and those whom you might supervise (hence a 360-degree view). I do recommend going through whatever feedback you receive with a coach, if possible. Some people even create a personal "board of directors" to whom they look for advice and inspiration as they contemplate their next moves.

Get out of the Building and Talk to the Future That Is Happening Now

Just as Steve Blank says that "there are no answers in the building" for the entrepreneurs he advises, there aren't going to be many insights about your future in the same tried-and-true places where you typically spend time. In the same way that Gisbert Rühl tried — and failed — to get inspiration for digital transformation at corporate headquarters, it's very hard to see around the next corner for yourself without introducing some sort of new and challenging thinking. It's also unlikely that your normal surroundings are going to expose you to where the future that's just not evenly distributed yet is already happening.

You need to develop a fresh perspective. Fortunately, there are any number of ways to do that. You might attend a conference of an industry that isn't directly related to what you do all day. Events such as the Digital Dozen competition at Frank Rose's Digital Storytelling Lab can be incredibly eye-opening (see Chapter 1). Local universities often host seminars and lectures that are open to the public. Even joining a club based on an interest of yours can expose you to people you wouldn't normally run across. And, of course, courses on topics you find personally interesting can provide the seeds of new ideas.

Scenarios and Leading Indicators for Yourself

The process I described in Chapter 2 for creating future scenarios and time zero events can be very useful on a personal level as well. It's worth asking what a future scenario might hold as you make pivotal decisions about what steps you want to take next. Even asking about the key uncertainties in your own life can be a valuable exercise to explore. What you might learn is that even if there is nothing particularly wrong with how your future looks, you might consider a change that could bring even greater opportunities.

This was a big part of Julie Sweet's journey from working at a top-tier law firm to becoming Accenture's CEO for North America. She was working at Cravath, Swaine & Moore, was one of the top attorneys there, and had enjoyed considerable success. And yet, she was beginning to feel as if she wasn't going to fulfill her potential by staying in the same role she currently had. So she left. As she has said, "If you can see your future, then you probably are not challenging yourself enough. I have this little plaque that my husband hung on our wall at home. It says, 'If your dreams don't scare you, they're not big enough.'" She now cites "curiosity" as one of the most significant traits she looks for in the people she hires.

PREPARING TO NAVIGATE

Just as an organization succeeds best when it builds its capability to address inflection points before it is absolutely necessary, you can succeed when you learn to look around corners in your own life. As Tom Kolditz will tell you, the time to get resources in the bank is *before* you desperately need them.

The Winding Path of Successful Careers

In the world of traditional careers (think Dustin Hoffman's character in *The Graduate*, who was told that his future lay in plastics), the dominant assumption was that we would climb a very linear ladder to the top and advance up a hierarchy. Today, of course, the assumptions in that type of career planning are often simply not relevant. Instead, we are much more likely to be facing career paths that have us moving in and out of what Reid Hoffman has called "tours of duty."

In other words, rather than thinking of a lifetime of advancement in a single organization, we are likely to be working in situations in which a team of people with the right skills and abilities are pulled together to accomplish a specific outcome, and then they are disbanded when that outcome has been achieved. This, in fact, is the way that some industries (think motion pictures) and some companies (think large consulting firms) already work.

How we construct careers in such an environment, with frequent inflection points changing what we need to be doing, is not always clear. One interesting conclusion from research done using LinkedIn data is that those who rise to the top often accumulate diverse skills and show an ability to learn about areas they are not comfortable with. Indeed, Marc Andreessen, the well-known inventor, investor, and venture capitalist, has gone so far as to call this capability the "secret formula to becoming a C.E.O." The most successful corporate leaders, he wrote, "are almost never the best product visionaries, or the best salespeople, or the best marketing people, or the best finance people, or even the best managers, but they are top 25 percent in some set of those skills, and then all of a sudden they're qualified to actually run something important."

The implications of this insight, based on a study of 459,000 people, are several. First, most of those who made it to senior-level positions started in jobs that required solving complex problems and having multiple skill sets, rather than more straightforward jobs that leaned on one set of skills. Second, the people who were willing to take on these different career roles also tended to be those who were willing to take on the modest risk of being somewhat incompetent and to get help from those around them. Finally, opportunities for what the researchers call "hybrid jobs" are on the rise. Organizations are looking for team members with more than one specialization or skill.

So, if you've been in your comfort zone doing the same thing for a while, it might be worth considering how to take on some kind of new role that could teach you a lot. Julie Sweet, for instance, after joining Accenture, had to learn how to be a general manager, a very different set of skills than she needed to be a partner in a major law firm.

Bricolage

In art or literature, "bricolage" means to assemble a diverse range of things to create something new. Increasingly, having a successful career involves different combinations of skills that come together in sometimes unexpected ways.

A great example of this is the career of my colleague and collaborator Ryan McManus, whose thinking on digital transformation I mentioned in Chapter 5. When McManus went to the University of Iowa for his undergraduate degree, he had, as many of us did, "a very limited idea of what I wanted to do." After some time there, though, he realized that he wanted to somehow gain international experience and have an international career. As he says now, the idea came to him while he was standing on a street corner in Iowa City, and that decision became a driver for many subsequent choices. While at Iowa, he also had the chance to study in the world-class Iowa Writers' Workshop, which he found to be rewarding. He imagined a future as some kind of creative worker.

With a desire to do something about gaining international exposure, he ended up spending a year abroad, in Paris. To make that happen, he had to major in French (in which he had limited experience at that point). Arriving in Paris, he was plunged into an overwhelmingly challenging situation at the Sorbonne. Without fluency in French, he faced entirely French-based classes and was assigned rather sophisticated French novels to read. Eventually, he mastered enough of the language to get by, and then eventually he became fluent.

McManus graduated as valedictorian of his class at Iowa and was hired by a large global accounting firm to help coordinate global marketing functions, a role for which his experience in Paris and his French communications skills had inadvertently prepared him. The next big inflection point he participated in was the advent of the Internet and digitization. He started working on projects that included building digital properties for the firm and went on to create entirely new digital businesses with new business models. This added competency in digitization to his portfolio. (As we saw earlier, digital first showed up in a significant way in the marketing side of organizational life.) Clearly, McManus was sensing that the digital revolution was something that was coming in the near future, something that he could see around the corner.

Next, he decided that it was perhaps time to hone his business capabilities, so he earned an executive MBA at the University of Chicago. He then joined Accenture and added a new skill—strategic direction—to his portfolio. At that point, he had a major "Aha!" moment during a conversation with one of the high-level consultants there. As he told me, the consultant observed that "in many of our business strategy conversations with our clients, they are asking us about technology, and in many of our technical conversations, clients are asking us how this connects to business strategy. The light went on immediately, and I realized, *We have to build a practice at the intersection of these things.*" That led to his leading the development of Accenture's digital transformation strategy business.

As the digital revolution went through several evolutionary stages, beginning with what was easy (digital books, for example) and progressing to more complex activities (such as automating business models), McManus realized that there was going to be a sea change in how companies operated and he wanted to have a hands-on role in that development. He left Accenture to join a fifty-person startup in the Internet of Things space, where, as he described it, "you had the opportunity to work directly with all of the company's teams, across multiple areas of development." Today, he has a broad portfolio of activities, including advisory roles, Internet startups, and board service, all of which have built on the unlikely capabilities he put together previously. He told me that he is still extraordinarily motivated by learning: "My career has always included an element of what I could learn and help to build next."

Generate Options

One reason that people can get stuck in their personal situations is that they feel it is too risky to make a big bet on a speculative next step for themselves. That may well be true, but remember that building skills and capabilities does not have to mean abandoning everything you know and starting from scratch. Just as I would advise corporations, I tell people to build up options for the future without taking big, risky bets.

An option is a small investment that buys you the right, but not the obligation, to make a choice in the future. Often, when we are thinking about what we want to do personally, we don't spend enough time generating new and fresh options, experimenting with them, and learning what they have to teach us. Just as McManus's experiences generated choices that proved to be hugely valuable as his career evolved, you can invest in choices that expand the opportunities you may find later on.

A useful way to think about this is to apply the principles of design thinking to your choices, as Paula Davis-Laack found when she felt she had arrived at a dead end in her job as a high-powered lawyer. Today, she is a professional life coach and helps people address issues around burnout.

The first step in any design challenge is to specify the problem you are trying to solve and the constraints that you will be operating under. In the case of your own career, you might couch the challenge in terms of a question such as "How might I find something I would love to do next at work?" or "How will I best take advantage of this trend that I'm seeing?"

Notice, we're just framing the problem here, not yet jumping to solutions. Add any constraints that you need to bear in mind — financial, locational, family, or others. Don't let those get too overwhelming, but do include them, as they can be creativity triggers later. Good designers will tell you that constraints are incredibly valuable, as they shape the context for design decisions and also challenge you to find ways around them.

The next step in design is observation. Since you are doing this for yourself, it's very much worth considering what activities you find rewarding, fun, or exciting.

The third step is to generate some ideas about what kinds of options you might want to take out and what your assumptions about those are. Davis-Laack realized she had failed to articulate and test her assumptions when she quit her job and took an internship as a pastry chef. She hated every minute of it. That sent her back to step two to figure out what kinds of things she really enjoyed doing. She developed what she calls "the list" — qualities that she felt were positive about previous experiences, whether work related or not.

Designers at this point will often create prototypes — sometimes *many* prototypes — in order to test their assumptions. Obviously, you're not going to build something to represent your future self, but you can start having conversations about it. Just as Nat Turner and Zach Weinberg did with Flatiron, don't be afraid to talk to people who have roles that you think might reflect the ones on your own list. In my case, for instance, before committing to get a PhD, I spoke with dozens of people who had academic jobs to see if that would be a suitable career for me to make a long-term commitment to. Yes, you may well find that a number of potential options aren't of interest to you. But you also may start to uncover other ideas that could be viable.

This is the personal equivalent of running experiments. You can also do things such as see if you can shadow someone at work and observe what the environment is like. You can test several ideas until one or more start to gel for you. Getting buy-in from your stakeholders is valuable here as well. I've sometimes paired executives with different capabilities who take time to observe each other. Recall how Satya Nadella of Microsoft learned from observing Reed Hastings of Netflix about faster decision-making and difficult choices by becoming a Netflix Insider for a time.

After sufficient testing and experimentation, it's time to move into the implementation phase. That's where you revisit the constraints, evaluate your options, and commit to any changes that you decide make sense. By following a process such as this, you won't have to make a huge, risky bet before you feel you've learned enough to proceed.

WHERE ARE YOU HEADING?

A good way to start thinking about how you might orchestrate your journey through a personal inflection point is to articulate a perspective on the shape you would like your life to take at some point in the future — perhaps ten or even twenty years hence. The greater the clarity of that calling, the more helpful it can be.

Don't Mix Up the Destination with the Vehicle You Use to Get There

One of the most common mistakes I see in this regard is that people sometimes become mixed up between the future state they think would be attractive to them and the vehicles they think will get them there.

For example, one of my clients is an exceptionally hierarchy-dependent organization that is going through a massive transformation. I've been working on helping its leaders see how they can make necessary and timely changes to shift them toward that future. "What," I asked one of them, "would you like to see for yourself if this all goes well?" "Oh," he replied with confidence, "I'd like to get to be an E-band 4-level officer." I continued to probe, asking him why he thought that would be such a great outcome and got pretty much nowhere. Regardless, he had convinced himself that this outcome would be nirvana.

And that's very risky. Let's say this company merges with another, its arena collapses, a flatter management structure comes along, or some other major inflection point takes place and the whole E-band idea disappears. If that's how you are thinking about your future state, it creates a potential vulnerability due to a lack of imagination. Instead, focus on the kinds of outcomes you'd like to surround yourself with in a future state.

I had a similar conversation with a woman who thought her nirvana was going to be becoming a senior director of marketing. As we
probed more deeply into why she envisioned that, it became clear that
the reason she thought that would be a wonderful position was because it would give her creative latitude, allow her to connect with and
develop other people, and give her the chance to interact with high-
level decision-makers. The exercise after that was for her to envision
multiple ways in which she could achieve those outcomes.

This is a much less risky path. The woman could conceive of different positions in different sectors in which this would be possible. She
could start her own business. She could join a creative consultancy or
a not-for-profit. The point is that by framing her goals in terms of *outcomes* rather than *positions,* she opened up many more options for
herself — very useful in the context of potential inflection points.

Pursue Your Own Leadership Journey

At Columbia Business School, we use an exercise called the Leadership Lifeline to make students' personal and professional journeys ex-
plicit and to bring forth the unique lessons that each of us has drawn
from them. We first ask individuals to reflect on the experiences that
have shaped who they have become as people and to make these lessons as concrete as possible. In the many years we've done this, no
one's journey has ever been a straight path. What this exercise can do
for you is illustrate and pinpoint where and how you've leveraged inflection point building blocks to create opportunities in your life.

Traversing inflection points leads to unique experiences. Connecting to others in an authentic and genuine way can provide an enormous impetus for making it through the challenges of navigating an
inflection point. One useful exercise is to consider and document your
journey. The goal is to reflect on the patterns you've seen in your life,
so that you can better recognize and build on similar patterns in the
future. This is a general process that I have found helpful — feel free to
elaborate or adjust as you see fit.

Step 1: Create Your Lifeline

Get a big piece of flip chart paper. Beginning with your birth, draw
your own "lifeline," or picture of the important events in your life from

your birth to the present. Try to include key events, relationships, suc-
cesses, failures, accomplishments, and disappointments. What you are
doing is creating the raw material to help you understand the critical
events and experiences that have influenced your current beliefs and
behaviors.

For each of the key events, note how it affected you. Did it shape
your values and what you believe to be important in some meaningful
way? Are there lessons you took from the experience that continue to
have an influence on you? Do these experiences reinforce one another?

Step 2: Identify Your Own Building Blocks

As you are preparing your lifeline, note any common themes that seem
to occur again and again, particularly with respect to the building
blocks for resilience in the face of inflection points. For instance, one
participant noted a common theme of always persevering in the face of
adverse events, leading to a firm belief in the power of hard work and
persistence. Capture these key values, and note some of the stories that
reflect them in your own life experiences.

It is also worthwhile to be clear about where your boundaries are,
given your experiences. Are there practices or beliefs that you would
stick with, even in the face of temptation? My friend the famous management scholar Clayton Christensen has observed that as he attended
successive Harvard Business School graduations, he discovered that
many of his classmates were living lives that none of them had intended to live — divorced, alienated from their children and families,
stuck in roles that had become stale, or even, as in the case of Enron's
Jeff Skilling, in jail. As Christensen said in 2012, "It became clear that
a lot of my classmates implemented a strategy that they never planned
to!" That same year, he encouraged all of us to, "in a deliberate way, articulate the kind of people we want to become. We can articulate the
culture that we would want to exist in our family, and you can then, as
the rest of life happens to you, you can utilize those things to help you
become the kind of person you want to be."

Step 3: Start Creating Your Own Story Up to This Point

With your lifeline and key themes documented, you're ready to reflect
on what this journey has taught you. Imagine if you were assigned the

task of writing about your story as though it were someone else interviewing you. Make it as authentic as you can. Use lots of examples and specifics — that will help keep it vivid in your mind. Remember, the purpose of this is to keep you connected with the forces that have been meaningful in your life by reflecting on them.

Step 4: Write an Article About Yourself from the Future

This is an exercise that my colleague Ian MacMillan and I developed for executives studying in Columbia's Advanced Management Program (AMP), a several-weeks-long immersion in personal and executive development. Here's how it goes.

Imagine it is fifteen years from now, and you are writing an article about yourself in a popular magazine or newspaper, such as *Fortune*. The article will say that five years before, you launched a set of activities that led to a significant and positive change in your personal trajectory. As a result of this strategic accomplishment, you achieved a massively fulfilling role that would have been inconceivable to you before you got started. Describe the program that you undertook to create such a positive trajectory.

Now think about your key stakeholders. What do the people you interact with appreciate most about the change that you made? How has the positive change you made for yourself resulted in a positive change for them? Describe this in your article.

The bulk of the article should reflect, with admiration, on your personal style. How do you spend your time — literally, what is on your agenda? How do you make decisions? What activities do you put your time and attention into? What kind of people do you have around you? What kind of people have you elected not to have around you anymore, and why?

The last part of the article should talk about the accomplishments of your family while all this was going on. What can you say about them?

Step 5: Get Feedback on Your Article

As with the stakeholder-centered feedback process described earlier in this chapter, getting input from others can help you strengthen and sharpen your article. It can also be useful, as those stakeholders can often help you bring the life described in your article into being! Reflect on and review your article every so often, especially when you have a big decision to make that could represent a personal inflection point.

The Impact an Article from the Future Can Have

This excerpt from an article that appeared in the *Wharton Magazine* describes how completing your article can become a catalyst for your life, as one participant in their version of the AMP discovered.

> It was the middle of a night in 2009 — at the very end of a five-week Advanced Management Program . . . when Olivier Bottrie turned a brief nightmare into the foundation of his life's dream.
>
> Bottrie, a leading executive at the New York–based cosmetics giant Estée Lauder, had fallen asleep for only about a half-hour when he bolted upright in a bit of a panic at 1 a.m. — suddenly remembering one last homework assignment for the program. He was supposed to write a mock *Fortune* magazine profile of himself, set 15 years in the future, spelling out his accomplishments and how he'd reached his cherished goals. Barely awake, Bottrie wrote quickly.
>
> "So I spoke of my career, of course, brilliant," he says, "and after two-and-a-half pages of job and profession and career, I started something else."
>
> He wrote that in 2011, which was two years away, he would launch a foundation that would be called The Brain Train. It would attract funding from billionaire Bill Gates, open its first school in Haiti — his wife's native country — in 2013 and be educating 150,000 students worldwide by 2025.
>
> Six years later — spurred on by the tragedy of Haiti's deadly 2010 earthquake — Bottrie is farther along in reality than he could possibly have imagined on that sleepless night. It was actually October 2011 when he and his philanthropic partners opened the doors to Lycée Jean-Baptiste Point du Sable, a nonprofit school in Saint Marc, Haiti, an isolated community with a high rate of poverty and few education options. He credits the exercise of self-reflection with crystallizing what had been a vague sense of "doing something for children" into a much more specific and actionable plan.

Take the time for a bit of self-reflection. You never know where it might lead you. Remember, you're looking to hone and sharpen your ability to see around the corner in terms of your own personal career. These exercises — which force you to look back and see where you have been — are a terrific and novel way to help prepare yourself to achieve a much more precise view of where you want to go — and whether you are on the right track.

THE NEXT STEP IN THE JOURNEY

Louis Pasteur is often quoted as saying "Fortune favors the prepared mind." My hope is that this journey through the world of strategic inflection points has been illuminating and perhaps inspiring for you. As you have seen, there are specific and predictable things that you can do to see around the corners of the next major shift.

The first part of seeing around corners is creating a vantage point. Inflection points don't happen instantly — they take a while to take hold. Since snow melts from the edges, it's vital to be curious and open to what is going on out there, long before it's obvious what actions should be taken. Picking up on and interpreting weak signals is another skill that you can use to determine when to make a move. Thinking in terms of total arenas, rather than artificially created topics such as "industries," can help broaden what you are looking for and at. And you can never go wrong with an external focus, paying attention to customers rather than assuming the world will operate in a way that you most prefer.

Moving on to taking action, you can contain the risk and exposure of leaping on a looming inflection point too early by using a discovery-driven approach. Learn from little bets, try early experiments, and question your own assumptions — they can be your worst enemy.

Then you have the challenge of bringing a critical mass of people along with you as the organization starts to respond to new inflection points. I've suggested that getting people focused on leading indicators of future success can be very helpful.

The organization, too, needs to be different after the inflection passes over it. Building innovation proficiency can be enormously helpful in making sure it doesn't collapse or get overrun by competitors with a better grasp of things.

Finally, inflection points can be very personal. They have an impact on how you need to lead, particularly in "wartime." They also can serve as opportunities for you to thrive in an entirely different way than you might have been expecting, leading to a life of outcomes that you genuinely desire.

The good news is that inflection points always represent opportunities for someone. There is no reason that shouldn't be you.

Key Takeaways

Recognizing inflection points early on can lead to positive personal outcomes.

Look at changes in the arenas that you or your organization depend on to acquire insights into how these changes might offer opportunities or create risks.

Expanding your network beyond the usual suspects you spend time with can help you see things you couldn't otherwise.

Deliberately getting feedback (and listening to it) can help you avoid blind spots you aren't aware of.

Getting out of the building by finding and investing in different perspectives can give you great ideas.

You can easily build scenarios and weak signal detection mechanisms for yourself.

Often the most successful career path is one that builds diverse skills. It may be windy, but that can be surprisingly effective.

Skills can come together in unexpected ways to create great value.

You can use the principles of options and design thinking to plan your next set of moves.

Reflecting on your goals, life lessons, and journey thus far can be enormously powerful if you take the time to write down the key moments.

Acknowledgments

This is so daunting. I thought it would be nice to go beyond the Oscars-style thank-yous and shout-outs to all the people involved in this book and in my life and to give my readers a little glimpse into the story behind the book.

PERSONAL THANKS

Books are awkward to live with — or, more precisely, book authors in the midst of producing one are awkward to live with. My husband, John, refers to my "hedgehog" periods — when a deadline approaches or a submission gets rejected, and its back to the drawing board. He went so far as to buy me a delightful little stuffed hedgehog (fortunately one without sharp quills). When it makes it to the corner of my desk at home, well, you can't say you weren't warned.

John was more of an advocate for the book than I was at times. "How is the book?" he would ask when I appeared to be getting distracted by yet another appealing-looking project or side activity. "You can't let this slide," he would remind me. Or when we were debating how I should be spending my time, he'd ask, "How will that affect the book?" Every author should have such an ardent book champion on their side.

The rest of my family is well used to the book process, and they have perfected the fine art of being distantly curious (lest too specific a set of questions send the author into a deadline-induced panic) while still maintaining a level of normalcy that is deeply comforting. Our children, Matt and Anne, gave me some very interesting insights that never would have emerged had I just lumbered along on my own. Anne, who was working on her MBA as the book moved along, made important observations about the intersection between personal motivations and business decisions that proved influential. Matt had some great ideas about including examples of companies that got things wrong (and why). Both of them serve as reminders that the world they were born into is a different place than the one I grew up in.

My dad, Wolfgang Gunther, had a front-row seat to observe the collapse of Kodak and the eventual irrelevancy of Xerox. He delights in sending me stories of business muddleheadedness that provide a lot of grist for the mill. Although my mom, Helge-Liane Gunther, passed away before the book was published, she was very encouraging as it got started. Both my parents provided examples of how to take some smart risks in the face of major inflection points and how to create pockets of safety, even while stretching out beyond what is comfortable.

Keeping the wheels on the bus while I was in book mode fell to my team. Marion Reinson brought much-needed marketing savvy into the mix and moved critical projects along. Pam Ryan is a genius – she truly earns her "virtual ringmaster" moniker and makes keeping everything going smoothly look easy. If there were Nobel Prizes for travel magic, Josette Carrizzo should receive one. And now we have Theresa Braun, Christine Andrewes, and Missy Pirrera to help bring this book into the world.

I'd be remiss if I didn't tip a hat to our "Forge family." Forge is a boutique local gym founded by Jack Molesko with partner coaches Ryan Carsia and Rebecca Swan. My good friend Eileen thought John and I would like working with them, and we do! We are there three or more times per week, and the coaches and the other members have been following the twists and turns in the book's progress. It's a great break from being hunched over a desk.

My wonderful colleagues at Columbia Business School provided lots of encouragement, good cheer, and support. It has been an honor to have been part of the institution for so many years now. The dialogues and discussions with our Executive Education clients enriched the examples in the book considerably. A special thanks to Trish Gorman, who delights in sparring about all things strategy and who emphasized the importance of the "right time" for making strategy choices.

THE STORY OF THIS BOOK

Seeing Around Corners follows on my first solo book, *The End of Competitive Advantage: How to Keep Your Strategy Moving as Fast as Your Business.* That book made the argument that if you can't count on competitive advantages lasting for long periods of time, you need to be able to continuously create new advantages and withdraw from exhausted ones on an ongoing basis. It was a bit of a challenge to strategy orthodoxy, but many people said that they found it a better fit for the world they were actually confronting than what they found in strategy textbooks.

Back in early 2016, my editor at *Harvard Business Review*, Melinda Merino, provided the initial impetus for this fifth book. She suggested that while a whole host of characters were circling around a new way to think about strategy and innovation, it was all still rather confusing and disjointed. As she said, "We have all this talk about ecosystems, platforms, digital, lean, agile, and so on, but it still feels as though people really don't know what to do . . . There is some recognition that the environment has totally changed, and we need some way of making sense of it all." Perhaps, she suggested, the follow-on to *The End of Competitive Advantage* could tackle some of this.

So I did a lot of reading, which is referenced in the main text. Still, having the seeds of an idea for a book is a rather long way from formulating a compelling proposal that can carry it. The core concept of inflection points crystallized in my mind when Martin Weil, our financial planner and a good friend, happened to send me an article called "When You Change the World and No One Notices." The article describes how it took over three years for the *New York Times* to even mention the Wright brothers' first flight, and nearly five years for the importance of their accomplishment to be more generally recognized. *Wow,* I thought. *If you combine the idea that it takes a long time for the world to actually change with Andy Grove's notion of strategic inflection points, that could be a very interesting jumping-off point. Inflection points happen — to quote Mike Campbell in Hemingway's* The

Sun Also Rises – *"Gradually, then suddenly." That's the opportunity for those who see them early enough.*

I spent most of the rest of 2016 pulling together assorted notes and trying to shape them into something, but it wasn't really gelling. Meanwhile, back in the rest of my life, I'd developed a very nice working relationship with the team at the speakers bureau Leading Authorities. Mark French, Matt Jones, and Rainey Foster couldn't have been better partners in helping to get the word out about the previous book. When Matt said that they were partnering with Ross Yoon, a literary agency, I thought it would be a good idea to reach out to them, which we did in January of 2017. Howard Yoon, a literary agent and principal at Ross Yoon, and I clicked immediately, and we agreed to start working together. I was a little concerned that my "stuff" at that stage was in assorted piles and heaps, but he assured me that a "data dump" was the best thing to send him.

Howard is amazing. Smart, blunt, honest, and candid, he has an uncanny ability to figure out where the bright threads are in the writing and help you ditch the rest. (Oh, the mess on my personal cutting-room floor . . .) One of the big turning points for this project came when he asked me to do the whole book as a PowerPoint presentation. (I think he was a little fed up with wading through my prose – one of the downsides of being a really fast typist.) The requirement to boil everything down into short presentation snippets was incredibly powerful. We got into a rhythm in which he would give me "assignments" and I would do my best to complete them, and eventually after more than a year, we had something he felt comfortable moving forward with.

Next came the arrangement with Houghton Mifflin Harcourt and working closely with my editor, Rick Wolff. What I appreciate very much about Rick is that he is such a staunch advocate for our readers. Like Howard, his feedback is blunt but inevitably helpful. There was one chapter that I wasn't sure either of us would be able to wrestle to the ground, but ultimately we landed on content that both of us were comfortable with. Rick, I can't thank you enough.

The rest of the HMH team is a publishing powerhouse. Lori Glazer and Michelle Triant in publicity masterfully laid out a complete campaign, with ideas I'd certainly never thought of. (Who knew there might be a specifically female angle to the book?) Brooke Borneman and Brianna Yamashita in marketing very quickly figured out the essence of the book's "brand" and created marketing materials that would do it justice. Debbie Engel handled "subrights"—the agreements with publishers working in other languages—to have the book translated and marketed in their territories. We have had more than a few chuckles over the unpredictable process of guessing who is going to be interested in what internationally. Katie Kimmerer oversaw the book in production. As an author, you really don't know how complicated this can be beyond getting the thing written. Michaela Sullivan took charge of the cover design, and I have to say her work was marvelous. Not only did she come up with a design that we all love, she came up with *three* of them! Rosemary McGuinness in editorial seems to thrive on detail-oriented and unforgiving tasks like getting footnotes in all the right places.

THE PEOPLE IN AND AROUND THE BOOK

Of course, the mechanics around the book wouldn't amount to anything without the insights and stories of the people who provided the real-life stories and inspiration that bring it to life. Ryan McManus has taught me a tremendous amount about how strategy, innovation, and digital transformation are all coming together and has been a pleasure to work with. We're busy now figuring out how to help organizations cope with inflection points while building capability at the same time.

Ron Boire offered deep insights from the front lines of retail and the pragmatic activities needed to move a large organization along. Michael Sikorsky, Tracey Zimmerman, and the team at Robots & Pencils are helping us design and automate strategy and innovation tools. We're blessed with many other collaboration partners, each of whom has a secret talent with respect to some aspect of the strategy and innovation challenge. Alex Osterwalder at Strategyzer, Mike Burn and Greg Galle at Solve Next, Christian Rangen at Engage/Innovate, Kaihan Krippendorff at Outthinker, Linda Yates and the bold accelerators at Mach49, and the team at Innosight, among others, have been fabulous co-creators and partners.

There are also whole communities of authors and thinkers that I'm so grateful to be part of. My colleagues in the Silicon Guild are an inspiring group, and it's a privilege to be among them. Marshall Goldsmith and his 100 Coaches group are committed to helping clients get better and to helping one another grow and develop. Richard Straub has single-handedly (it seems) created a vibrant community of thinkers honoring the legacy of Peter Drucker, celebrated annually at the Drucker Forum in Vienna. It's become an annual pilgrimage site for John and me. And every other year, we enjoy the glitter of the Thinkers50 annual event.

Finally, to those whose stories provided me with the inspiration to learn how to see around corners and benefit from capitalizing early on inflection points, I am so grateful.

Notes

INTRODUCTION

page

1 *"are about to change":* Andrew S. Grove, *Only the Paranoid Survive: How to Exploit the Crisis Points That Challenge Every Company and Career* (New York: Doubleday, 1996).

discovery-driven growth playbook: Rita Gunther McGrath and Ian C. MacMillan, *Discovery-Driven Growth: A Breakthrough Process to Reduce Risk and Seize Opportunity* (Boston: Harvard Business Review Press, 2009).

2 *"perennial gale of creative destruction":* Joseph A. Schumpeter, *Capitalism, Socialism, and Democracy* (New York: Harper Perennial, 1942).

"'I can't afford hearing aids'": Paula Span, "Hearing Aids at the Mall? Perhaps Congress Could Make It Happen," *New York Times,* June 12, 2017.

3 *seems like overkill:* Kim Cavitt, "2016: Will It Be the Year of the Disruption? Gosh, I Hope So," HearingHealthMatters.org, February 26, 2016, https://hearinghealthmatters.org/hearinprivatepractice/2016/hearing-aid-industry-disruption-2016-gosh-i-hope-so/.

problem of epidemic proportions: "The Hidden Risks of Hearing Loss," Johns Hopkins Medicine, n.d., https://www.hopkinsmedicine.org/health/healthy_aging/healthy_body/the-hidden-risks-of-hearing-loss.

5 *"every word of your conversations":* "Hear Better," Bose, 2019, https://www.bose.com/en_us/products/wellness/conversation_enhancing_headphones/hearphones.html.

self-fitting hearing aid: "FDA Allows Marketing of First Self-Fitting Hearing Aid Controlled by the User," FDA, press release, October 5, 2018, https://www.fda.gov/NewsEvents/Newsroom/PressAnnouncements/ucm622692.htm.

7 *fundamentally altered forever:* Morgan Housel, "When You Change the World and No One Notices," Collaborative Fund, September 3, 2016, http://www.collaborativefund.com/blog/when-you-change-the-world-and-no-one-notices/.

8 *how technologies are commercialized:* "Gartner Hype Cycle," Gartner,

https://www.gartner.com/en/research/methodologies/gartner-hype
-cycle.

making the same decision: William A. Sahlman and Howard Stevenson, "Capital Market Myopia," *Journal of Business Venturing* 1 (1985):
7–30.

9 *"at the periphery":* Grove, *Only the Paranoid Survive.*

10 *Amazon in 1996:* Michael H. Martin, "The Next Big Thing: A Book-
store?," *Fortune,* December 9, 1996.

need to transform: Clayton M. Christensen, *The Innovator's Dilemma: When New Technologies Cause Great Firms to Fail* (Boston: Harvard
Business School Press, 1997).

1. SNOW MELTS FROM THE EDGES

13 *"doesn't know what to do":* Shona Ghosh, "'Christ, This Guy Has the
Fate of European Democracy in His Hands,'" Business Insider Australia,
May 24, 2018, https://www.businessinsider.com.au/mark-zuckerberg
-facebook-power-democracy-2018-5.

business model pushback: Russell Brandom, "Google's Bad Day in
Congress Came at the Worst Possible Time," The Verge, September 6,
2018, https://www.theverge.com/2018/9/6/17827854/google-congress
-regulation-facebook-twitter-ftc-complaints.

14 *"where it is most exposed":* Andrew S. Grove, *Only the Paranoid Survive: How to Exploit the Crisis Points That Challenge Every Company
and Career* (New York: Doubleday, 1996).

"access to information": "Privacy: An Interpretation of the Library
Bill of Rights," American Library Association, amended July 1, 2014,
http://www.ala.org/advocacy/intfreedom/librarybill/interpretations
/privacy.

15 *$88 billion in 2017:* Sarah Sluis, "Digital Ad Market Soars to $88
Billion, Facebook and Google Contribute 90% of Growth," AdExchanger,
May 10, 2018, https://adexchanger.com/online-advertising/digital-ad
-market-soars-to-88-billion-facebook-and-google-contribute-90-of
-growth/.

16 *"Do you have pets?":* Steve Kroft, "The Data Brokers: Selling Your Personal Information," *60 Minutes,* first aired March 9, 2014, CBS, https://
www.cbsnews.com/news/the-data-brokers-selling-your-personal
-information/.

any privileged information: Alessandro Acquisti, "Privacy and Market Failures: Three Reasons for Concern, and Three Reasons for Hope,"
Journal on Telecommunications and High Technology Law 10, no. 2
(2012): 227–33, http://jthtl.org/content/articles/V10I2/JTHTLv10i2_
Acquisti.PDF.

accountable to no one: Samantha Schmidt, "This Site Will Remove Your Mug Shot—for a Price, Authorities Say. Its Owners Are Charged with Extortion," *Morning Mix* (blog), *Washington Post,* May 18, 2018, https://www.washingtonpost.com/news/morning-mix/wp/2018/05/18/this-site-will-remove-your-mug-shot-for-a-price-now-its-owners-are-charged-with-extortion/.

17 *"third-party cookies":* "Disable Third-Party Cookies in Firefox to Stop Some Types of Tracking by Advertisers," Mozilla Support, n.d., https://support.mozilla.org/en-US/kb/disable-third-party-cookies.

you've been doing on the web: Jason Murdock, "Facebook Is Tracking You Online, Even If You Don't Have an Account," *Newsweek,* April 17, 2018, https://www.newsweek.com/facebook-tracking-you-even-if-you-dont-have-account-888699.

network having my data: David Nield, "Here's All the Data Collected from You as You Browse the Web," *Field Guide,* Gizmodo, December 6, 2017, https://fieldguide.gizmodo.com/heres-all-the-data-collected-from-you-as-you-browse-the-1820779304.

"connection between the two events": Katherine Bindley, "Why Facebook Still Seems to Spy on You," *Wall Street Journal,* February 28, 2019, https://www.wsj.com/articles/facebook-ads-will-follow-you-even-when-your-privacy-settings-are-dialed-up-11551362400?mod=hp_lead_pos7.

sharing highly personal information with Facebook: Sam Schechner and Marc Secada, "You Give Apps Sensitive Personal Information. Then They Tell Facebook," *Wall Street Journal,* February 22, 2019, https://www.wsj.com/articles/you-give-apps-sensitive-personal-information-then-they-tell-facebook-11550851636?mod=searchresults&page=1&pos=4&mod=article_inline.

18 *connected to the same network:* Gordon Whitson, "How to Stop Your Smart TV from Tracking What You Watch," *New York Times,* July 26, 2018.

"a little magical": Sapna Maheshwari, "TVs That Find an Audience for Your Data," *New York Times,* July 5, 2018.

19 *elsewhere in their homes:* Sarah Perez, "47.3 Million U.S. Adults Have Access to a Smart Speaker, Report Says," TechCrunch, March 7, 2018, https://techcrunch.com/2018/03/07/47-3-million-u-s-adults-have-access-to-a-smart-speaker-report-says/.

hundreds of miles away: Corky Siemaszko, "Little Did She Know, Alexa Was Recording Every Word She Said," NBC News, May 24, 2018, https://www.nbcnews.com/tech/tech-news/little-did-she-know-alexa-was-recording-every-word-she-n877286.

20 *"Dumb fucks":* Nicholas Carlson, "Well, These New Zuckerberg IMs

Won't Help Facebook's Privacy Problems," Business Insider, May 13, 2010, https://www.businessinsider.com/well-these-new-zuckerberg-ims -wont-help-facebooks-privacy-problems-2010-5.

outside academic institutions in 2006: Saul Hansell, "Site Previously for Students Will Be Opened to Others," *New York Times,* September 12, 2006.

which they hoped would "dominate": Adam Fisher, "Sex, Beer, and Coding: Inside Facebook's Wild Early Days," *Wired,* July 10, 2010, https://www.wired.com/story/sex-beer-and-coding-inside-facebooks -wild-early-days/. See also Adam Fisher, *Valley of Genius: The Uncensored History of Silicon Valley* (New York: Twelve, 2018).

forays into targeted ads: Rebecca Greenfield, "2012: The Year Facebook Finally Tried to Make Some Money," *Atlantic,* December 14, 2012, https://www.theatlantic.com/technology/archive/2012/12/2012-year -facebook-finally-tried-make-some-money/320493/.

automated access to advertisers: Natasha Lomas, "A Brief History of Facebook's Privacy Hostility Ahead of Zuckerberg's Testimony," TechCrunch, April 10, 2018, https://techcrunch.com/2018/04/10/a-brief -history-of-facebooks-privacy-hostility-ahead-of-zuckerbergs-testi mony/.

"one can find": Julia Angwin and Terry Parris Jr., "Facebook Lets Advertisers Exclude Users by Race," ProPublica, October 28, 2016, https:// www.propublica.org/article/facebook-lets-advertisers-exclude-users-by -race.

"more choices for everyone": Rita Gunther McGrath, "The EU's $5 Billion Fine Is Bad News for Google — but It's Not About the Money," *Fortune,* July 20, 2018, http://fortune.com/2018/07/20/google-android-chrome -eu-fine-antitrust-laws/.

21 *poor crisis response:* James F. Haggerty, "Commentary: How Facebook's Response Ignited the Cambridge Analytica Scandal," *Fortune,* March 27, 2018, http://fortune.com/2018/03/27/facebook-cambridge -analytica-data-scandal-crisis-investigation/.

targeting political ads: Kevin Granville, "Facebook and Cambridge Analytica: What You Need to Know as Fallout Widens," *New York Times,* March 19, 2018, https://www.nytimes.com/2018/03/19/technology /facebook-cambridge-analytica-explained.html.

has emerged: Lindsey Bever, "Why Apple Co-Founder Steve Wozniak Is Joining the #DeleteFacebook Movement," *The Switch* (newsletter), *Washington Post,* April 9, 2018, https://www.washingtonpost.com/news /the-switch/wp/2018/04/09/why-apple-co-founder-steve-wozniak-is -joining-the-deletefacebook-movement/.

the way of Myspace: John Herrman, "What Happens When Facebook Goes the Way of Myspace?," *New York Times Magazine*, December 12, 2018.

declared #DeleteFacebook: Ed Mazza, "Apple Co-founder Steve Wozniak Ditches Facebook After Data Scandal," HuffPost, April 9, 2018, https://www.huffingtonpost.com/entry/steve-wozniak-quits-facebook_us_5acaf56ee4b09d0a119529bf.

"at war": Madison Malone Kircher, "Facebook Is at War and Mark Zuckerberg Is Its General," *Intelligencer,* November 19, 2018, http://nymag.com/intelligencer/2018/11/mark-zuckerberg-declared-facebook-at-war.html.

"days are numbered": Olivia Solon, "George Soros: Facebook and Google a Menace to Society," *Guardian,* January 26, 2018, https://www.theguardian.com/business/2018/jan/25/george-soros-facebook-and-google-are-a-menace-to-society.

22 *"answers to such questions":* Tim Berners-Lee, "The World Wide Web: Past, Present and Future," August 1996, https://www.w3.org/People/Berners-Lee/1996/ppf.html.

Facebook's News Feed feature: Danah Boyd, "Will Facebook Learn from Its Mistake?," *Apophenia* (blog), September 7, 2006, http://www.zephoria.org/thoughts/archives/2006/09/07/will_facebook_l.html; Danah Boyd, "Facebook's 'Privacy Trainwreck': Exposure, Invasion, and Drama," *Apophenia* (blog), September 8, 2006, https://www.danah.org/papers/FacebookAndPrivacy.html.

"Friend Is a Fake": Nick O'Neill, "7 Surefire Signs Your New Facebook Friend Is a Fake," *Adweek,* March 3, 2011, https://www.adweek.com/digital/fake-facebook-friend/.

23 *"inside the company":* James Jacoby and Anya Bourg, "Facebook Insider Says Warnings About Data Safety Went Unheeded by Executives," *Frontline,* first aired March 20, 2018, PBS, https://www.pbs.org/wgbh/frontline/article/facebook-insider-says-warnings-about-data-safety-went-unheeded-by-executives/.

"ripping apart society": James Vincent, "Former Facebook Exec Says Social Media Is Ripping Apart Society," The Verge, December 11, 2017, https://www.theverge.com/2017/12/11/16761016/former-facebook-exec-ripping-apart-society.

social media addiction: Nellie Bowles, "Early Facebook and Google Employees Form Coalition to Fight What They Built," *New York Times,* February 5, 2018.

24 *all around the Internet:* Antonio García Martínez, *Chaos Monkeys: Obscene Fortune and Random Failure in Silicon Valley* (New York: HarperCollins, 2016).

"as to be un-mutable": Antonio Garcia-Martinez, "I'm an Ex–Facebook

Exec: Don't Believe What They Tell You About Ads," *Guardian*, May 2, 2017, https://www.theguardian.com/technology/2017/may/02/face book-executive-advertising-data-comment.

primary source of income: Brian Mastroianni, "Survey: More Americans Worried About Data Privacy Than Income," CBS News, January 28, 2016, https://www.cbsnews.com/news/truste-survey-more-americans -concerned-about-data-privacy-than-losing-income/.

claw back access: Paul Mozur, Mark Scott, and Mike Isaac, "Facebook Is Navigating a Global Power Struggle," *New York Times*, September 18, 2017.

for Facebook's business: Larry Elliott, "Is It Time to Break Up the Tech Giants Such as Facebook?," *Guardian*, March 25, 2018, https:// www.theguardian.com/business/2018/mar/25/is-it-time-to-break-up -the-tech-giants-such-as-facebook.

25 *their thin margins:* Sapna Maheshwari, "Senators Urge Investigation of Smart TV Industry, Citing Privacy Concerns," *New York Times*, July 13, 2018.

on the right track: Deepa Seetharaman, "Facebook Morale Takes a Tumble Along with Stock Price," *Wall Street Journal*, November 14, 2018, https://www.wsj.com/articles/facebook-morale-takes-a-tumble-along -with-stock-price-1542200400.

work at other organizations: Casey Newton, "Facebook's Morale Problem Is Getting Worse," The Verge, December 6, 2018, https://www .theverge.com/2018/12/6/18128267/facebook-morale-uk-parliament -emails-privacy-competition.

turn into purchases: Leo Sun, "Amazon Becomes a Major Contender in Digital Advertising: A Foolish Take," *USA Today*, October 2, 2018, https://www.usatoday.com/story/money/markets/2018/10/02/amazon -contender-digital-advertising-sales/37920325/b.

"something new": Salvador Rodriguez, "Former Instagram CEO on Why He Quit Facebook: 'No One Ever Leaves a Job Because Everything's Awesome,'" CNBC, October 15, 2018, https://www.cnbc.com/2018/10/15 /instagram-former-ceo-kevin-systrom-on-why-he-left-facebook.html.

27 The Signals Are Talking: Amy Webb, *The Signals Are Talking: Why Today's Fringe Is Tomorrow's Mainstream* (New York: PublicAffairs, 2016).

as a "family": Sara Salinas, "Facebook's 'Family' Is Getting Smaller, as Several Executives Head for the Exits in a Turbulent Year," CNBC, September 3, 2018, https://www.cnbc.com/2018/09/01/all-the-facebook -executives-who-announced-departure-so-far-in-2018.html.

28 *"had on the world":* Nick Bilton, "'Oh My God, What Have I Done': Some Early Facebook Employees Regret the Monster They Created,"

Vanity Fair, October 12, 2017, https://www.vanityfair.com/news/2017 /10/early-facebook-employees-regret-the-monster-they-created.

creating blind spots: Salvador Rodriguez, "Inside Facebook's 'Cult-Like' Workplace, Where Dissent Is Discouraged and Employees Pretend to Be Happy All the Time," CNBC, January 8, 2019, https://www.cnbc .com/2019/01/08/facebook-culture-cult-performance-review-process -blamed.html.

29 *had access to it:* Aarti Shahani, "Mark Zuckerberg's Big Blind Spot and the Conflict Within Facebook," *All Tech Considered* (blog), NPR, October 31, 2017, https://www.npr.org/sections/alltechconsidered/2017 /10/31/560667628/mark-zuckerbergs-big-blind-spot-and-the-conflict -within-facebook.

"anything to hide": Jose Antonio Vargas, "The Face of Facebook," *The New Yorker,* September 20, 2010, https://www.newyorker.com /magazine/2010/09/20/the-face-of-facebook.

unsavory conduct: Jen Chung, "After Porn & Masturbation Incidents, LinkNYC Removes Web Browsing from WiFi Kiosks," Gothamist, September 14, 2016, http://gothamist.com/2016/09/14/free_porno_ spigots_cut_off.php.

conventional bureaucracy: Stephen Denning, *The Age of Agile: How Smart Companies Are Transforming the Way Work Gets Done* (New York: AMACOM, 2018).

30 *"They just build":* Chris Zook and James Allen, "Reigniting Growth," *Harvard Business Review,* March 2016.

most critical lesson for a while: Motley Fool Staff, "Home Depot Is Doing Everything Right," The Motley Fool, May 23, 2017, https://www .fool.com/investing/2017/05/23/home-depot-is-doing-everything-right .aspx.

31 *his book* Little Bets: Peter Sims, *Little Bets: How Breakthrough Ideas Emerge from Small Discoveries,* repr. ed. (New York: Simon & Schuster, 2013).

new ideas to the surface: Mark Wilson, "Adobe's Kickbox: The Kit to Launch Your Next Big Idea," *Fast Company,* February 9, 2015, https:// www.fastcompany.com/3042128/adobes-kickbox-the-kit-to-launch -your-next-big-idea.

32 *give it a try:* "Discover Kickbox," Adobe, n.d., https://kickbox.adobe .com/what-is-kickbox.

33 *by an executive:* Noam Scheiber, "Steady Shifts for Workers Help Stores, Too," *New York Times,* March 28, 2018.

34 *immensely liberating:* John Bielenberg, Mike Burn, and Greg Galle, *Think Wrong: How to Conquer the Status Quo and Do Work That Matters* (San Francisco: Instigator Press, 2016).

did not want to listen: Reza Moaiandin, "How Facebook Ignored Security Warnings for 3 Years," *CPO Magazine,* April 20, 2018, https://www.cpomagazine.com/2018/04/20/how-facebook-ignored-security-warnings-for-3-years.

"gave their consent": Claudia Geib, "Here's Why That Recent Abuse of Facebook Data Matters," Futurism, March 20, 2018, https://futurism.com/abuse-facebook-data-cambridge/.

"blog posts and research": Shahani, "Mark Zuckerberg's Big Blind Spot."

35 *illegal behavior:* Dan Ackman, "Pay Madness at Enron," *Forbes,* March 22, 2002, https://www.forbes.com/2002/03/22/0322enronpay.html#3cec42dd7a6d.

US Supreme Court: Bill Chapell, "Aereo's TV Streaming Service Is Illegal, Supreme Court Says," *The Two-Way* (blog), NPR, June 24, 2014, https://www.npr.org/sections/thetwo-way/2014/06/25/325488386/tech-firm-aereo-performs-an-illegal-service-supreme-court-says.

Securities and Exchange Commission report: Jeff John Roberts, "Facebook Has Been Hit by Dozens of Data Lawsuits. And This Could Be Just the Beginning," *Fortune,* April 30, 2018, http://fortune.com/2018/04/30/facebook-data-lawsuits/.

2016 presidential election: Zeynep Tufekci, "Mark Zuckerberg Is in Denial," *New York Times,* November 15, 2016.

stories on the platform: Karen Zraick, "Mark Zuckerberg Seeks to Clarify Remarks About Holocaust Deniers After Outcry," *New York Times,* July 18, 2018.

voters in the midterm elections: John Markoff, "Social Networks Can Affect Voter Turnout, Study Says." *New York Times,* September 13, 2012.

36 *"Patriarch Partners in 2007":* Dave Carpenter, "Rand McNally Adapts to New Age with Software, Gadgets," *Houston Chronicle,* October 18, 2006, https://www.chron.com/business/technology/article/Rand-McNally-adapts-to-new-age-with-software-1511674.php.

representatives of the future: See Scott D. Anthony, Clark G. Gilbert, and Mark W. Johnson, *Dual Transformation: How to Reposition Today's Business While Creating the Future* (Cambridge: Harvard Business Review Press, 2017).

37 *tie the messaging together:* "Hi, We're . . . Nice to Meet You," Mailchimp, n.d., https://mailchimp.com/did-you-mean/.

2. EARLY WARNINGS

39 "than will actually happen": Patrick Marren, email communication with author, February 28, 2019.

40 *"Uh, sure":* Clifford Stoll, "Why the Web Won't Be Nirvana," *News-*

week, February 26, 1995, http://www.newsweek.com/clifford-stoll-why -web-wont-be-nirvana-185306.

41 *"at least 20 years":* Claire Cockburn and T. D. Wilson, "Business Use of the World-Wide Web," *Information Research* 1, no. 2 (1995), http:// www.informationr.net/ir/1-2/paper6.html.

43 *"lulled into inaction":* Bill Gates, with Nathan Myhrvold and Peter Rinearson, *The Road Ahead* (New York: Viking, 1995).

"OS share is 1%": Stephen G. Blank, "Why Tim Cook Is Steve Ballmer and Why He Still Has His Job at Apple," blog post, October 24, 2016, https://steveblank.com/2016/10/24/why-tim-cook-is-steve-ballmer -and-why-he-still-has-his-job-at-apple/.

47 *"catch these signals":* Sanjay Purohit, interview with author, December 14, 2018.

48 *employee satisfaction and engagement:* See, for example, Mark Heymann, "Spotlight on Service: Integrating Workforce Management with Employee Engagement to Optimize Customer Satisfaction and Profitability," *Global Business and Organizational Excellence* 34, no. 5 (2015): 6–12; Lisa Cain, Sarah Tanford, and Lenna Shulga, "Customers' Perceptions of Employee Engagement: Fortifying the Service-Profit Chain," *International Journal of Hospitality & Tourism Administration* 19, no. 1 (2018): 52–77; Ieva Martinaityte, Claudia Sacramento, and Samuel Aryee, "Delighting the Customer: Creativity-Oriented High-Performance Work Systems, Frontline Employee Creative Performance, and Customer Satisfaction," *Journal of Management* 45, no. 2 (2019): 728–51; and Dharmendra Mehta and Naveen K. Mehta, "Employee Engagement: A Literature Review," *Economia: Seria Management* 16, no. 2 (2013): 208–15.

more recently reconfirmed: Amy Edmondson, "Psychological Safety and Learning Behavior in Work Teams," *Administrative Science Quarterly* 44 (1999): 350–83; Peter Cauwelier, "Building High-Performance Teams Through Action Learning," *Action Learning: Research and Practice* 16, no. 1 (2019): 68–76.

"Customer love": Matt Weinberger, "Satya Nadella: 'Customer Love' Is a Better Sign of Success Than Revenue or Profit," Business Insider, October 7, 2015, http://www.businessinsider.com/microsoft-ceo-satya -nadella-on-culture-2015-10.

52 *"put food into boxes":* Sam Harnett, "How Delivery Apps Are Changing the Restaurant Industry," Marketplace, November 19, 2018, https:// www.marketplace.org/2018/11/19/business/how-delivery-apps-are -changing-restaurant-industry.

envision the future: P. Schoemaker and C. A. J. M. van der Heijden, "Integrating Scenarios into Strategic Planning at Royal Dutch/Shell," *Planning Review,* May/June, 1992.

three future scenarios: Andrew S. Grove, "Surviving a 10X Force," *Strategy & Leadership* 25, no. 1 (1997): 35–37.

57 *existing model for education:* Derek Alexander Muller, "This Will Revolutionize Education," YouTube, December 1, 2014, https://www .youtube.com/watch?v=GEmuEWjHr5c.

mover on the World Wide Web: Paula J. Hane, "Fathom This: Academic and Cultural Institutions Partner to Create Interactive Knowledge Company," Information Today, April 10, 2000, http://newsbreaks .infotoday.com/nbreader.asp?ArticleID=17822.

at all unusual: Karen Hua, "Education as Entertainment: YouTube Sensations Teaching the Future," *Forbes,* June 23, 2015, https://www .forbes.com/sites/karenhua/2015/06/23/education-as-entertainment -youtube-sensations-teaching-the-future/#73ea596247c2.

58 *four-year degree:* "37 Percent of May 2016 Employment in Occupations Typically Requiring Postsecondary Education," US Department of Labor, Bureau of Labor Statistics, June 28, 2017, https://www.bls.gov /opub/ted/2017/37-percent-of-may-2016-employment-in-occupations -typically-requiring-postsecondary-education.htm?view_full.

"risk of degree inflation": Joseph B. Fuller and Manjari Raman, "Dismissed by Degrees: How Degree Inflation Is Undermining U.S. Competitiveness and Hurting America's Middle Class" (report, Accenture, Grads of Life, and Harvard Business School, October 2017), https://www.hbs .edu/managing-the-future-of-work/Documents/dismissed-by-degrees .pdf.

within four years: Jeffrey J. Selingo, "Wanted: Factory Workers, Degree Required," *New York Times,* January 30, 2017.

59 *overall consumer price index:* Timothy McMahon, "College Tuition and Fees vs Overall Inflation," InflationData.com, June 14, 2012, https:// inflationdata.com/articles/charts/college-tuition-fees-inflation/.

owed a decade earlier: Anthony Cilluffo, "5 Facts About Student Loans," Pew Research Center, August 24, 2017, http://www.pewresearch .org/fact-tank/2017/08/24/5-facts-about-student-loans/.

"a dead end": Selingo, "Wanted: Factory Workers."

60 *alternative certification systems:* Dan Schawbel, "10 Workplace Trends You'll See in 2018," *Forbes,* November 1, 2017, https://www.forbes.com /sites/danschawbel/2017/11/01/10-workplace-trends-youll-see-in-2018 /#68a0ecc4bf22.

ongoing skepticism: Cathy Sandeen, "The Emerging World of Alternative Credentials," *Higher Education Today* (blog), American Council on Education, October 1, 2013, https://www.higheredtoday.org/2013/10 /01/the-emerging-world-of-alternative-credentials/.

traditional credentials are "boring": Mordy Golding, "What's Next in

L&D: Experts Reveal Predictions for 2017," *The Learning Blog*, LinkedIn, January 19, 2017, https://learning.linkedin.com/blog/learning-thought -leadership/what_s-next-in-l-d--experts-reveal-predictions-for-2017.

for their workers: Ainsley Harris, "Say Hello to the University of Microsoft," *Fast Company*, June 17, 2015, https://www.fastcompany.com /3046941/say-hello-to-the-university-of-microsoft.

61 *large research universities:* John Holusha, "Steel Mini-Mills Could Bring Boon or Blood Bath," *New York Times*, May 30, 1995.

the book Disrupting Class: Clayton Christensen, Michael B. Horn, and Curtis Johnson, *Disrupting Class: How Disruptive Innovation Will Change the Way the World Learns*, exp. ed. (New York: McGraw-Hill Education, 2016).

"intellectual values": Michael M. Harmon, "Business Research and Chinese Patriotic Poetry: How Competition for Status Distorts the Priority Between Research and Teaching in U.S. Business Schools," *Academy of Management Learning & Education* 5, no. 2 (2006): 234–43.

obsolete lessons to their students: Stephen Denning, "Why Business Schools Teach Yesterday's Expertise," *Forbes*, May 27, 2018.

62 *an increasing rate:* Scott Jaschik, "When Colleges Rely on Adjuncts, Where Does the Money Go?," Inside Higher Ed, January 5, 2017, https:// www.insidehighered.com/news/2017/01/05/study-looks-impact -adjunct-hiring-college-spending-patterns.

63 *"Impossible":* Jillian D'Onfro, "Jeff Bezos' Brilliant Advice for Anyone Running a Business," Business Insider, January 31, 2015, https://www .businessinsider.com/jeff-bezos-brilliant-advice-for-anyone-running-a -business-2015-1.

3. ON THE LOOKOUT FOR WEAK SIGNALS: DEFINING YOUR ARENA

65 *"no longer true":* Matthew S. Olson, Derek van Bever, and Seth Verry, "When Growth Stalls," *Harvard Business Review*, March 2008.

66 *potential bad news:* Rita Gunther McGrath, *The End of Competitive Advantage: How to Keep Your Strategy Moving as Fast as Your Business* (Boston: Harvard Business Review Press, 2013).

"for the market": Michael E. Porter, *Competitive Advantage: Creating and Sustaining Superior Performance* (New York: Free Press, 1985).

67 *"Design for Action":* Tim Brown and Roger L. Martin, "Design for Action," *Harvard Business Review*, September 2015.

69 *hair removal and its importance decline:* Kaitlyn Tiffany, "The Absurd Quest to Make the 'Best' Razor," Vox, December 11, 2018, https:// www.vox.com/the-goods/2018/12/11/18134456/best-razor-gillette-har rys-dollar-shave-club.

71 *digital devices "addictive":* Adam Alter, *Irresistible: The Rise of Addictive Technology and the Business of Keeping Us Hooked* (New York, Penguin Press, 2017).

73 *"periods of profitable performance":* Alexei Agratchev, "New Metrics for a New Retail Industry," The Robin Report, May 2, 2016, https://www.therobinreport.com/new-metrics-for-a-new-retail-industry.
   social websites and the Internet: "The Teens Market in the U.S.," Packaged Facts, June 1, 2007, https://www.packagedfacts.com/Teens-1493744/.
   approval on a purchase: Ylan Q. Mui, "As the Kids Go Buy," *Washington Post,* June 4, 2007.
   a major inflection had arrived: Ryan Knutson and Theo Francis, "Basic Costs Squeeze Families," *Wall Street Journal,* December 1, 2014.
   "'stay connected,' she said": Elizabeth A. Harris and Rachel Abrams, "More Plugged-In Than Preppy," *New York Times,* August 28, 2014.

74 *"online since last October":* Vanessa Friedman, "Stepping Off the Runway," *New York Times,* February 11, 2016.

75 *conventional apparel industry:* Walter Loeb, "Zara Leads in Fast Fashion," *Forbes,* March 30, 2015, https://www.forbes.com/sites/walterloeb/2015/03/30/zara-leads-in-fast-fashion/#6b316b759447.
   total US growth in 2016: Lauren Thomas, "Amazon's Shoe Business Sees Double-Digit Growth, and the Year Is Only Halfway Over," CNBC, August 3, 2017, https://www.cnbc.com/2017/08/03/amazons-shoe-business-sees-double-digit-growth-and-the-year-is-only-halfway-over.html.

76 *"mostly in offshore wind":* Nerijus Adomaitis, "Statoil to Become Equinor, Dropping 'Oil' to Attract Young Talent," Reuters, May 15, 2018, https://www.reuters.com/article/us-statoil-agm-equinor/statoil-to-become-equinor-dropping-oil-to-attract-young-talent-idUSKCN1IG0MN.

4. CUSTOMERS, NOT HOSTAGES

78 *"hardly blame them":* Stu Woo, "Under Fire, Netflix Rewinds DVD Plan," *Wall Street Journal,* October 11, 2011.
   would consume content: Ashley Rodriguez, "Netflix Was Founded 20 Years Ago Today Because Reed Hastings Was Late Returning a Video," Quartz, August 29, 2017, https://qz.com/1062888/netflix-was-founded-20-years-ago-today-because-reed-hastings-was-late-a-returning-video/.

79 *"at the right time":* Charlie Gaudet, "6 Strategies Netflix Can Teach Us for Dominating Our Market," Predictable Profits, n.d., https://

predictableprofits.com/6-strategies-netflix-can-teach-us-dominating
-market/.

one of Sony's early models: Ashlee Kieler, "On This Day in 1984, the
Supreme Court Saved the VCR from Certain Death," Consumerist, January 17, 2014, https://consumerist.com/2014/01/17/on-this-day-in-1984
-the-supreme-court-saved-the-vcr-from-certain-death/.

80 *"time it would take":* E. Scott Mayfield, "Netflix (2000)" (case study,
Harvard Business School, September 2000; revised January 2016).

81 *"use by other firms":* Rumble Press, "If Only Blockbuster Had Listened to Enron . . . : How Blockbuster Blew a Chance to Dominate Video-on-Demand," Medium, n.d., https://medium.com/@rumblepress/if-only
-blockbuster-had-listened-to-enron-4166752a78de.

decide to take action: Jason Del Ray, "This Is the Jeff Bezos Playbook for Preventing Amazon's Demise," Recode, April 12, 2017, https://
www.recode.net/2017/4/12/15274220/jeff-bezos-amazon-shareholders
-letter-day-2-disagree-and-commit.

82 *more than $6 billion:* "Blockbuster: Its Failure and Lessons to Digital Transformers," submission, Digital Initiative, Harvard Business
School, February 2, 2017, https://digit.hbs.org/submission/blockbuster
-its-failure-and-lessons-to-digital-transformers/.

16 percent of its revenue: Michael Liedtke and Mae Anderson,
"Blockbuster Tries to Rewrite Script in Bankruptcy," Boston.com, September 23, 2010, http://archive.boston.com/business/articles/2010/09
/23/blockbuster_tries_to_rewrite_script_in_bankruptcy/.

"tolerable" attribute: Ian MacMillan and Rita Gunther McGrath,
"Discover Your Products' Hidden Potential," *Harvard Business Review*,
June 1996.

83 *"simply can't match":* W. Sean Owen, "Why Netflix Can't Match
Blockbuster's Competitive Advantage," Seeking Alpha, March 27, 2007,
https://seekingalpha.com/article/30771-why-netflix-cant-match
-blockbusters-competitive-advantage.

easing Antioco out: John Antioco, "Blockbuster's Former CEO on
Sparring with an Activist Shareholder," *Harvard Business Review*, April
2011.

went bankrupt in 2010: Greg Satell, "A Look Back at Why Blockbuster Really Failed and Why It Didn't Have To," *Forbes*, September 5, 2014, https://www.forbes.com/sites/gregsatell/2014/09/05/a
-look-back-at-why-blockbuster-really-failed-and-why-it-didnt-have-to
/#6f0d31ac1d64b.

84 *"take the first step":* "Netflix Offers Subscribers the Option of Instantly
Watching Movies on Their PCs," Netflix, press release, January 16, 2007,

https://media.netflix.com/en/press-releases/netflix-offers-subscribers
-the-option-of-instantly-watching-movies-on-their-pcs-migration-1.

"subscribes to Netflix": Ryan Lawler, "Netflix: The Future Is Streaming," Gigaom, May 27, 2010, https://gigaom.com/2010/05/27/netflix
-the-future-is-streaming/.

86 *began to appear:* Rex Crum, "Netflix Facing a Fight Against Obsoles-
cence," MarketWatch, October 25, 2011, https://www.marketwatch.com
/story/netflix-facing-a-fight-against-obsolescence-2011-10-25.

defected from the service: Nick Wingfield and Brian Stelter, "How
Netflix Lost 800,000 Members, and Good Will," *New York Times,* October 24, 2011, https://www.nytimes.com/2011/10/25/technology/netflix
-lost-800000-members-with-price-rise-and-split-plan.html.

for "defensive" reasons: Rebecca Greenfield, "Netflix Snaps Up DVD.com
Domain," *Atlantic,* March 30, 2012.

creation of original content: Rani Molla, "Netflix Now Has Nearly
118 Million Streaming Subscribers Globally," Recode, January 22, 2018,
https://www.recode.net/2018/1/22/16920150/netflix-q4-2017-earnings
-subscribers.

87 *"will cut the cord":* Gerry Smith, "Who Killed the Great American Cable Bundle?," Bloomberg, August 8, 2018, https://www.bloomberg.com
/news/features/2018-08-08/who-killed-the-great-american-cable-tv
-bundle.

subscribe to the streaming service: Sarah Perez, "Netflix Reaches 75%
of US Streaming Service Viewers, but YouTube Is Catching Up," Tech-
Crunch, April 10, 2017, https://techcrunch.com/2017/04/10/netflix
-reaches-75-of-u-s-streaming-service-viewers-but-youtube-is-catching
-up/.

"multitude of other options": Alex Sherman, "Reed Hastings Won by
Studying Amazon — Then Running in the Opposite Direction," CNBC,
June 16, 2018, https://www.cnbc.com/2018/06/13/netflix-reed-hastings
-inspiration-amazon.html.

88 *they already had:* Wingfield and Stelter, "How Netflix Lost 800,000
Members."

89 *"if we can keep improving":* Matthew Ball, "Netflix Isn't Being Reckless, It's Just Playing a Game No One Else Dares (Netflix Misunderstand-
ings, Pt. 3)," Redef, July 8, 2018, https://redef.com/original/5b400a2779
328f4711d5675e?curator=MediaREDEFb.

90 *overwhelmingly via cell phone:* Kis Leswing, "Two Photos of Tiger Woods Taken 16 Years Apart Show How Much Smartphones Have
Changed the World," Business Insider, August 11, 2018, https://www
.businessinsider.com/tiger-woods-photos-show-how-smartphones
-changed-the-world-2018-8.

91 *some guarantee of quality:* Lawrence Van Gelder, "Medallion Limits Stem from the 30's," *New York Times,* May 11, 1996, https://www.nytimes .com/1996/05/11/nyregion/medallion-limits-stem-from-the-30-s.html.

92 *$1.3 million by 2013:* Ameena Walker, "In NYC, 139 Prized Yellow Taxi Medallions Will Hit the Auction Block," Curbed New York, June 11, 2018, https://ny.curbed.com/2018/6/11/17450366/nyc-taxi-medallions -bankruptcy-auction.

the customer's point of view: Megan McArdle, "Why You Can't Get a Taxi," *Atlantic,* 2012.

94 *the city's yellow cabs:* Winnie Hu, "Uber, Surging Outside Manhattan, Tops Taxis in New York City," *New York Times,* October 12, 2017, https://www.nytimes.com/2017/10/12/nyregion/uber-taxis-new-york -city.html?module=inline.

on to its next phase: Shona Ghosh, "Underpaying Drivers Is 'Essential' to Uber's Business Model, According to a New Study on Low Wages," Business Insider, March 7, 2018, https://www.businessinsider.in /Underpaying-drivers-is-essential-to-Ubers-business-model-according -to-a-new-study-on-low-wages/articleshow/63202511.cms.

over $2 billion: Dan Primack, "Scooter Startup Bird Is Seeking a $2 Billion Valuation," Axios, June 12, 2018, https://www.axios.com/scooter -startup-bird-is-seeking-a-2-billion-valuation-1528813078-11187061 -2a49-440c-a2e6-65e74faad5ec.html.

"hungry tapeworm" affecting the economy: Associated Press, "Amazon, Buffett, JPMorgan Chase Tackle US Health Care Tapeworm," Marketplace, January 30, 2018, https://www.marketplace.org/2018/01/30 /health-care/amazon-buffett-jpmorgan-chase-tackle-us-health-care -tapeworm.

95 *world's fifth-largest economy:* "Why Is Health Care So Expensive?," *Consumer Reports,* September 2014.

96 *"pharmacies and health plans":* "Pharmacy Benefit Managers (PBMs) 101," National Community Pharmacists Association, n.d., http://www.ncpa .co/pdf/leg/nov12/pbm_one_pager.pdf.

"over the past two years": Charley Grant, "Hidden Profits in the Prescription Drug Supply Chain," *Wall Street Journal,* February 24, 2018.

according to Pembroke Consulting: Adam J. Fein, "The Outlook for Pharmacy Benefit Management: Evolution or Disruption?" (handout, 2018 National Conference of the Pharmacy Benefit Management Institute, Palm Springs, CA, March 5, 2018), http://drugchannelsinstitute .com/files/PBMI-PBM_Outlook-Drug_Channels-Fein-Mar2018 -Handouts.pdf.

$4 in other countries: Neil Weinberg and Robert Langreth, "Drug Costs Too High? Fire the Middleman," Bloomberg, March 3, 2017,

https://www.bloomberg.com/news/articles/2017-03-03/drug-costs-too
-high-fire-the-middleman.

"operations and cash flows": Jared S. Hopkins, "Drug-Price Plan Echoes
a Regulatory Remnant of Financial Crisis," Bloomberg, May 17, 2018,
https://www.bloomberg.com/news/articles/2018-05-17/drug-price
-plan-echoes-a-regulatory-remnant-of-financial-crisis.

97 *the discounted price"*: Briana Montalvo, "Many Overpay for Prescriptions When Co-pays Are Higher Than Drug Prices: Study," ABC News,
March 15, 2018, https://abcnews.go.com/Health/overpay-prescriptions
-pays-higher-drug-prices-study/story?id=53767651.

evaluate banning it: Michael Hiltzik, "The 'Clawback': Another
Hidden Scam Driving Up Your Prescription Prices," *Los Angeles Times*,
August 9, 2017, http://www.latimes.com/business/hiltzik/la-fi-hiltzik
-clawback-drugs-20170809-story.html.

98 *lawyers and legislators:* Jacklyn Wille, "Prescription Drug Clawbacks
Under Fire from Lawmakers, Lawyers," Bloomberg, March 23, 2018,
https://www.bna.com/prescription-drug-clawbacks-n57982090234/.

99 *10 to 25 percent waste:* Todd N. Bisping, "Caterpillar Breaks New
Ground Managing the Prescription Drug Supply Chain," *American Journal of Pharmacy Benefits* 2, no. 2 (2010): 103–5.

transparency in pricing: Eileen Koutnik-Fotopoulos, "Coalition Fights
for Total Transparency," *Pharmacy Times,* February 1, 2006.

Brought the decision in-house: John Carroll, "Having Mined Gold
in Pharmacy Deal, Caterpillar Sets Sights on Gold-Standard Therapies,"
Biotechnology Healthcare 6, no. 2 (2009): 49–50.

lower than those in 2004: Staff Report, "Bulldozing Pharmacy Benefit Managers, Caterpillar Engineers Drug Cost Savings," *Workforce*, December 1, 2009, http://www.workforce.com/2009/12/01/bulldozing
-pharmacy-benefit-managers-caterpillar-engineers-drug-cost-savings/.

other parts of the economy: "Amazon Is Likely to Succeed at Healthcare and Have Lasting, Disruptive Impact: Five Scenarios Show How It
Will Enter and Prevail," Cision PR Newswire, March 26, 2018, https://
www.prnewswire.com/news-releases/amazon-is-likely-to-succeed-at
-healthcare-and-have-lasting-disruptive-impact-five-scenarios-show
-how-it-will-enter-and-prevail-300619075.html.

5. WHAT MUST BE TRUE?
CREATING A PLAN TO LEARN FAST

101 *"disconfirm their beliefs":* "Jeff Bezos: People Who Are Right a Lot
Listen a Lot," Conversation Agent, n.d., https://www.conversationagent
.com/2016/11/jpeople-who-are-right-a-lot-listen-a-lot.html.

102 *written about extensively elsewhere:* Rita Gunther McGrath and Ian

C. MacMillan, *Discovery-Driven Growth: A Breakthrough Process to Reduce Risk and Seize Opportunity* (Boston: Harvard Business Review Press, 2009).

"hold strong opinions weakly": Paul Saffo, "Six Rules for Effective Forecasting," *Harvard Business Review*, July–August 2007.

103 *"little bets":* Peter Sims, *Little Bets: How Breakthrough Ideas Emerge from Small Discoveries*, repr. ed. (New York: Simon & Schuster, 2013).

worth to us: McGrath and MacMillan, *Discovery-Driven Growth*.

104 *"the reverse is fragile":* Nassim Nicholas Taleb, *Antifragile: Things That Gain from Disorder* (New York: Random House, 2012).

so clearly explained: Pierre Leroy and Ryan P. McManus, "Value Creation and Corporate Survival in the Digital Revolution," Venture Lab, July 12, 2016, http://theventurelab.blogspot.com/2016/07/value -creation-and-corporate-survival.html; Ryan P. McManus, "Understanding the Past, Present, and Future of the Digital Revolution," *BoardTalk* (blog), NACD, September 26, 2017, https://blog.nacdonline.org/posts /digital-past-present-future.

105 *the ensuing dot-com crash:* Douglas Galbi, "U.S. Annual Advertising Spending Since 1919," Galbi Think!, September 14, 2008, https://www .galbithink.org/ad-spending.htm.

106 *$70 million in revenue:* Thomas Bagshaw, "The Evolution of Google AdWords – A $38 Billion Advertising Platform," *WordStream* (blog), April 3, 2015, https://www.wordstream.com/blog/ws/2012/06/05/evolution -of-adwords.

a small surcharge: Elisa Gabbert, "How Does the AdWords Auction Work? [Infographic]," *WordStream* (blog), July 27, 2018, https://www .wordstream.com/blog/ws/2011/11/16/how-adwords-works.

likely to have seen the ad: John E. Lincoln, "How Does Pay-Per-Click Work?," Ignite Visibility, 2019, https://ignitevisibility.com/how-does -ppc-work/.

$50 billion in 2017: Suzanne Vranica and Jack Marshall, "Plummeting Newspaper Ad Revenue Sparks New Wave of Changes," *Wall Street Journal*, October 20, 2016, https://www.wsj.com/articles/plummeting -newspaper-ad-revenue-sparks-new-wave-of-changes-1476955801.

109 *pull the plug on it:* Barry M. Staw, "Knee-Deep in the Big Muddy – A Study of Escalating Commitment to a Chosen Course of Action," *Organizational Behavior and Human Performance* 16, no. 1(1976): 27.

show for that expenditure: "BBC Was 'Complacent' over Failed £100m IT Project," BBC News, April 10, 2014, https://www.bbc.com /news/entertainment-arts-26963723.

110 *"completely tapeless" production workflows:* Peter Brightwell, "Standardising Media Delivery in a File-Based World" (research white paper,

no. WHP 158, BBC, December 2007), http://downloads.bbc.co.uk/rd
/pubs/whp/whp-pdf-files/WHP158.pdf.

£99.6 million: Robert N. Charette, "BBC Blows £98 Million on Digital Media Initiative," *IEEE Spectrum,* May 30, 2013, https://spectrum
.ieee.org/riskfactor/computing/it/bbc-blows-984m-on-digital-media
-initiative-project.

"new and emerging services": "Siemens Selects Cinegy for BBC's
Digital Media Initiative," TV Technology, April 23, 2008, https://www
.tvtechnology.com/opinions/siemens-selects-cinegy-for-bbcs-digital
-media-initiative.

111 *"distant":* House of Commons, Committee of Public Accounts, "The
BBC's Management of Its Digital Media Initiative," Twenty-Ninth Report
of Session 2010–11 (London: Stationery Office, April 7, 2011), https://
publications.parliament.uk/pa/cm201011/cmselect/cmpubacc/808/808
.pdf.

112 *"privately voicing them":* Elizabeth Daniel and John Ward, "BBC's
DMI Project Failure Is a Warning to All Organisations," *Computer
Weekly,* June 2013, https://www.computerweekly.com/opinion/BBCs
-DMI-project-failure-is-a-warning-to-all-organisations.

"design and development work": House of Commons, Committee of
Public Accounts, "The BBC's Management of Its Digital Media Initiative."

113 *"spending on this initiative":* Dominic Coles, "The BBC Announces
the Closure of the Digital Media Initiative – DMI," *About the BBC*
(blog), May 24, 2013, http://www.bbc.co.uk/blogs/aboutthebbc/entries
/1b3fa3ed-9775-32e7-a68c-9a8272d7c23c.

Advancement of Science in 2018: Becky Ham, "Scientists Must Adapt
to 'Inflection Point' in Cancer Research, Says Biden," American Association for the Advancement of Science, February 18, 2018, https://www
.aaas.org/news/scientists-must-adapt-inflection-point-cancer-research
-says-biden.

114 *$81 million in 2010:* Nicholas Carlson, "After Selling a Startup to
Google for $81 Million, 26-Year-Old Nat Turner Now Wants to Solve
Healthcare," Business Insider, June 5, 2012, https://www.businessinsider
.com/after-selling-a-startup-to-google-for-81-million-26-year-old-nat
-turner-now-wants-to-solve-healthcare-2012-6.

nearly $2 billion in 2018: Sarah Buhr, "Swiss Pharma Company
Roche Is Buying Flatiron Health for $1.9 Billion," TechCrunch, February
15, 2018, https://techcrunch.com/2018/02/15/swiss-pharma-company
-roche-is-buying-flatiron-health-for-1-9-billion/.

115 *"build a big business":* "How Invite Media's Founder Is Making Sure
Success 'Wasn't a Fluke,'" *Financial Post,* February 8, 2012, https://

business.financialpost.com/entrepreneur/fp-startups/how-invite-me dias-founder-is-making-sure-success-wasnt-a-fluke.

"dollar flow": Ibid.

116 *"inviting you to do something":* "Nat Turner: Young, Entrepreneurial and Google-Owned," interview with Knowledge@Wharton High School, February 5, 2011, http://kwhs.wharton.upenn.edu/2011/02/nat-turner -young-entrepreneurial-and-google-owned/.

117 *"insight into the health care industry":* Mary Woods, "Nat Turner Disrupts the Health Care Industry," YPO, February 2017, https://www .ypo.org/2017/02/entrepreneur-nat-turner-shakes-up-the-health-care -industry/.

"find any information": Richard Feloni and Daniel Richards, "The 32-Year-Old Who Sold His First Company for $80 Million and a Second for $2 Billion Talks About Writing to Richard Branson, How He's a Terrible Employee, and Why He Never Intends to Build Companies to Sell Them," Business Insider, March 12, 2018, https://www.businessinsider .com/nat-turner-flatiron-health-interview-2018-3.

"why is it that way?": Ibid.

118 *they possibly could:* Ibid.

"'get their feedback early'": Woods, "Nat Turner Disrupts the Health Care Industry."

"more reliable treatment decisions": Jennifer Bresnick, "FDA: Real-World Data, Machine Learning Critical for Clinical Trials," HealthIT Analytics.com, January 31, 2019, https://healthitanalytics.com/news /fda-real-world-data-machine-learning-critical-for-clinical-trials.

"regulatory-grade" information: "Pivotal Study Validates Real-World Mortality Endpoint for Oncology Research," Flatiron, press release, May 14, 2018, https://flatiron.com/press/press-release/validates-real-world-mor tality-endpoint/.

119 *in an advanced study:* C. H. Bartlett, J. Mardekian, M. Cotter, et al., "Abstract P3-17-03: Concordance of Real World Progression Free Survival (PFS) on Endocrine Therapy as First Line Treatment for Metastatic Breast Cancer Using Electronic Health Record with Proper Quality Control Versus Conventional PFS from a Phase 3 Trial," in *2017 San Antonio Breast Cancer Symposium,* supplement, *Cancer Research* 78, no. 4 (2018), http://cancerres.aacrjournals.org/content/78/4_Supplement/P3-17 -03.

cost of conducting such trials: David Shaywitz, "The Deeply Human Core of Roche's $2.1 Billion Tech Acquisition — and Why It Made It," *Forbes,* February 18, 2018, https://www.forbes.com/sites/davidshaywitz /2018/02/18/the-deeply-human-core-of-roches-2-1b-tech-acquisition -and-why-they-did-it/#6395534029c2.

120 *"It's called 'experienced'":* Jake Cook, "Steve Blank: Lessons from 35 Years of Making Startups Fail Less," 99U, November 29, 2012, http://99u.com/articles/7256/steve-blank-lessons-from-35-years-of-making-startups-fail-less.

121 *other strategic partners:* Carol Seagle and Lisa Jones Christensen, "Case Study: Procter & Gamble's Pur," *Financial Times,* March 2, 2011, https://www.ft.com/content/1415f250-44fe-11e0-80e7-00144feab49a.

123 *an upgradable object:* Yuting Su, "Octobo — a Toy That Can Actually Respond to Feedback from Children and Truly Engage Them in Genuine Interactive Play," OpenIDEO, February 14, 2018, https://challenges.openideo.com/challenge/ecprize/submission/octobo.

124 *"tactile objects":* "Meet the Entrepreneur Revolutionizing Toys by Blending Physical and Digital Play," Comcast NBCUniversal LIFT Labs for Entrepreneurs, August 27, 2018, https://lift.comcast.com/2018/08/meet-the-entrepreneur-revolutionizing-toys-by-blending-physical-and-digital-play/.

6. GALVANIZING THE ORGANIZATION

127 *"organizations to embrace":* Adam Lashinsky, "What Makes Amazon CEO Jeff Bezos Such a Visionary Leader," *Fortune,* April 14, 2017, http://fortune.com/2017/04/14/data-sheet-be-like-jeff-bezos/.

129 *fundamentally complex:* Gokce Sargut and Rita Gunther McGrath, "Learning to Live with Complexity," *Harvard Business Review,* September 2011.

130 *"for the Internet":* Dean Takahashi, "The Rise and Fall of Microsoft's Xbox Champions, Robbie Bach and J Allard," VentureBeat, May 25, 2010, https://venturebeat.com/2010/05/25/microsofts-longtime-entertainment-executives-robbie-bach-and-j-allard-resign/.
"information-browsing technologies": Steve Lohr, "Microsoft Says Internet Browser Idea Arose Long Before Netscape," *New York Times,* August 6, 1998, https://www.nytimes.com/1998/08/06/business/microsoft-says-internet-browser-idea-arose-long-before-netscape.html.
an "evangelist": Ibid.
"big bet on the Internet": Ibid.

131 *carrying them around:* "405 Million Mobile Phones Sold in 2000, and Makers Still Get Stung," *Los Angeles Times,* January 10, 2001, http://articles.latimes.com/2001/jan/10/business/fi-10497.
"great user experience": Jason Duane Hahn, "The History of the Sidekick: The Coolest Smartphone of All Time," *Complex,* September 11, 2015, https://www.complex.com/pop-culture/2015/09/history-of-the-sidekick.
fee for every user: Chris DeSalvo, "The Future That Everyone For-

got — Some of the Work We Did at Danger," Medium, January 5, 2014, https://medium.com/@chrisdesalvo/the-future-that-everyone-forgot -d823af31f7c.

132 *"a really bad idea":* Donna Kardos, "Microsoft to Acquire Danger, Maker of Sidekick Technology," *Wall Street Journal,* February 11, 2008, https://www.wsj.com/articles/SB120274323781658967.
"internet-connected smartphone": Ibid.

133 *"(or pricing)":* Joshua Topolsky, "What Killed the Kin?," Engadget, June 30, 2010, https://www.engadget.com/2010/06/30/what-killed -the-kin/.
reportedly cost $500 million: Jay Yarrow, "Meet Andy Lees, the Man in Charge of Saving Microsoft," *Forbes,* May 26, 2010, https://www.forbes .com/sites/velocity/2010/05/26/meet-andy-lees-the-man-in-charge-of -saving-microsoft-read/#2e85454878c8.
"withering": Chris Ziegler, "Life and Death of Microsoft Kin: The In- side Story," Engadget, July 2, 2010, https://www.engadget.com/2010/07 /02/life-and-death-of-microsoft-kin-the-inside-story/.

134 *"forced into the background":* Ibid.
delayed the project: Ibid.
cut in half that year: Preston Gralla, "Microsoft's Ballmer Loses Big Bonus over Kin, Phone, Tablet Failures," *Computerworld,* October 1, 2010, https://www.computerworld.com/article/2469355/mobile-apps /microsoft-s-ballmer-loses-big-bonus-over-kin--phone--tablet-failures. html.
people working together: Ziegler, "Life and Death of Microsoft Kin."
edging it out: Derek Thompson, "Why Steve Ballmer Failed," *At- lantic,* August 23, 2013, https://www.theatlantic.com/business/archive /2013/08/why-steve-ballmer-failed/278986/.

135 *he said at the time:* "Ballmer Laughs at iPhone," YouTube, September 18, 2007, https://www.youtube.com/watch?v=eywi0h_Y5_U.
"think they have to use": Derek Thompson, "Why Steve Ballmer Failed."
"very different from Ballmer": Nicholas Thompson, "Why Steve Ballmer Failed," *The New Yorker,* August 23, 2013, https://www .newyorker.com/business/currency/why-steve-ballmer-failed.
"people-centric" IT: Charles Cooper, "Satya Nadella Promises Cus- tomers a 'People-Centric IT,'" CNET, February 4, 2014, https://www.cnet .com/news/satya-nadella-promises-customers-a-people-centric-it.

136 *"And its culture":* Matt Weinberger, "Satya Nadella: 'Customer Love' Is a Better Sign of Success Than Revenue or Profit," Business Insider, October 7, 2015, http://www.businessinsider.com/microsoft-ceo-satya -nadella-on-culture-2015-10.

work of Frederick Winslow Taylor: Frederick Winslow Taylor, *The Principles of Scientific Management* (New York: Harper & Brothers, 1911).

optimize workers' behavior: Sarah O'Connor, "When Your Boss Is an Algorithm," *Financial Times,* September 8, 2016, https://www.ft.com /content/88fdc58e-754f-11e6-b60a-de4532d5ea35.

137 *every voice might matter:* Rita Gunther McGrath, *The End of Competitive Advantage: How to Keep Your Strategy Moving as Fast as Your Business* (Boston: Harvard Business Review Press, 2013).

"bring things together": Simon London, "Microsoft's Next Act," podcast, April 2018, *McKinsey Quarterly,* https://www.mckinsey.com /industries/high-tech/our-insights/microsofts-next-act.

"from these trips": Andrew Nusca, "The Man Who Is Transforming Microsoft," *Fortune,* November 11, 2016, http://fortune.com/satya -nadella-microsoft-ceo.

"fixed mindset": Satya Nadella, Greg Shaw, and Jill Tracie Nichols, *Hit Refresh: The Quest to Rediscover Microsoft's Soul and Imagine a Better Future for Everyone* (New York: HarperCollins, 2017).

getting better: Carol Dweck, *Mindset: The New Psychology of Success* (New York: Random House, 2007).

"spectacular": Harry McCracken, "Satya Nadella Rewrites Microsoft's Code," *Fast Company,* September 18, 2017, https://www.fastcompany .com/40457458/satya-nadella-rewrites-microsofts-code.

138 *"in a constrained world":* Nusca, "The Man Who Is Transforming Microsoft."

"there's the quest": Adam Bryant, "Satya Nadella, Chief of Microsoft, on His New Role," *New York Times,* February 20, 2014, https://www .nytimes.com/2014/02/21/business/satya-nadella-chief-of-microsoft-on -his-new-role.html.

139 *over $8.6 billion:* Gregg Keizer, "Microsoft's Enterprise Phone Strategy Flops as Revenue Evaporates," *Computerworld,* May 1, 2017, https:// www.computerworld.com/article/3193644/microsofts-enterprise -phone-strategy-flops-as-revenue-evaporates.html.

"to achieve more": Bryant, "Satya Nadella."

books for the blind: McCracken, "Satya Nadella Rewrites Microsoft's Code," https://www.fastcompany.com/40457458/satya-nadella-rewrites -microsofts-code.

140 *"Microsoft had built up":* Ibid.

"inside of Redmond": Ibid.

"strong supporter ever since": Ibid.

141 *had passed Microsoft by:* Nick Wingfield, "A $7 Billion Charge at Microsoft Leads to Its Largest Loss Ever," *New York Times,* July 21, 2015,

https://www.nytimes.com/2015/07/22/technology/microsoft-earnings
-q4.html.

"now I love it": Liam Tung, "Ballmer: I May Have Called Linux a Cancer but Now I Love It," ZDNet, March 11, 2016, https://www.zdnet.com
/article/ballmer-i-may-have-called-linux-a-cancer-but-now-i-love-it/.

"I am with you": McCracken, "Satya Nadella Rewrites Microsoft's Code."

142 *"profit by segment"*: McGrath, *The End of Competitive Advantage.*

7. HOW INNOVATION PROFICIENCY DEFANGS
THE ORGANIZATIONAL ANTIBODIES

144 *"they practice it"*: Peter Drucker, *Innovation and Entrepreneurship* (New York: Harper & Row, 1985).

145 *steel business worldwide:* OECD Steel Committee, "Presentation for the Council Working Party on Shipbuilding," July 9, 2009, https://www
.oecd.org/sti/ind/43312347.pdf.

"negative market trend": "Klöckner & Co SE," Boersengefluester, July 8, 2013, https://boersengefluester.de/newarticle/?newsId=13529.

146 *"A Global Perspective"*: World Economic Forum, "Fostering Innovation-Driven Entrepreneurship: A Global Perspective" (private session, Dalian, China, September 11, 2013), http://www3.weforum.org/docs
/AMNC13/WEF_AMNC13_FosteringInnovationDrivenEntrepreneurs
hip_SessionSummary.pdf.

had gone mainstream: Sangeet Paul Choudary, "The Billion Dollar Startup Disruption," Medium, May 30, 2013, https://medium.com/@
sanguit/the-billion-dollar-startup-disruption-67d82e91281f.

147 *"where we started"*: Gisbert Rühl, "From Steel Distributor to Digital Industry Platform," YouTube, December 10, 2015, https://www.youtube
.com/watch?v=RJrKjxsze0s.

industries they had touched: "It Will Revolutionize the Entire Industry," Vodafone Institute, n.d., https://www.vodafone-institut.de/event
/will-revolutionize-entire-industry.

148 *metals service center:* Gisbert Rühl, "Disrupting the Steel Industry Through Platforms," SlidesLive, May 8, 2018, https://slideslive.com
/38907723/disrupting-the-steel-industry-through-platforms.

149 *new approach was necessary:* Gisbert Rühl, "We Want to Revolutionise the Industry," interview by Hansjörg Honegger, Swisscom, October 16, 2017, https://www.swisscom.ch/en/business/enterprise/themen
/digital-business/digitalisierung-im-stahlhandel.html.

"minimum viable product": Eric Ries, *The Lean Startup: How Today's Entrepreneurs Use Continuous Innovation to Create Radically Successful Businesses* (New York: Crown Business, 2011).

150 *disappointing results:* Alex Moazed, "Why GE Digital Failed," *Inc.,* January 8, 2018, https://www.inc.com/alex-moazed/why-ge-digital -didnt-make-it-big.html.

151 *"non-hierarchical communication":* Klöckner & Co., "Annual General Meeting 2017" (presentation, Düsseldorf, May 12, 2017), https://www .kloeckner.com/dam/kco/files/en/investors/annua-general-meeting /2017/Kloeckner_Co_presentation_AGM2017.pdf.
"Fuck-up nights": Klöckner & Co., "Leading the Digital Transfor-mation of Metal Distribution" (presentation, December 2017), https:// www.kloeckner-i.com/wp-content/uploads/2017/12/Kloeckner_Co_ Digitalization_December-2017.pdf.

152 *"more agile overall":* Rühl, "We Want to Revolutionise the Industry."
profitability and growth: Martin Wocher, "A Metal Marketplace," *Handelsblatt Today,* July 11, 2017, https://global.handelsblatt.com /companies/a-metal-marketplace-795869.

153 *useful tools and perspectives:* Scott D. Anthony, Clark G. Gilbert, and Mark W. Johnson, *Dual Transformation: How to Reposition Today's Business While Creating the Future* (Cambridge: Harvard Business Re-view Press, 2017).

158 *Steve Blank and Bob Dorf:* Steve Blank and Bob Dorf, *The Startup Owner's Manual: The Step-by-Step Guide for Building a Great Company* (Pescadero, CA: K & S Ranch, 2012).
Alexander Osterwalder and Yves Pigneur: Alexander Osterwalder and Yves Pigneur, *Business Model Generation* (Hoboken, NJ: John Wiley & Sons, 2010).
Ian MacMillan and Zenas Block: Zenas Block and Ian C. MacMillan, *Corporate Venturing: Creating New Businesses Within the Firm* (Boston: Harvard Business School Press, 1993).

159 *Clay Christensen and the Innosight folks:* Scott D. Anthony, *The Lit-tle Black Book of Innovation: How It Works, How to Do It* (Boston: Har-vard Business Review Press, 2011); Clayton M. Christensen, Scott D. Anthony, and Erik A. Roth, *Seeing What's Next: Using the Theories of In-novation to Predict Industry Change* (Boston: Harvard Business School Press, 2004); Clayton Christensen, David S. Duncan, and Taddy Hall, *Competing Against Luck: The Story of Innovation and Customer Choice* (New York: Harper Business, 2016).
Cindy Alvarez: Cindy Alvarez, *Lean Customer Development: Build Products Your Customers Will Buy,* The Lean Series, ed. Eric Ries (Sebas-topol, CA: O'Reilly Media, 2014).
Curtis Carlson: Curtis Carlson, interview with author, January 10, 2019.
and me: Rita Gunther McGrath and Ian C. MacMillan, *The Entre-*

preneurial Mindset: Strategies for Continuously Creating Opportunity in an Age of Uncertainty (Boston: Harvard Business School Press, 2000). *(tomorrow's business):* Rita Gunther McGrath, Alexander B. van Putten, and Ron Pierantozzi, "Does Wall Street Buy Your Growth Story? For How Long?," *Strategy & Leadership* 46, no. 2 (2108): 3–10.

160 *an incentive for action:* Rita Gunther McGrath and Ian C. Mac-Millan, *Discovery-Driven Growth: A Breakthrough Process to Reduce Risk and Seize Opportunity* (Boston: Harvard Business Review Press, 2009).

opportunity portfolio analysis: Nancy Tennant Snyder, *Unleashing Innovation: How Whirlpool Transformed an Industry,* ed. D. L. Duarte (San Francisco: Jossey-Bass, 2008).

no consumer found exciting: McGrath and MacMillan, *Discovery-Driven Growth.*

162 *the rest is history:* Meg Godlewski, "How Skunk Works Got Its Name," *General Aviation News,* November 4, 2005, https://generalaviationnews.com/2005/11/04/how-skunk-works-got-its-name.

The Soul of a New Machine: Tracy Kidder, *The Soul of a New Machine* (Thorndike, ME: Thorndike Press, 1981).

continuous innovation: Steve Blank, "Why Corporate Skunk Works Need to Die," *Forbes,* November 10, 2014, https://www.forbes.com/sites/steveblank/2014/11/10/why-corporate-skunk-works-need-to-die/#498e6ea83792.

"customer discovery" process: Steven G. Blank, *The Four Steps to the Epiphany: Successful Strategies for Products That Win* (Foster City, CA: Cafepress.com, 2006).

165 *in other assets:* William Lazonick, "Profits Without Prosperity," *Harvard Business Review,* September 2014.

8. HOW LEADERSHIP CAN AND MUST
LEARN TO SEE AROUND CORNERS

167 *"the pressure skyrockets":* Thomas Kolditz, email communication with author, December 29, 2018.

169 *at work all day:* Sally Helgesen, *The Female Advantage: Women's Ways of Leadership,* 1st ed. (New York: Doubleday, 1990); Henry Mintzberg, *The Nature of Managerial Work* (New York: Harper & Row, 1973).

170 *rather than hierarchies:* Helgesen, *The Female Advantage.*

172 *"and pre-funding":* Gail Goodman, "Founders Can't Scale: Gail Goodman at TEDxBeaconStreet," YouTube, December 6, 2013, https://www.youtube.com/watch?v=0NzBgfyRbho. Unless otherwise noted, all the quotes from Goodman in this section are from this talk or from Gail Goodman, "How to Negotiate the Long, Slow, SaaS Ramp of Death"

(address, Business of Software USA 2012), blog post by Mark T. Little-
wood, February 26, 2013, https://businessofsoftware.org/2013/02/gail
-goodman-constant-contact-how-to-negotiate-the-long-slow-saas-ramp
-of-death/.

173 *"use your resources more effectively":* Gail Goodman, interview with
author, September 13, 2018.

174 *"team alignment and prioritization":* Ibid.

175 The Advantage: Patrick Lencioni, *The Advantage* (San Francisco:
Jossey-Bass, 2012).

177 *"get it right":* Ibid.

178 *different approaches to leadership:* L. J. Bourgeois and David R.
Brodwin, "Strategic Implementation: Five Approaches to an Elusive Phenomenon," *Strategic Management Journal* 5, no. 3 (1984): 241–64.

179 *"previously inconceivable":* "Everything We Do Starts by Blending
the Sciences with the Humanities, the Robots with the Pencils," Robots &
Pencils, n.d., http://www.robotsandpencils.com/#expertise.
"new and frontier technologies": Ibid.
"benefit our clients": Ibid.

181 *"state of global capitalism":* Andrew Ross Sorkin, "World's Biggest
Investor Tells C.E.O.s Purpose Is the 'Animating Force' for Profits," *New
York Times,* January 27, 2019, https://www.nytimes.com/2019/01/17
/business/dealbook/blackrock-larry-fink-letter.html.
community creation: Steve Denning, "Resisting the Lure of
Short-Termism: Kill 'the World's Dumbest Idea,'" *Forbes,* January 8, 2017, https://www.forbes.com/sites/stevedenning/2017/01/08
/resisting-the-lure-of-short-termism-how-to-achieve-long-term-growth
/#6e5f03931ca0.
Martin Wolf of the Financial Times: Martin Wolf, "The Long and
Painful Journey to World Disorder," *Financial Times,* January 5, 2017,
https://www.ft.com/content/ef13e61a-ccec-11e6-b8ce-b9c03770f8b1.
what happens to companies: William Lazonick, "Profits Without
Prosperity," *Harvard Business Review,* September 2014.
management teams and boards: "BlackRock Investment Stew-
ardship's Approach to Engagement on Human Capital Management," BlackRock, March 2018, https://www.blackrock.com/corporate
/literature/publication/blk-commentary-engagement-on-human-cap
ital-march2018.pdf.

182 *work on strategic inflection points:* Andrew S. Grove, "Navigating
Strategic Inflection Points," *Business Strategy Review* 8, no. 3 (1997): 11–
18.
could be significant: See, for example, Ram Charan, "Conquering a
Culture of Indecision," *Harvard Business Review,* April 2001; Don Sull,

The Upside of Turbulence: Seizing Opportunity in an Uncertain World (New York: Harper Business, 2009); and Nassim Nicholas Taleb, *Antifragile Things That Gain from Disorder* (New York: Random House, 2012).

"not at risk": Taleb, *Antifragile Things.*

183 *"regardless of their seniority"*: Stanley McChrystal, with Tantum Collins, David Silverman, and Chris Fussell, *Team of Teams: New Rules of Engagement for a Complex World* (New York: Portfolio/Penguin, 2015).

"objectives you do": Adam Pisoni, "What Startups Can Learn from General McChrystal About Combining Strategy and Execution," First Round Review, n.d., http://firstround.com/review/what-startups -can-learn-from-general-mcchrystal-about-combining-strategy-and -execution/.

184 *"heavy digital component"*: Columbia Entrepreneurship, "@sgblank, @rgmcgrath, & @HarperCollins on Corp Innovation: Refactoring the Crazies," YouTube, January 23, 2017, https://www.youtube.com/watch ?v=i2bvNB5G_eQ&feature=youtu.be.

meticulously documented: Bryce G. Hoffman, *American Icon: Alan Mulally and the Fight to Save Ford Motor Company* (New York: Crown, 2012).

185 *"putting together a plan"*: Dinah Eng, "How Maxine Clark Built Build-A-Bear," *Fortune*, March 16, 2012, http://archive.fortune. com/2012/03/16/smallbusiness/build-bear-maxine-clark.fortune /index.htm.

186 *"we will make it happen"*: Veneta Rizvic, "Life in Balance: Sharon Price John Solves Work Challenges by Running," *St. Louis Business Journal*, October 26, 2018, https://www.bizjournals.com/stlouis /news/2018/10/26/life-in-balance-sharon-price-john-solves-work .html.

187 *nonetheless fail*: Phil Rosenzweig, *The Halo Effect . . . and the Eight Other Business Delusions That Deceive Managers* (New York: Free Press, 2007); Annie Duke, *Thinking in Bets: Making Smarter Decisions When You Don't Have All the Facts* (New York: Portfolio/Penguin, 2018).

188 *"peacetime" leaders*: Ben Horowitz, *The Hard Thing About Hard Things: Building a Business When There Are No Easy Answers* (New York: Harper Business, 2014).

leadership in crisis: Thomas Kolditz, *In Extremis Leadership: Leading as Though Your Life Depended on It* (New York: John Wiley and Sons, 2007).

"how they were different": Jena McGregor, "The Extreme Leadership That Got the Thai Soccer Boys out of the Cave Alive," *Washington Post*, July 10, 2018, https://www.washingtonpost.com/news/on-leadership

/wp/2018/07/10/the-extreme-leadership-that-got-the-thai-soccer-boys
-out-of-the-cave/?utm_term=.930a16f8d991.

189 *"deny the possibility of failure"*: Kolditz, *In Extremis Leadership*.

"I've got your back": Justin Bariso, "Microsoft's CEO Sent an Extraordinary Email to Employees After They Committed an Epic Fail," *Inc.*,
February 23, 2017, https://www.inc.com/justin-bariso/microsofts-ceo
-sent-an-extraordinary-email-to-employees-after-they-committed-an
-.html.

190 *"demands of wartime"*: Kolditz, email communication with author.

9. SEEING AROUND CORNERS IN YOUR OWN LIFE

191 *"more desirable direction"*: Eric C. Sinoway, *Howard's Gift: Uncom-
mon Wisdom to Inspire Your Life's Work* (New York: St. Martin's Press,
2012).

194 *"joint ventures"*: "Our Story," Parliament, n.d., https://www.parliamen
tinc.com/conspire/.

195 *"Stakeholder Centered Coaching"*: "Guaranteeing Measurable Results
in Leadership Development on a Global Scale," Marshal Goldsmith
Stakeholder Centered Coaching, n.d., https://sccoaching.com/.

197 *"'not big enough'"*: David Gelles, "Living as an Example of 'Leading
by Example,'" *New York Times*, January 6, 2019.

198 *"tours of duty"*: Reid Hoffman, Ben Casnocha, and Chris Yeh, "Tours
of Duty," *Harvard Business Review*, June 2013.

not comfortable with: David Egan, "Here Is What It Takes to Become a CEO, According to 12,000 LinkedIn Profiles," *Talent Blog*, Linked
In, https://business.linkedin.com/talent-solutions/blog/trends-and
-research/2018/what-12000-ceos-have-in-common.

199 *"run something important"*: Neil Irwin, "A Winding Path to the Top,"
New York Times, September 10, 2016.

"what I wanted to do": Ryan McManus, interview with author, December 6, 2018. All the quotes from McManus in this section are from
this interview.

201 *high-powered lawyer:* Paula Davis-Laack, "I Used Design Thinking
to Reinvent My Career: Here's Why It Worked," *Fast Company*, October 16, 2017, https://www.fastcompany.com/40481175/i-used-design
-thinking-to-reinvent-my-career-heres-why-it-worked.

202 *Netflix Insider for a time:* Harry McCracken, "How Microsoft's Satya
Nadella Became a Netflix Insider," *Fast Company*, September 18, 2017,
https://www.fastcompany.com/40469252/how-microsofts-satya-nad
ella-became-a-netflix-insider.

205 *"never planned to"*: Clayton Christensen, "How Will You Measure

Your Life?," TedxBoston, 2012, https://tedxboston.org/speaker/chris tensen-1.

"you want to be": Drake Baer, "Clayton Christensen's Personal Quest to Help You Measure Your Life," *Fast Company*, May 18, 2012, https://www.fastcompany.com/1837732/clayton-christensens-personal-quest -help-you-measure-your-life.

207 *"actionable plan"*: Matthew Brodsky, "Alum 'AMP'ed' to Support Education," *Wharton Magazine*, October 6, 2015, http://whartonmagazine .com/blogs/alum-amped-to-support-education/#sthash.fWUNKSXY .dpbs.

ACKNOWLEDGMENTS

213 *"No One Notices"*: Morgan Housel, "When You Change the World and No One Notices," Collaborative Fund, September 3, 2016, http://www .collaborativefund.com/blog/when-you-change-the-world-and-no-one -notices/.

Index

Page numbers in italics refer to figures.

Abraham, Jack, 30
acceleration, 125
actions, staggered, 104–8
Acton, Brian, 21
addiction, Facebook, 23
Adobe, Kickbox program, 31–32
The Advantage (Lencioni), 175
advertising. *See also* privacy
   digital tracking, 18–19, 25
   discovery-driven planning,
     114–17
   discriminatory, 20
   evolution of digital, 105–6
AdWords (Google), 105–6
Aereo, 35
Aetna, 170
agile methodology, 29–31, 38, 112–
   13. *See also* discovery-driven
   planning
AI (artificial intelligence), 141
Airbnb, 146
Allard, J, 130–34
Allen, James, 30
Allgood, Greg, 121
Alvarez, Cindy, 159
Amazon
   agile decision-making, 29–30
   competition from, 25
   privacy, 19
   Web Services, 146
America Online (AOL), 41
Andreessen, Marc, 198

Anthony, Scott, 36, 153
*Antifragile: Things That Gain from
   Disorder* (Taleb), 103–4
Antioco, John, 82–83
antitrust allegations, 23–25
AOL (America Online), 41
Apatoff, Robert S., 35–36
apparel industry, 71–75
Apple
   AirPods, 5
   iPhones, 132, 133
   Siri, 19
apprenticeships, 59
arena-based analysis, 10, 208. *See
   also* customers
   attribute map lens, 88
   changes in conditions, 192–93
   changing customer needs,
     71–75
   constraints, 91–94, 152–53
   consumption chain lens, 88
   customer motivation lens, 88
   non-consumer businesses, 76
   response to market share loss,
     69–71
   signs of decline, 65–67
   strategies, 67–69, 100
article from the future exercises,
   206–8
artificial intelligence (AI), 141
Atria, 79
AT&T, 89

attributes
  maps, 88
  negative, 56–62, 82–83, 87, 91–94,
      100, 166
  types, *67*
automotive industry, 107
Azure (Microsoft), 140

Bach, Robbie, 133
Bain & Company, 30
Ballmer, Steve, 43, 48, 133–35, 141
Barnard College, 167–69
BBC Digital Media Initiative,
      109–13
benchmarks, 103, 111–12, 121–25
Berkshire Hathaway, 94
Berners-Lee, Tim, 21–22
Bertolini, Mark, 170
Bezos, Jeff
  healthcare venture, 95, 99
  seeing inflection points, 81, 171
  type 1/type 2 decisions, 29–30
  unchangeables, 63
Bid Manager, 116–17
Biden, Joe, 113–14
Bird (scooter company), 94
Bisping, Todd, 99
BlackRock, 180–82
Blank, Steve
  customer discovery, 162
  on "get out of the building," 32,
      119–20, 196
  on Microsoft, 43, 48
  on skunk works, 162
  as thought leader, 158
Block, Zenas, 158
Blockbuster, 78, 81–83, 88
Boeing, 196
Bourgeois, Jay, 178
Boyd, Danah, 22, 183
Brand Takeover exercise, 34
Breeggemann, Hank, 86
bricolage, 199–201

Britt, Joe, 131
Brodwin, David, 178
Brown, Tim, 67
bubbles, 8
Buffalo Wild Wings, 160
Buffett, Warren, 94, 95, 99
Build-A-Bear Workshop, 169,
      185–87
building block exercise, 205
business models, 107–8
"Business Research and Chinese
      Patriotic Poetry" (Harmon), 61

Cambridge Analytica, 21
cameras, 91
cancer research, 113–19
career trajectories, 198–201, 209
Carlson, Curtis, 159
Cassandras. *See* forecasting;
      information gathering
Caterpillar, 98–99
CEMEX, 106
Center for Humane Technology, 23
change. *See also* edges
  in arena conditions, 192–93
  in consumption chains, 68–73,
      76–81
  forecasting, 36–38
  slow pace, 62–63
  what won't, 63–64
  willingness of customers to, 83–86
Chaos Monkeys (Martínez), 24
Charan, Ram, 182
checkpoints, 103, 111–12, 121–25
China, 24
Christensen, Clayton, 61, 62, 159,
      200
Cigna Corp., 96, 97
Citi Bike, 94
civil rights violations, 20. *See also*
      privacy
claims business models, 108
Clark, Maxine, 185

clothing industry, 71–75
Coles, Dominic, 112–13
collaboration
  executives, 172–77
  Mulally's principles, 184–85
  non-hierarchical communication,
    28, 151, 165–66, 170, 180
  strategic planning, 9–10
  support of development teams,
    131–36, 184–85
  talent reallocation, 163–64
Columbia Business School, 168,
  204–5
Comcast, 89
"command-and-control" mindset, 11,
  170, 175–76, 183, 189
communication
  bad news to leadership, 34–36,
    171, 175–76, 182–83
  executive isolation, 27–28
  non-hierarchical, 28, 151, 165–66,
    170, 180
company culture
  alignment around, 127–28, 171,
    175–76
  people-centric, 135–36
  resiliency, 136–38
  shared risk, 189
Constant Contact, 172–77
constraints
  arena-based analysis, 91–94,
    152–53
  customers, 10
  innovation, 152–55, 166
  internal, 154–55
consumption chains. *See also*
  customers
  changes, 68–73, 76–81
  definition, 88
context analysis, 160
cookies, 16–17
credentialing, 56–62
crises, 145–46, 187–90

culture, company
  alignment around, 127–28, 171,
    175–76
  people-centric, 135–36
  resiliency, 136–38
  shared risk, 189
current indicators, 45–46, 64
customers. *See also* arena-based
  analysis
  changing needs, 71–75
  connecting with, 135–36, 150,
    177
  constraints, 10
  consumption patterns, 68–73,
    78–81
  data collection, 14–19
  discovery, 162
  exploitation of, 94–99
  "get out of the building"
    leadership, 32–34, 38, 131–36
  keeping, 89–90
  leading indicators, 177
  motivations, 85–86, 88, 90–94,
    100
  pain points, 56–62, 82–83, 87,
    91–94, 100, 166
  satisfaction, 48
  willingness to change, 83–86
CVS Health, 96

Danger (technology company),
  131–33
Dash, Anil, 29
data. *See also* metrics; surveillance
  capitalism
  acquisition of, 14–21, 140–41
  combining databases, 15–16
  in discovery-driven planning,
    113–19
  energy-use, 46
  looking for inflection points in, 141
  revenue, 45
Davis-Laack, Paula, 201–2

decline
    changing customer needs, 71–75
    early warning signs, 65–69
    response to, 69–71
    separation of operations from
        growth, 83–89, 100
degree inflation, 57–59
#DeleteFacebook campaign, 21
Deloitte, 110
denial, 35–36, 38
Denning, Steve, 61
DeSalvo, Chris, 132
"Design for Action" (Brown and
        Martin), 67
design thinking, 10, 67–71, 202–3,
        209. *See also* discovery-driven
        planning
Deutsche Telekom, 132
development, inflection point, 7–9
Digital Dozen, 36–37, 197
Digital Media Initiative (DMI),
        109–13
Digital Storytelling Lab, 36–37,
        197
digitization
    definition, 104
    evolution, 42, 105–8, 200–201
    health records, 118–19
    innovation, 123–25, 147–52
    publishing industry, 183–84
    steel industry, 147–52
DiLandro, Christine, 18
Dimon, Jamie, 95, 99
discovery-driven planning, 1, 208
    caveats, 101–2
    learning from failures, 108–13
    practices, 119–25, 126
    staggering actions, 104–8
    timing, 104, 125
    using data, 113–19
dismissive stage, 8–9
Disney Studios, 89
Disrupting Class (Christensen), 61

disruption, 2
    hearing aid industry, 2–6
distribution business models,
        107–8
diversity
    degree requirements, 58
    importance of, 28–29, 38
dollar flow, 115
Dollar Shave Club, 69
Donahoe, John, 30
Dorf, Bob, 158
Dual Transformation (Anthony, et
        al.), 153
Dweck, Carol, 137

early warning signs
    customer pain points, 56–62
    decline, 65–69
    freedom to signal strength ratio,
        49–51
    ignoring, 26–27, 34–36, 183
    importance, 39
    indicators, 44–49
    optimum warning period, 51
    time zero event identification,
        51–56, 64
    weak, 40–43, 62–63, 208–9
    what won't change, 63–64
eBay, 30
ecosystems, 42
edges, 9, 208
    agile processes, 29–31
    candor, 34–36, 182–83
    customer connections, 27–28
    definition, 26
    diversity, 28–29
    forecasting, 36–37
    "get out of the building," 32–34,
        38, 131–36, 196–97
    little bets, 31–32
    personal, 191–97, 209
    styles of, 27–28, 38
Edmonson, Amy, 48

education
  alternatives, 56–57, 59–61
  degree inflation, 57–59
  universities, 61–62
emergent stage, 9
employees. *See* management
  empowerment of, 28, 30, 38,
    139–42
  innovation training, 158–59
  listening to, 112, 127–29, 137–38,
    143, 183
  non-hierarchical communication,
    28, 151, 165–66, 170, 180
  shielding management, 32–34
  training, 151
The End of Competitive Advantage
  (McGrath), 66
energy industry, 53–56, 76
energy-use data, 46
Enron, 34–35, 81
Enron Broadband Services (EBS),
  81
entrepreneurs. *See also* innovation
  networking, 119–20, 126
  practices of habitual, 126
Equinor (was Statoil), 76
experimentation. *See also* innovation
  design thinking, 10, 67–71
  fun, 179–80
  learning from failure, 10, 108–13,
    151, 152–54
  little bets, 31–32, 38, 103, 125
Express Scripts Holding Co., 96

Facebook
  challenges to, 23–25
  data acquisition, 16–21
  decision making at, 30–31
  emotional impacts of, 22–23
  executive isolation, 27–28, 32–34
  ignoring early warnings, 26–27,
    34–36, 183
  lack of diversity, 28–29

  little bets, 31
  "move fast and break things,"
    30–31
  News Feed feature, 22
  reach, 146
failure
  learning from, 10, 108–13, 151,
    152–54
  proof of concept, 161–62
  response to market share loss,
    69–71
fast fashion, 75
Fathom, 57
FDA (Food and Drug
  Administration), 3–4, 5, 118
feedback
  bad news to leadership, 34–36,
    171, 175–76, 182–83
  leading through, 175–76
  personal, 195–96, 209
Fink, Larry, 180–82
first-mover advantage, 148
Flatiron Health, 114–19, 202
Food and Drug Administration
  (FDA), 3–4, 5, 118
forecasting, 9, 208. *See also*
  discovery-driven planning
  personal, 196–97, 203–9
  scenario planning, 52–56
  SPARK (See it, Plan it, Action
    it, Repeat it, Keep the faith),
    186–87
  spotting change, 36–38
  starting from future focus, 149
freedom, to adjust, 49–51, 64
front-line employees
  empowerment of, 28, 30, 38,
    139–42
  listening to, 112, 127–29, 137–38,
    143, 183
  shielding management, 32–34
Fuller, Joseph, 58
FunLabs, 179–80

future thinking. *See* forecasting
Futures Strategy Group (was Futures
 Group), 49

Gap, 33
Gartner Hype Cycle, 8, 43
Gates, Bill, 43, 130–31
GDPR (General Data Protection
 Regulation), 23–24
GE (General Electric), 150
General Electric (GE), 150
Gerstner, Lou, 28, 182
"get out of the building"
 consequences of failing to, 134–35
 customer discovery, 32–34, 38
 empathy, 135–36
 personal applications, 196–97,
  209
Ghosn, Carlos, 187–88
Gibson, William Ford, 36, 98
Gilbert, Clark, 153
Gillette, 69–71
goals
 alignment, 170, 174
 clarity, 138–39, 175, 180–82
 elements, 9–10
 intersection with technology,
  200
Goldsmith, Marshall, 169, 184,
 195–96
Goodman, Gail, 172–77, 183, 195
GoodRx, 97
Google
 AdWords, 105–6
 Amazon as competitor, 25
 purchase of Bid Manager, 116–17
 radio, 161
 regulations, 13, 20
Gottlieb, Scott, 118
Gratton, Lynda, 62
green energy, 53–56, 76
Grove, Andy, 1, 9, 14, 52, 182, 188,
 192

growth mindset, 137–38
growth stalls, 65

Haas Act of 1937, 91–92
Hanson, Kaaren, 120
The Hard Thing About Hard Things
 (Horowitz), 188
Harmon, Michael, 61
HarperCollins, 183
Hastings, Reed, 78–79, 84–86,
 88–89, 202
Health Transformation Alliance, 99
healthcare industry, 94–99, 113–19
hearing aids, 2–6
Helgesen, Sally, 169–70
Hershenson, Matt, 131
higher education
 alternatives, 56–57, 59–61
 degree inflation, 57–59
 universities, 61–62
Highfield, Ashley, 110
Hit Refresh (Nadella), 137, 139
Hoffman, Reid, 198
HoloLens (Microsoft), 140
Home Depot, 30
Horowitz, Ben, 188
How Women Rise (Helgesen and
 Goldsmith), 169
hybrid jobs, 199
Hype Cycle, 8, 43

IBM, 28
ideation, 162–63
Imagination Premium, 159–60
In Extremis Leadership (Kolditz), 188
incentives
 consumption-based, 142
 helpful *vs.* harmful, 34–35, 38
 realignment, 95–98
income share agreements (ISA),
 60–61
incumbents, negative attributes of,
 82–83, 87

indicators
  building into incentives, 142, 143
  current, 45–46, 64
  lagging, 44–45, 64
  leading, 46–47, 64, 142–43, 177,
    197, 208
  outcomes and, 47–49
Inditex, 75
inflection points. *See also* early
    warning signs
  arena-based analysis, 65–77, 88,
    94, 100, 152–53, 192–93
  customer indicators, 78–100
  definition, 1
  development, 7–9
  discovery-driven planning, 1,
    101–26
  employee empowerment, 139–42
  information gathering, 9, 13–38
  innovation, 144–66
  leadership, 10–11, 127–43
  leadership models, 167–90
  leveraging, 9–10
  matching inside to outside,
    152–54
  negative, 65
  personal, 11, 191–209
  stages, 64
  use of, 208–9
information gathering, 9
  agile processes, 29–31
  candor, 34–36, 182–83
  challenges to, 23–25
  customer connections, 27–28
  diversity, 28–29
  forecasting, 36–37
  "get out of the building," 32–34,
    38, 131–36, 196–97
  little bets, 31–32
  online tracking, 15–19
  social media, 19–23
  styles of, 27–28, 38
  surveillance capitalism, 14–19

Infosys, 47
Innosight, 36, 159
innovation. *See also* leadership
  constraints, 152–55, 166
  design thinking, 10, 67–71
  digitization, 122–25, 147–52
  from failure, 152–54
  fostering, 31–32, 38, 125, 170–72
  fun, 179–80
  legacy IT, 149–50
  organizational systems, 10
  problem-focused *vs.* solution-
    focused, 120–21, 126
  women, 167–70
innovation proficiency
  building, 154–56, 165–66,
    208–9
  level challenges, 158–65
  scale, 155, 156–58
innovation theater, 125, 156
Instagram, 25
insurance industry, 107–8
Internet. *See also* social media
  data collection, 14–21, 140–41
  evolution, 40–43
  impact on teen market, 71–75
  online education, 57
  predicted effects of, 21–22
  regulations, 13, 20, 23–25
Internet tracking, 15–18
Invite Media, 114–15
iPhones, 132, 133
iterative processes, 10, 67–71, 202–3,
    209. *See also* discovery-driven
    planning

Jet.com, 154
jobs to be done
  changing customer needs, 71–75
  customer motivations, 85–86, 88,
    90–94, 100
  lenses, 88
John, Sharon Price, 169, 185–87

Johnson, Mark, 153
Johnson, Peggy, 140

Kelley, Barbara, 2
Keyes, Jim, 83
Kickbox program, 31–32, 161
Kickstarter, 123–25
Kin (Microsoft), 129–36
Kipman, Alex, 140
Klöckner
   digitization, 147–52, 165–66
   restructuring, 145–46
Kolditz, Thomas, 188–90

lagging indicators, 44–45, 64
LaserDisc, 80
leadership. *See also* teams
   agile, 29–31, 38
   clarity of strategy, 138–39
   collaboration, 172–77
   "command-and-control" mindset,
      11, 170, 175–76, 183
   crescive, 178–87
   diversity of, 28–29, 38
   empowerment of employees, 28,
      30, 38, 139–42
   flexibility, 136–38
   "get out of the building," 32–34,
      38, 134–36
   incentives, 142
   inflection points, 10–11
   innovation theater, 125
   innovation training, 158–59
   isolation of, 27–28, 38
   listening to front-line employees,
      112, 127–29, 137–38, 143, 183
   non-hierarchical communication,
      28, 151, 165–66, 170, 180
   support of development teams,
      131–36, 184–85
   in uncertain times, 10–11
   using feedback, 175–76

wartime *vs.* peacetime, 187–90,
   209
women, 167–70
leading indicators
   building into incentives, 142, 143
   explanation of, 46–47, 64
   external focus, 177
   helpful, 208
   personal, 197
Lees, Andy, 133–34
legal challenges, 34–35
Lencioni, Patrick, 175
lenses, analytical, 88
level-skipping communication, 28,
   151, 165–66, 170, 180
lifeline exercise, 204–5
Lin, Frank, 3
LinkedIn, 140–41
LinkNYC, 29
Linux Foundation, 141
little bets, 31–32, 38, 103, 125, 208
Little Bets (Sims), 31, 194
Lore, Marc, 154
Lövgren, Pähr, 193–94
Lyft, 91

MacMillan, Ian, 115, 119, 158, 206
Mailchimp, 37
management. *See also* leadership
   agile, 29–31, 38
   executive collaboration, 172–77
   inflection points, 10–11
   isolation of, 27–28
   Mulally's principles, 184–85
   non-hierarchical communication,
      28, 151, 165–66, 170, 180
   peripheral information gathering,
      56
   strategic planning, 9–10
   support of development, 131–36,
      184–85
   talent reallocation, 163–64

Martin, Roger, 67
Martínez, Antonio García, 24
massive open online courses
    (MOOCs), 57
maturity stage, 9
McArdle, Megan, 92
McChrystal, Stanley, 170, 183
McCracken, Harry, 139
McGrath, Rita, 66, 159
McManus, Ryan, 104, 199–201
Megaron, 193
metrics
    consumption, 142
    helpful *vs.* harmful, 34–35, 38
    indicators, 44–49, 64, 142–43,
        177, 197
Microsoft
    company culture, 127–28, 135–36,
        171, 189
    Kin mobile phone, 129–36
    overlooking trends, 43
    Vista operating system, 134–35
Microsoft Band, 141
mindset, 137
MOOCs (massive open online
    courses), 57
"More Plugged-In Than Preppy," 73
Morfit, G. Mason, 140
Mulally, Alan, 170, 182, 184–85, 196
Murray, Brian, 183–84

Nadella, Satya
    company culture, 127–28, 135–36,
        171, 189
    customer focus, 177
    employee empowerment, 139–42
    leading indicators, 48
    learning from Netflix, 140, 202
National Cancer Moonshot, 114
Netflix
    vs. Blockbuster, 81–83
    competition, 88–89

    influence on Microsoft, 140
    origin, 78–80
    switch to streaming, 83–88
networking
    entrepreneurial, 119–20, 126
    personal, 193–95, 209
Nissan, 187–88
noise, 49–51
Nokia, 26, 139, 141
non-hierarchical communication,
        28, 151, 165–66, 170, 180
Norway, 76

Obama, Barack, 114
Octobo, 123–25
Olson, Matthew, 65
Only the Paranoid Survive (Grove),
        1, 188
opportunity portfolio analysis, 160
optimum warning, 51
OptumRx, 96
Organisation for Economic Co-
        operation and Development,
        145
organizational systems, 10, 109–13
Osterwalder, Alexander, 158
outcomes
    indicators and, 47–49
    lagging indicators, 45

pain points
    early signs of inflections, 56–62
    identifying, 87–88
    as opportunities, 82–83, 91–94,
        100, 166
Palihapitiya, Chamath, 23
Parakilas, Sandy, 23
Parliament, 194–95
Payless ShoeSource, 185
PBMs (pharmacy benefit managers),
        96–99
"peacetime" CEOs, 187–90

personal inflection points
  connection to greater inflections,
    11
  finding edges, 191–97
  forecasting, 196–97, 203–9
  preparation, 198–203
personal sound amplification
    products (PSAPs), 4–6
personal story exercise, 205–6
Pfizer, 118
pharmacy benefit managers (PBMs),
    96–99
Pigneur, Yves, 158
planning, discovery-driven, 1
  caveats, 101–2
  learning from failures, 108–13
  practices, 119–25, 126
  staggering actions, 104–8
  timing, 104, 125
  using data, 113–19
prescription drugs, 94–99
pricing business models, 108
privacy
  consumer attitudes towards, 24
  data collection as invasion, 14–19
  regulations, 13, 20, 23–25
  rights to, 14–15
privilege, 28–29, 38
problem-focused planning, 120–21,
    126
Procter & Gamble, 121
product fatigue, 74
proficiency, innovation
  building, 154–56, 165–66
  level challenges, 158–65
  scale, 155, 156–58
Progressive, 108
proofs of concept, 161–62
prototypes, 202
PSAPs (personal sound amplification
    products), 4–6
PuR, 121

Pure Atria, 79
Pure Software, 79
Purohit, Sanjay, 47

qualitative indicators, 46–47
Quirky platform, 161
Qwikster, 85–86

rallying cries, 175
Raman, Manjari, 58
Rand McNally, 35–36
Randall, Mark, 31–32
Randolph, Marc, 78–79
regulation
  data collection, 13, 20, 23–25
  FDA clinical trials, 118
renewable energy, 53–56
resource pools. *See* arena-based
    analysis
Revlon, 161
ride-hailing companies, 91–94
Ries, Eric, 149
risk, shared, 189
The Road Ahead (Gates), 43
Robots & Pencils, 178–80
Rose, Frank, 36, 197
Rubin, Andy, 131, 133
Rühl, Gisbert
  aspirations, 144
  context analysis, 160
  digitization of steel supply chain,
    147–52
  inspiration, 197
  restructuring at Klöckner, 145–46
  step-by-step innovation, 165–66

SaaS (software as a service), 172–73
Saffo, Paul, 102
Sahlman, William, 8
Samba, 18–19
Say Media (was VideoEgg), 115
scalability, 162

scenario planning, 52–56, 209
Schumpeter, Joseph, 2
SDSS ("Stop doing stupid stuff"), 187
"See it, Plan it, Action it, Repeat
    it, Keep the faith" (SPARK),
    186–87
Shahani, Aarti, 34
Siemens, 110–11, 112
signal strength
    interpreting weak, 40–43, 62–63,
        208–9
    ratio to freedom, 49–51
signal-to-noise ratios, 49, 51
Sikorsky, Michael, 178–80
silos. *See also* "get out of the
    building"
    breaking down, 28, 151, 165–66,
        170, 180
    internally imposed constraints,
        154–55
Sims, Peter, 31, 103, 194
skepticism, 40–43
skill-based credentialing, 56–62
skunk works, 161–62
Slack, 180
smart devices
    early, 131–32
    impact on teen market, 71–75
    Microsoft Kin, 129–36
    privacy, 18–19
    shifting constraints, 90–91
Smith, Adam, 136
social media. *See also* Facebook
    blind spots, 13–14
    challenges to, 23–25
    emotional impacts of, 22–23
    fakes, 22
    impact on teen market, 71–75
    Instagram, 25
    LinkedIn, 140–41
    Twitter, 141
    warnings, 21–23

software as a service (SaaS), 172–73
solar energy, 53–56
solution-focused planning, 120–21,
    126
Solve Next, 34
Sorkin, Andrew Ross, 181
Soros, George, 21
Spar, Debora, 168–69
Sparapani, Tim, 15
SPARK ("See it, Plan it, Action it,
    Repeat it, Keep the faith"),
    186–87
stability, 63–64. *See also* change
stages, inflection point, 8–9
Stakeholder Centered Coaching,
    195–96
Statoil (now Equinor), 76
steel industry
    Great Recession of 2008, 145–48,
        165
    mini-mills, 61–62
    service centers, 144–45
    supply chain digitization, 147–52
Stevenson, Howard, 8
Stoll, Clifford, 40
"Stop doing stupid stuff" (SDSS),
    187
strategic inflection points. *See*
    inflection points
strategy
    alignment, 170, 174
    clarity, 138–39, 175, 180–82
    elements, 9–10
    intersection with technology,
        200
streaming media
    antecedents, 79–80
    customer influence, 82–87
    early inflection points, 81–82
Su, Yuting, 123–25
success, defining, 121–22
Sull, Don, 182

surveillance capitalism. *See also* data
   challenges to, 23–25
   combining databases, 15–16
   extent, 14–19
   financial value, 15
Sweet, Julia, 197, 199
systems, innovation, 163–65
Systrom, Kevin, 25

Take5 Solutions, 16
Taleb, Nassim Nicholas, 103–4, 122,
   182
taxi services, 91–92
Tay chatbot, 141, 189
Taylor, Frederick Winslow, 136
Team of Teams (McChrystal), 183
teams
   executive collaboration, 172–77
   Mulally's principles, 184–85
   non-hierarchical communication,
      28, 151, 165–66, 170, 180
   strategic planning, 9–10
   support of development, 131–36,
      184–85
   talent reallocation, 163–64
televisions, smart, 18
10X. *See* inflection points
Thinkers50 rankings, 62
Thinker-Tinker, 123–25
Thompson, Derek, 135
Time Warner, 41
time zero
   event identification, 51–56, 64
   freedom to signal strength ratio,
      49–51
timing
   of digitization, 104–8
   moving too early, 104
T-Mobile Sidekick, 131–32
toy industry, 122–25, 169, 185–87
Toys "R" Us, 123
triggers, inflection point, 7
Turner, Nat, 114–19, 193, 202

21st Century Cures Act of 2016, 114
Twitter, 141
type 1/type 2 decisions, 29–31, 38

Uber, 91–94
underwriting business models, 108
UnitedHealth Group, 96
universities. *See* higher education

value chains, 66
van Bever, Derek, 65
vantage points, monitoring, 9, 208
   agile processes, 29–31
   candor, 34–36, 182–83
   customer connections, 27–28
   definition, 26
   diversity, 28–29
   forecasting, 36–37
   "get out of the building," 32–34,
      38, 131–36, 196–97
   little bets, 31–32
   personal, 191–97, 209
   styles of, 27–28, 38
Verry, Seth, 65
VHS (Video Home System), 79
Victor Company, 79
Video Home System (VHS), 79
VideoEgg (now Say Media), 115
Vista operating system (Microsoft),
   134–35
VoiceStream Wireless, 132

Walmart, 153–54
Warner Media, 89
warning signs
   customer pain points, 56–62
   decline, 65–69
   freedom to signal strength ratio,
      49–51
   ignoring, 26–27, 34–36, 183
   importance, 39
   indicators, 44–49
   optimum warning period, 51

time zero event identification,
 51–56, 64
  weak, 40–43, 62–63, 208–9
  what won't change, 63–64
"wartime" CEOs, 187–90, 209
waterfall methodology, 111
webbing, 119–20, 126, 193–95
Weinberg, Zach, 114–19, 193,
 202
Whirlpool, 160
Whitwam, David, 160
"Why You Can't Get a Taxi"
 (McArdle), 92
wind energy, 53–56
"Windows: The Next Killer
 Application for the Internet"
 (Allard), 130
Wintel, 134

Wolf, Martin, 181
women, in leadership, 167–70
Women in Leadership: Expanding
 Influence and Leading
 Change, 168–69, 186
World Wide Web. *See* Internet
Wozniak, Steve, 21
Wright, Orville, 6
Wright, Wilbur, 6

Xbox (Microsoft), 131

YouTube, 146

Zara, 75
Zook, Chris, 30
Zuckerberg, Mark, 19–20, 27–28, 31.
 See also Facebook